Sitting Pretty

Violet Valentine

Published by Violet Valentine 2013
http://www.facebook.com/Violet.Valentine2

Published with the assistance of
Publicious Pty Ltd
www.publicious.com.au

Cataloguing-in-Publication Data available on request

ISBN: 978-0-9873144-0-6

Also available as an ebook
ebook ISBN: 978-0-9873144-1-3

Cover Photo by Martin Atkinson
Cover and book layout design
by Publicious Pty Ltd
www.publicious.com.au

To Anna, Kay, Kerrie, Lisa, Lee and
Colin, Rick and Di, my sweetheart
Marty and our family.

There are none more beautiful and pure,
than the souls that surround me.

There are none richer than these,
for their riches cannot diminish, with the
rise and fall of Wall Street.

Their riches are everlasting and shine
brilliantly with each day.

These people are gifts, and I am
grateful for the diamonds they are!

Table of Contents

Allow me to introduce myself

"Whether you think you can or think you can't, you are right."
Henry Ford
(Founder of the Ford Motor Company)

I have a couple of quotes that I live by, like mantras, and this is one of them. It is forever etched into my brain (by choice) so that I can't get away with anything. I call it my mantra, because I cannot count the number of times I have repeated this phrase to myself since the accident. I find it utterly amazing how simple words can change a person's life, because these twelve words have given me courage to step out of my comfort zone and given me resolve when I have been low.

I do not profess to be anything that I am not. I do not pretend to be oblivious to pain, and I do not aspire to be a superwoman. I have cried, I have screamed, and I have felt the depths of depression.

Look, life will throw all sorts of things at us throughout our lifetime and everybody will have a story, or two. Some will be sad, some will be terrible, and some will be just heart-breaking. However, the story is not the point, the point is what we do and make of each moment! I say this because when we are sitting in our house at eighty years of age, the only person we will have to thank or blame for our life - is us!

Allow me a few minutes here.....

The day is January 26 1980, Australia Day, and I am ten years old at this point in time. My best friend has come around to my place, and we (Mum, Dad and the two of us) are all relaxing in the lounge room enjoying the parades on television. There weren't many times when my Dad would sit down to watch television, I guess that is why this day felt so like a real family day to me. For once, we were all together. Then this moment was disrupted by a sound... an unfamiliar noise. I look around to see what was making the noise, and it was my Mum. I couldn't understand the gurgling noise, yet before I knew it, my mum looked right back at me. Then, what seems like two minutes later I heard the noise again, so I turned to look at her again, but this time she doesn't look back at me and the gurgling noise continued. I screamed to Dad to look at Mum and he ran over to her. He tried to get her to wake up, but she doesn't. She just keeps on making that noise, and then Dad asks me to run next door to the granny flat for the neighbour. I race back to Mum and her head is on my dad's chest. He has her in his arms. When my Dad and brother returned from the hospital, I was told that Mum had gone to heaven.

That could have made me bitter, and then came the accident.

Up until this day I had gone to hospital twice only, once for tonsillitis and the second for appendicitis. I was definitely not a thrill seeker, nor a risk-taker. Don't get me wrong, I love having fun and I have a few stories to tell, but I was not and still am not, an adrenalin junkie.

As fate turned out, I met who I thought was to be my Prince Charming (Miles) in a nightclub, of all places. At that point in my life, I was where I wanted to be (England), had a job that I enjoyed, had friends around me, and had now met a wonderful man who really loved and lived life. Things could not have possibly been any better.

I was not crazy about motorbikes and even though my brother was a self-made mechanic owning and repairing countless bikes – they never held any interest for me whatsoever. It was my decision to join Miles on his bike because I wanted to spend time with him doing the things he loved. I can recall that I climbed on to the back of his bike only four times beforehand. Five times was a charmer, because I found myself waking up to the blinding lights of a hospital. Two doctors came to the end of my bed when I opened my eyes, and began to inform me that I had been involved in a very bad accident. They told me that I may never be able to walk again because of the damage to my spinal cord, and lastly, that my boyfriend had not survived. All this within ten minutes of waking up...... good bedside manner, NOT!

During the seven months that I was incarcerated in the spinal unit for rehabilitation, I received two calls from my father in Australia. The first call was just when the accident happened and the second call was to ask if I was coming home, and to inform me that the cancer that had been cut out of his body (two years earlier) had returned, and was now terminal.

Of course, I made the decision to give up what I had in England and return home to be with my father, for as long as I had him. That turned out to be six months after I landed in Australia in December 1999. Yet, when I arrived home I also discovered that my brother had been diagnosed with a brain tumour since I last visited him in February 1999. By the time I arrived home post my own trauma, the tumour had a very firm grip on my brother, and I learnt that he had decided not to have any operations. Saddened by his choice, I respected that it was his mind, his experience, and his right to choose.

So, as you can see, within the space of only one year I had lost my boyfriend, buried my only brother as well as my father, and not to mention, I had lost my life as I knew it. I had lost the lifestyle, privileges and freedom that I had previously been born with. That in itself, is a death – the death of my life and the person I was.

I think you would agree that I probably have every right (and reason) to be bitter and twisted at life and God, but instead, I choose not. Instead of sitting down and feeling sorry for myself (which gets me nowhere) I choose to gather the diamonds out of these experiences/ events, I choose to learn, and I choose to live!

I know, without a shadow of a doubt, that I would not be the person that I am today, if not for all of the events and experiences that I have faced, felt and walked forward through – both positive and not-so positive.

I have chosen to share this information with you to make a point. I do not ask or seek, in any way, pity, sympathy or mercy.

I do not pretend to know anything about the complex dimensions of the mind, how it works or how to fool it. I do not pretend to know anything about medicine, occupational therapy or counselling for that matter. But what I do know about is living with a wheelchair. And so, I offer all that I know to you. It is my hope to be of some form of help, no more, no less.

Warmest Regards, Violet

We choose our mood,

we choose how we see life,

we choose to look for the diamonds,

and

we choose to move forward.... or backward.

Chapter one

Create the life you want!

bit one – the Beach

I just came back from the beach with my friends and it was a wonderful day!

Some of you might be thinking – 'beach, I can't go to the beach now that I use a wheelchair!' But I have three words for you - 'Wrong, wrong and still wrong!'.... (maybe five words, heehee).

I will agree with you that we can no longer get into the ocean alone anymore, but, I want to let you know that we can still go to the beach.

I want to tell you a story about how a friend and her partner helped me get back into the beach. If I was to describe my friend and her partner as a type of coffee, it would be Mr and Mrs Straight Black – this is a really strong, punchy coffee.

So Mr and Mrs Straight Black made it possible for me to go to the beach for the first time in nine plus years and it was nothing short of fabulous. I cannot put into words what it was like to actually be in the ocean again, to smell the salt water around me, to be doing something that everyone else can enjoy, to feel the waves crash over me, and to experience the life that is in the ocean.

First, I am going to tell you my story, and then I will share with you what I realised from that experience.

After I drove to Mr and Mrs Straight Black's place, they packed the car and I followed them to the beach at North Burleigh; a beautiful part of the Gold Coast. After we found car parks, Mr Straight Black checked out the ocean and the rips to make sure it was a safe part of the beach. While he was doing that Mrs Straight Black came over to my car to take my towel, sunscreen and keys.

Mrs Straight Black and I talked about the best way to do the whole beach excursion a couple of days earlier. We thought about me pushing my chair as close as possible to the beach before getting out and leaving it on the side lines, but I wasn't comfortable with that idea. After all, that chair is my legs, and if it goes missing I am literally and physically 'stuck'. I didn't think it was practical for me to push close to the beach and then get Mrs Straight Black to carry the chair back and put it into the car, either. So, the only logical and practical solution we could come up with was just carrying me directly from the car to the water.

Lucky for me, Mr Straight Black is a nice bloke, because Mrs Straight Black kindly offered her partners services in order to get me into the ocean. Lucky for me Mr Straight Black's work is very physical, making it easy for him to carry me.

So when Mr Straight Black returned from checking out the ocean and its movements, he confirmed that it was a good area and said, 'Let's go'. So next, I turned my entire body, including moving my legs and feet, so that I was now facing the car parked next to my car. My legs were now hanging over the side of my car seat and my feet were resting on the ground. Mr Straight Black bent his knees, with his back to me, so that I could put my arms around his neck in a piggy-back method. When he stood up, I asked him to grab my legs while I made sure that my swimwear was all in place and we headed towards the beach. Mrs Straight Black had the keys to my car which she locked after I was out of it. As you can imagine, I was super excited (and a tad nervous too).

Mrs Straight Black wanted to lay out the towels and set things up before we got into the ocean, so her man patiently waited, still carrying me all the while – poor guy. After that we all headed to the surf. As Mr Straight Black was walking into the water, I could see by the look on Mrs Straight Black's face that it was a tad fresher than what she had hoped for. By the time the water reached my waist, I too had the same look on my face.

After about five minutes in the ocean, I wondered if the waves were coming in particularly strong and frequent or if it was just that I was not used to what everyone else enjoys on a frequent basis. But either way, I was not going to complain about anything, after all, this experience was a beautiful gift.

Mrs Straight Black had brought her boogie board so that I could use it for floatation assistance. I was holding onto that and both Mr and Mrs Straight Black were around me. As the waves came in, I noticed that I was easily pulverised but that didn't deter me either. Mrs Straight Black suggested I climb more onto the board so that I could ride over the waves with her holding onto it. Mr Straight Black watched what was happening and thought it might help if he held the tip of the board so that he could lift it up over the waves as they came. It was a top idea and made the whole experience better, as I was not being dunked so much anymore.

I had no idea how long I was out there, the time flew by, yet I noticed that I was getting dumped more and more frequently, so I decided to get into some more shallow water. I also wanted to give Mr and Mrs Straight Black some time together.

Ah, the shallow waters, no more thrashing around. Mrs Straight Black ended up joining me less than a few minutes later and together we lay basking in the frothy shallow water. After a while it occurred to me that we must of looked like two white girls trying to do those sexy beach poses, you know like on Bay *Watch*... (Heehee, that's hillarious).

Actually, I was laughing myself silly because as the sand was being dragged out from under us, I was being tossed around like I was a piece of fluff in a washing machine. My legs don't have much weight to them so they were being thrown around all over the shop. And yes, the top half of my body is strong, but in the ocean, I am but a mere leaf, heehee. Do you like that one? No seriously, I wish we had had a video camera filming because I think we could of made a lot of money from a television show like, *Funniest Home Videos.*

Now, in order for me to get out of the ocean, Mr Straight Black had to squat next to me so that I could climb on his back as best as possible. Actually Mrs Straight Black also helped me onto Mr Straight Black's back and we headed again for the deeper waters, so that we could clean out all the sand we had accumulated in our swimsuits.... Fun, fun, fun.

I tried to clear as much of the sand as possible, but there will always be a tonne or two left to wash out in the shower at home, not to mention your car and chair. Oh, just so that you know, today is about five days post going to the beach and I am still finding sand in and on my chair. I just thank God the sand is nowhere near my wheels. Now that is a pain in the neck! (Heehee). However, I have been out again to the beach, despite the sand!

I have to say that I was bewildered why I hadn't thought of going to the beach before now? And I think my girlfriend and I could handle the ocean by ourselves, if we could get a helping hand from one or two Lifesavers to get me into and out of the water. So I am going to make some calls and find out if Lifesavers do things like that or if I can bribe them with some sort of reward? (Get your mind out of the gutter girls, I was thinking more along the lines of beer).

Mrs Straight Black told me a story about a guy who is in a chair at Byron Bay who goes to the beach too, but completely by himself. Apparently he gets out of his chair and leaves it sitting on the nearest spot just on the grass, and then proceeds to 'bum' his way across the sand and into the water. And, I guess when he's had enough of the salt and sand, he does the same in reverse (he bums his way back across the sand to his chair). I'm going to see if I can locate him and put his story in the book, I haven't seen him when I've been in Byron before, but I will keep my fingers crossed. I would imagine though, that he would need serious protection on his bottom and legs while he is bumming his way about two hundred meters or more. I guess a wetsuit could be sufficient protection?

TIDBITS

- Lather your entire body up on 30+ Sunscreen and take it with you onto the beach, because I had forgotten how strong the Australian sun is. I am telling you this because you will probably need to re-apply it.

- Ensure your swimsuit bottoms remain in place as the water has the power to move your swimwear around, especially if your swimsuit is loose-fitting. I forgot how easily this happens.

- When your friends are eyeing the ocean, see if they can spot a part of the beach that is safe from rips and has a break between the waves.

- I would only recommend staying a couple of hours, because if you stay longer you will need to keep up your water intake and that means locating and accessing a wheelchair friendly bathroom. That means someone will need to get your chair from and return it to your car.

- Mrs Straight Black suggested purchasing one of those fold up mini-chairs that has a back rest to allow me sit up easier on the beach. I think that would be a good idea if you enjoy being part of the beach culture and like sitting and watching whatever is going on at the time.

As I wrap up this topic, I want you to remember to surround yourself with people who see possibilities, not limitations.

My next goal is to work out how I can do this with just my girls.

bit two - Swimming

Now we can move onto some more fun things, such as swimming. I love swimming for so many reasons, however I haven't always, like when I was younger.

Truth be told, when those swimming carnivals came around every year at high school, it was not my favourite time of year. Somehow I was always in the bathroom about the same time that my race was happening. I don't know how it always worked out that way, maybe it was just bad luck. It could have had something to do with the fact that I always seemed to come last in my races, which is probably part of the reason why I hated swimming for most of my life

But for some bizarre reason, I thought about swimming again for the first time in about fifteen years while I was in England, pre-accident. I have never been a hugely athletic type of person, but I have always enjoyed being active; whether it was aerobics, walking on the beach, roller-blading with girlfriends, karate or kung fu. But, then the accident happened, and I knew I couldn't go back to the Kung Fu classes I had been taking with a girlfriend. In fact, I had little idea about what sort of things I could do now in order to exercise, raise my heart-rate and have fun.

Side track

The Physiotherapists (from the Spinal Unit) took a few of us to the indoor pool not far from the unit and I hated it. Looking back, it wasn't that bad, but at the time, I recall using that word to describe the experience which is why I chose 'hated' as the adjective.

We were told to get dressed in our swimming costumes before leaving the spinal unit and to put something over the top of them that was really easy for us to take off, and then we met up with the physiotherapists at the Gymnasium and went from there. Each of the patients had their own physiotherapist; there were only three of us in-mates. It was only a five minute push until we arrived at the swimming pool. Someone mentioned that this was the site that the first ever Paralympics was held, knowing that was somewhat comforting.

After we undressed, we re-grouped and discussed how we were going to get into the pool. The physiotherapists introduced us to a machine that was going to lower each of us, one at a time down into the water safely. I have seen this machine a couple more times since that brief introduction, but personally, I don't intend to make that machine my new best friend any time soon. For me, if I can do it myself I will. Why? Well, because if I can do it myself then I will probably gain new skills, techniques and understanding as well as strength and independence. Machines to me, are kind of like chemical medication - at times it can be handy, but if you become dependent on them, they will only weaken the mind and the body, in turn making you more and more dependent.

It was not long before I found myself flapping my arms like crazy, just to stay above the water. The physiotherapist held me for a bit but wanted me to get used to what I would have to do if I wanted to be in the water. I asked the physio if he could show me how to swim again, but I did not get the answer that I wanted to hear. He could not give me any advice about swimming other than if I put my head down, my feet will lift behind me and if I put my head back they will raise in front of me. I attempted to do some freestyle movements but felt myself have one of those sinking sensations. I gave it two more attempts, with no success whatsoever. As we left the swimming complex to return to the unit, I hung my head and thought that I had to add swimming to the list of opportunities that I had lost in life.

See my TIDBITS on page 16

But, I want to get back to the story.

That was until I returned to Australia. It was a hot, sticky summer in Sydney and I knew that I couldn't get into the ocean by myself so I was going to give swimming pools another chance. At that point, I was very happy just to sit in the water. So I found a swimming pool with wheelchair access in a nearby suburb, at Willoughby. There was a beach-side entrance to the pool and the centre itself owned a plastic wheelchair that they wheeled into the pool. I just needed to approach one of the lifeguards on duty to request the plastic chair, ask them to hold it while I transferred onto it, and then ask them to take me into the pool. I knew that if I went to the centre at a time that was not busy, I wouldn't have to wait so long to get assistance.

So, I started going on a regular basis, relishing the opportunity to cool down while enjoying doing something normal. As I lazed around, watching families enjoying each other, children frolicking and individuals doing laps, suddenly just being there was not enough anymore. So I wondered if I could somehow work out how I could swim again. That was it, I already had my next objective and I was determined. I tried as many ways as I could think of but discovered that my feet would always drag on the tiles on the bottom of the pool. Finally, I came up with the idea to get one of those swimming buoys. You know, those yellow and blue foam floating things? I then made two holes in the middle of it, one under the other, like a snake bite – about 3 inches apart. Then I bought some thick elastic, from a fabric store, that I fed through the holes and sewed together at the ends. That way I could place my legs into the middle of the elastic circles and pull the buoy up and in between my legs. And voila! That's how I keep my legs and feet where I want them. You will be surprised how much of a difference this will make to your ability to balance face down in the water and swim in general, I definitely was.

Swimming is not only a compound exercise for the body, but I have found that it will also strengthen any muscles that you have functioning in your abs, obliques, back, and well, anywhere in your torso. You will feel great because you are out of your chair and doing something 'normal'. So your self-esteem and self worth will grow because you are doing something by yourself for yourself, you are expending energy, and we all know that exercise makes us feel good in general.

Oh, I guess it would be helpful if I talk about how I get from my chair and into the swimming pool now. Yes, ok then.

My daily routine changes from week to week, but it is my aim to swim every week. I would love to go swimming on a daily basis, yet, as you probably already realise our arms can only do so much, we can't expect our little arm muscles to do the job of both our arms and our legs..... it is just not realistic.

If you are going directly to the pool from home, you can change into your swimsuit at home so that you are not wasting time or freezing your legs off.... heehee. And, if you are anything like me, you will know that getting cold is not fun as it takes us twice as long to raise our body temperature – maybe it is because we are not able to run around as much or as easily? However, back to the point - it is not impossible to change into your swimsuit when you arrive at the swimming pool. You will just need a toilet or a change room, and if you can't close the door, it doesn't have to be a big deal as your body will be facing inwards anyway. As I have had to do this a couple of times, I can tell you that women won't be standing outside your cubicle watching you get changed - most people don't have enough hours in the day!

Oh, I just remembered that I have forgotten to tell you that I use an outdoor pool, which is why I don't go swimming in winter as much as I would like.

TIDBITS

- Some pools have those electric chair lifts that lower people with challenged mobility down into the water. If you do not see one, ask a staff member as some pools store them and only get them out as required.

- Then, there are those pools that have a wheel-in entry (similar to a beach) with a water-friendly wheelchair that is usually plastic. These chairs will also be stored, so again, ask if they provide these. Here is a photo of this plastic chair. When I used this type of pool I had to wait for a staff member to be free to get into the pool, and then catch a staff's attention to ask for their assistance to get out as well. I quickly became frustrated with this and devised how I could be more independent.

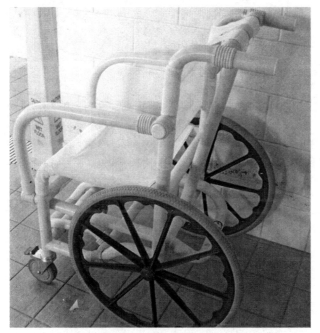

Plastic wheelchair for pools

- Other swimming pools will have ramps that lead down into the pool on one side. These pools will also have a water-friendly chair that can wheel down the ramp and stay in the water until you are ready to exit. I don't know how they get back out of the pool, reversing the chair themselves I suppose, or perhaps with a staff member's assistance. I have never used these ramps.

Pool with a ramp into it

- Then, there are those pools that are completely even with the ground, which is the new fad. I haven't quite worked out how to use these pools just yet as they have no raised edges for me to use as leverage for lifts. Unfortunately, they are becoming more and more popular and replacing the older-style pools that I prefer to utilise.

Pool with flat edge

- My favourite types of pool are the older ones that have a raised concrete edging, surrounding the entire pool. I like these the most, as the edging is wide enough for me to sit on, which permits me to get in and out when I want to, and not depend on others.

Getting into these type of pools involves three-steps, (a) the transfer from my chair to step, (b) the transfer from step down to the next step that is at water level and (c) the transfer from that step into the water.

Pool with raised edge

Process for getting into a pool at the steps:

- Position your chair directly in front of the railing (get as close as physically possible).

- Make sure all your bibs and bobs are reachable from the chair so that you can get to them when you get out.

- Try to get your castor wheels facing forward, this will help keep your chair in position.

- It is scary at first, but have persistence as it will get easier. Trust me.

- Secure your brakes.

- Lift your legs onto the ground in front of you, between the railings. Place your feet well in front as you want to leave yourself somewhere to land when you lift down.

- Then, grab the railings and slowly lower yourself down to the pools edge.

- Straighten your legs and place them into the water.

- And finally, lean into the water.

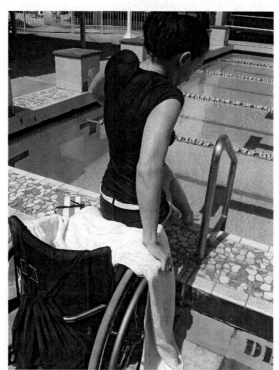

Me sitting on chair at the rails of a swimming pool

<u>Process for getting out of the above-mentioned swimming pool:</u>

- I swim up next to the steps and position my back to the steps.

- You can lift yourself up a couple of steps at a time or go the whole hog in one go.

- Use the rails to give you leverage for the lifts.

- The steps are tiny and it might be awkward to balance on, just be sure to hold on tight.

- Once you reach the top step – being the ground level, take a moment before you do the ground to chair transfer. You might want to pull your towel down to dry off a bit or keep you warm while you get your breath. This is the most difficult lift and your arms may be fatigued from the laps.

- I lay my towel back onto my chair with the length of the towel falling across my chair from left to right (big wheel to big wheel). I make sure that the towel covers the back rest so that it doesn't get soaked either.

- Finally, I move the chair so that it is directly behind me so that when I lift my bottom, it will find its way straight onto the cushion without too much trouble. This needs to be a good and strong lift.

Basically, there is no right or wrong way ladies and you will work out what works best for you. All I want to say is "don't give up before you start"(big cheesy smile).

bit three - Kayaking

I thought it might be fun to go kayaking with my friend while she was over here on holidays from England. Now, how shall I refer to her? What type of beverage would she be? Ah yes, Miss Lady Grey of course. Back to the story. As Miss Lady Grey loves outdoor activities and has been kyacking plenty of times, I thought it might be fun for her to do it here in Australia, and I wanted to share that experience with her (as this was my first time).

Fortunately, the operators came with us so we had a kayak each. I had no idea what it would be like or what to expect, I just knew if Miss Lady Grey can do it then so could I. I was just excited about the opportunity and open to the whole experience.

After we met up with the instructors we followed them to the location where they would put the kayaks into the water. We were all ready to go with our swimsuit, hats, sunscreen, long sleeve tops on and towels handy. We sat in the car and one by one, we were carried to and seated inside the kayaks.

I would suggest that you try a 'taster' first so that you're not wasting time and money on an entire day trip, just in case it is not what you imagined. What I discovered is that the point of your injury will determine how easy or tricky it is going to be for you to sit upright and paddle at the same time. My point of injury is at T8, and I will honestly say that kayaking is possible, but a bit of a challenge. We had really rough water apparently, making the paddling that bit more of a slog rather than an enjoyment. When they first sat me in the kayak, I felt like I would be falling all over the shop, so I asked for the cushion off my wheelchair and sat it behind me in the kayak, to help keep me upright and more stable, however it did not provide as much support as I had hoped.

I found it challenging to do the whole paddling thing as I don't have the best balance and I was working very hard on just being upright. My hands were sore from holding the paddle and my wrists were tired from the turning motion of paddling. When I have watched it on television it definitely appears more relaxing and tranquil, than what it was. Miss Lady Grey loved it though, and I'm very glad we did it together. It is do-able, and I would recommend it to anyone that loves water and team activities. I will say that when I was calling around, not a lot of operators were keen to take two people in wheelchairs. This was also the case with jet skis too; I don't know if it had more to do with lack of knowledge or fear of legal matters should something happen. I completely understand their risk, yet I feel that if we are doing it tandem with a qualified person then I don't understand their hesitation. I think it just comes from the fear of the unknown, like everything else, so please don't let that stop you (winks).

Me kayaking

bit four – Wheelchair Basketball

I mentioned in another chapter that I tried my hand at women's wheelchair basketball, and I think now is the perfect time to give you all the low-down on this sport.

As of this year, 2010, you will find you can play wheelchair basketball in almost every state of our big country (Australia). There are games for beginners who have absolutely no idea about what they're doing, and as you progress, you can join the regional games, and if you fall in love with the game, one day you might be invited to join the Paralympic Preparation Program and end up representing your country at the Paralympics. This website will give you all of the contact details you need - www.basketball.net.au/index.php?id=846

Wheelchair basketball is a great sport because you feel like you are a part of something bigger than yourself with a definite direction and purpose. Suddenly you are surrounded with like-minded people who have a desire for sport, thrive on competition, and aim at achieving their personal best – I think that was what I was drawn to. Oh, and the fun of the game too!

The only difference between the able-bodied version and the wheelchair version of this game is the fact that you need to bounce the ball every two pushes. The ring is at the same height, the court is the same size, and it is still not a contact sport - unlike what the able-bodied people seem to think about the game, I guess they hear all the clanging of the metal and think we are just running into each other.

You may, like I used to, think that there would be no way you could throw the ball into the ring at that height from a seated position. I'll agree because in the beginning the ring did look like it might as well have been Mars or Jupiter. I have to tell you that when I was walking I used to go to schools on the weekends and play hoop with a former boyfriend, and I rarely got anywhere near the hoop. If I did manage to hit the ring, I was over the moon. Then, when I attempted it in a basketball wheelchair to my surprise it didn't seem to be that impossible after all. I don't know if it was because I wanted to do it more than before or what, but I just want you to know that it is not nearly as difficult as it might seem right now.

Personally I believe the actual game of wheelchair basketball is far more skilful, challenging, and team-building than the able-bodied version of the sport – and no, I'm not biased! (I'm not!!!!)

Side track

Let me explain. The wheelchairs add a whole new dimension of complexity and challenge to the game, because, no matter how good your skills are at ball-handling, when you add a set of wheels that you have to control and direct simultaneously, it really stretches anybody. Wheelchair basketball is like a game of chess because it is all about out-witting the other team's players and their skills, not just about ball-handling. It is about putting 100% into the game, learning the strengths and weaknesses of yourself, your team members as well as your opponents, and never giving up. To me, regardless of the sport you play or watch – if the player/ team is beaten psychologically, the game is already over! End of story, it is that simple.

If only the top two teams of the Australian Basketball League could get a game televised on one of the main channels at a prime time, I know that anyone who likes sport would see that it is not just a "disabled sport", it is a fantastic, exciting and talented sport! But, I will keep my fingers crossed - what a game that would be.

Now, let's get back to the game of basketball.

The teams are made up of a diverse range of girls and guys, ages, cultures and backgrounds, skills, and people who also happen to have disabilities. Some you will like, others you will like less, yet, together you are a team, you are one and it is a great thing to be apart of something like that. You will be encouraged to spend hours in your basketball chair honing and becoming an expert in that piece of equipment, so your skills in your day chair will benefit hugely as a by product. It will be a benefit if you can get a basketball wheelchair of your own, but in the start you might be able to borrow one. I would suggest waiting to get your own until you talk to and watch a lot of other girls play in their chairs to find out which design factors will maximise your strengths and weaknesses the most. I took my time and the chair that I ended up with was a perfect fit for my level of function and my body.

You will need to attend training to learn the tools, skills and 'plays'. When I was playing I trained with the women on Monday nights and then I also went to training with the men's team on Wednesday evenings, and then most weekends were filled with games between February and September of each year. You can choose how much you want to be a part of the game.

I just want to give a shout-out here to the men's team that opened their arms to me – the Razorbacks. I really loved attending the men's training sessions – there's no room for excuses, it is not about who you like or who doesn't like you, it is simply about the game and pushing yourself. I just wish that more people had the chance to see both the women's and men's wheelchair basketball games on television in Australia (and of course around the world). I believe it is a shame that the Australian public lose out because it is not a main-stream sport like cricket or rugby. I'd be interested to see the statistics though, if the television networks were to take a chance and air a few games! (I dare them).

So, my advice is – if you like sport, contact one of the sporting associations in your state and get off to a game. You will have fun, I can guarantee it.

However, if basketball doesn't tickle your fancy, these wheelchair sporting organisations offer a vast variety of sports (about 12 more in fact), and I am sure there will be one out there that you will relish.

The Hornets team – Women's Wheelchair Basketball National League

bit five – the Gymnasium

When I was playing wheelchair basketball in Sydney, I also used to go to the gymnasium as any athlete needs to maximise their strength, fitness and body. We may not be able to use every piece of machinery in the gymnasium (which is somewhat frustrating), however, we will be able to use enough stations for our arms to get a substantial ache and enable us to hurt enough so that we know we've done a workout.

When you are with the gymnasium's personal trainer you will need to provide them with enough information so that he/she can accurately assess your capabilities with each piece of equipment and determine which pieces you can in fact access and utilise. Not many personal trainers have experience working with people who have physical challenges, but if they do, then you need to make sure that they are not assuming your functions and capabilities. And, sometimes we, the person with the disability, do that too; we create a box and mentally confine and restrict ourselves within that box for a lot of different reasons. I know this because I've done it. By trying new things we start breaking down the walls within our minds. So, I would tell you to try every piece of equipment there is, just give it a go. You might surprise yourself.

There are so many sports out there for you to join and I would fervently recommend that you try anything and everything you can think of. There are sports you can do by yourself (like swimming), sports you can play with a team (rugby, basketball, seated volleyball), and sports you can still enjoy with your able-bodied friends, (like tennis, ten pin bowling or snooker). I know that Australia is primarily a summer sport country, yet, don't forget the winter sports too, like sitted-skiing. I know I have said this before, but it is soooo true – we are only limited by our minds ladies!

Some of you might like just to enjoy your sport on a social level and that is great or some of you might like to see how far you can take it – like the Paralympics! That is great too. What is not great – is giving up before you even start. Look, I just want you to get back out there into this thing called "life". It can still be a whole lot of fun.

In fact, I would almost go so far to say that it should be compulsory that each new member (of the disabled community) is conscripted to participate in some form of sport within the first twelve months of injury, like teenagers are still conscripted to join the army for 12-24 months in some countries. Not only will participating in a sport do heaps for your self-worth, it will build your self confidence, give you wheelchair skills, and also give you great friends!

bit six - Zorbing

This was the next thing on my list!

As you can see from this picture, Zorbing requires a gigantic plastic ball and a person willing to jump inside it. What you don't see is the ball (and person) being pushed down the side of a hill.

Me inside the zorbing ball

The zorbing ball and moving vehicle

Ok, this story involves another close friend and her son, whom I think I will call Mrs Vienna and boy Vienna.

Sure the Zorbing experience came from a desire to give a present to one of Mrs Vienna's children. Yet I also saw it as a chance to do something for me too, a challenge, a thrill.

You see, I had just come out of a relationship that made me feel like I was living inside a box, and I think in order to help me psychologically I had to do something physically. And that is how I found myself Zorbing.

When I rang the company that provided this experience, a very kind gentleman advised me that they had previously had a lot of people with a disability participate, which suddenly gave me a sense of anxiety in the pit of my stomach. Because, as you will learn, when people say 'disabled', they are usually talking about walking sticks and broken legs. So, when I hear someone say that they have worked with 'disabled people', I need to find out exactly what they mean by that in order to get some peace of mind.

But you know what? Every single time a person with a disability steps outside of their comfort zone and works with someone in the community, another person learns, grows and sees our abilities, not disability (Smiles).

The gentleman at the other end of the line (telephone) gave me directions to parking that was closer and easier for me to access, which made me very happy after I arrived and saw how far I would have had to walk.

So after we arrived Mrs Vienna, boy Vienna and I made our way from the car across the dirt staff car park, up the way-too-steep ramp to the reception desk. Hey, at least a ramp existed right? Both boy Vienna and I had come prepared, we already had our swimsuit on, and we took several towels, and of course, a change of clothes for afterwards. I want to mention that the toilets and change rooms were all accessible, and I loved it.

We didn't have to wait long before the staff came to tell us 'we were up next'.

If you keep your weight within healthy parameters there are far more exciting adventures available for you, than if you don't. I am mentioning this because one of the staff members just scooped me up into his arms and sat me down into the 4WD; something that would not be possible if I was not conscious about what goes in my mouth.

Boy Vienna and I were both super hyped. Yet, as we climbed our way up the hill in the 4WD, towing the Zorb ball behind us, millions and millions of butterflies started doing somersaults in my stomach I can tell you. As you may have read before, I am not one of those girls that live for adrenalin, yet there I was about to put myself into a ball, put a bit of water in there too, and then get pushed down a hill.

Again, one of the staff members scooped me up and placed me feet first into the zorb ball. Boy Vienna was already in there and now I was too. They had already put a touch of water in the ball before either of us climbed inside. So there we were, boy Vienna and I, looking at each other when they said to us 'Ok, let's go', and then before I knew it we were falling over each other. We were not strapped down inside the ball and the water was a great idea as it provided a lubricant between the skin of the ball and the skin of our bodies. We were simply free-falling inside the ball for as long as it took to reach the bottom of the hill, which was about 3-4 minutes.

I can not think of a better way to describe this experience, other than tell you it felt like we were inside a front-loading washing machine. We did not know which way we were falling, as we could not see a thing outside the ball and we were spinning too quickly anyway. Yet, it was over all too quickly, and there we were, lulling the rattle of our heads at the bottom of the hill. I am sure boy Vienna was wishing it went for longer, while I was 'thanking God that it stopped'.

All in all, I would do it again in a heartbeat – it definitely put a smile on my face.

TIDBITS

- Definitely no food.

- No jewellery.

- Two towels (x1 for you and x1 for your chair).

- Take a deep breath and be present!

bit seven - Sewing

Sewing has been a love of mine since my mum introduced me to my first sewing machine at the age of five or six.

It was one of those gorgeous old steel Singer sewing machines that you can see in any antique stores nowadays. It had a lid that opened out to provide a side table, and then you needed to lift the machine out from the belly of the structure. In order to start the machine you needed to spin the handle and then pump the foot pedal on the ground to keep it moving. It was a simple machine, but one that was very solid and un-breakable. And, because it was such a simple design, there weren't too many things that could go wrong, unlike these plastic versions that we have in the stores in recent-times.

However, from a very young age, I fell in love with sewing machines because of their power to create. Be it a curtain, a blanket, a pair or trousers or a wedding dress, you are only limited by your mind.

When the accident occurred, thinking back to 1999, I didn't think that I could touch a sewing machine again. It wasn't even a question in my head until years later. Silly really, because it proves to you that we don't know what is possible until we give it a go.

One day when I was in Spotlight (a fabric store) drooling over the fabrics and their untapped possibilities, I started thinking about how much I used to love sewing. Then I asked myself why can't I still sew now? So I walked (figuratively speaking) over to the section where they sell machines and looked at them. Then I realised that the foot pedal was on a cable. I thought about the foot pedal and asked myself if there was another way I could use it to control the machine? This was when I came up with the idea of putting it up on the table and using my elbow to control it. It might look different but at least I can do what I want – and that is to sew again.

I had the opportunity to put this theory into practice and see how it worked and if it was practical and realistic – and it worked and it was.

Within the week I had purchased a sewing machine and overlocker and made my first garment. I was delighted and you couldn't wipe the smile off my face if you tried! Yes, doing this for myself was another step closer to being the 'old' me as well as gaining independence and freedom. I was over the moon with excitement and pride. I was excited because there was nothing that could stop me, I was proud of myself because I had accomplished something that I had previously wiped out of my life for good.

Moral to the story: Take the word, 'Impossible' out of your dictionary.

It doesn't do us any good. Because as soon as most people hear or think this word, they give up – many times without trying. Everything is possible, unless we can come up with two solid reasons why and how it can't be done. To me the word 'impossible' is for people who can't be bothered, or who just haven't thought about 'it' enough to find a way.

Now, I can only cover the sports or hobbies that I have personally tried but below are the contact details for sports and recreation organisations throughout Australia.

Me at the sewing machine

Sport and Recreation Organisations

INTERNATIONAL

Martial Arts for people with disabilities - UK

Disability Martial Arts Association (DMAA) -
www.disabilitymartialartsassociation.co.uk/

This link outlines alternative martial art moves for people who use
chairs -
www.fightingarts.com/reading/get_articles.php?cat=Martial%20
Arts%20and%20the%20Disabled

Shape - UK

Develops opportunities for artists (with disabilities), trains cultural
institutions to be more open to pwad, and runs participatory arts and
development programmes - www.shapearts.org.uk

Arts and Disability IRELAND

ADI is a national arts development organisation striving to
promote cultural equality for people with disabilities in the arts -
www.adiarts.ie

National Arts and Disability Center - USA
Promotes the full inclusion of artists and audiences with disabilities
into all facets of the arts community - www.nadc.ucla.edu

Kickstart – Disability, Arts and Culture – CANADA

Produces and promote artistic excellence among artists with disabilities
working in a variety of disciplines - www.kickstart-arts.ca

AUSTRALIA-WIDE

Fog Theatre - Is a drama group for people with a disability. It started in 1991 in St Kilda, Victoria. The members love playing music. They also like to act and dance. Fog recently performed a show called Forest of Gongs. It was a great show. After the show the performers enjoyed meeting the audience. Below is the link to where I discovered this theatre group.

www.divine.vic.gov.au/main-site/arts/artists-spotlight/performing-in-fog

Arts & Disability Organisations around Australia

Arts Access Australia is the national peak body of State and Territory arts and disability organisations working to increase access and participation in the arts for the one in five Australians with a disability.
Tel: 02 9518 0561
Email: ed@artsaccessaustralia.org
Website: www.artsaccessaustralia.org

New South Wales - Accessible Arts is the peak arts and disability organisations across New South Wales.
Tel: 02 9251 6499
Email: info@aarts.net.au
Website: www.aarts.net.au

Queensland - Access Arts Queensland is the peak body working with artists, cultural workers and their communities across Queensland.
Tel: 07 3358 6200
Email: info@accessarts.org.au
Website: www.accessarts.org.au

South Australia - Arts Access SA (AASA) is a key service organisation for arts and disability in South Australia.
Tel: 08 8224 0799
Email: info@artsaccess-sa.org.au
Website: www.artsaccess-sa.org.au

Western Australia - Primary Arts and Disability infrastructure in WA, providing cultural access to over 2000 West Australians with disabilities and or mental illness per year.
Tel: 08 9430 6616
Email: arts@dadaawa.asn.au
Website: www.dadaawa.org.au

Australian Capital Territory - Art Ability ACT is the peak arts and disability organisation in the ACT. Art Ability ACT is a source of information and advice for artists with disabilities living and working in the ACT.
Tel: 02 6247 1882
Email: DDAO@artsrec.org.au
Website: none

Tasmania - Arts Action is the statewide body in Tasmania with responsibility for information exchange, lobbying and policy development in arts and disability.
Tel: 03 6214 7634
Email: MTaylor@gcc.tas.gov.au
Website: none

Northern Territory - Arts Access Darwin works in the greater Darwin area to improve access to the arts for people with disabilities.
Tel: 08 8945 7347
Website: www.darwincommunityarts.org.au/node/30

Central Australia - Arts Access Central Australia is working in Alice Springs to improve access to the arts for people with disabilities.
Tel: 08 8952 6338
Email: monikam@bigpond.net.au
Website: none

Wheelchair Dancing

DanceSport Australia (DSA) is the governing body responsible for the rules and regulations around competition dancing, adjudication and coaching within the DanceSport sylabus. DSA is the National Member of the International DanceSport Federation (IDSF). www.wheelchairdancesport.com.au/home.php

This link will tell you more about the art of dancing in a wheelchair - www.wikipedia.org/wiki/Wheelchair_dance_sport

This is a link to classes and news about wheelchair dancing, South Australia - www.madeleine.com.au/Links.html

NEW SOUTH WALES

Wheelchair Sports NSW

The not-for-profit association conducts and supports a wide range of wheelchair sporting events in Sydney and across the state – 14 in fact! I'm sure there will be something that takes your fancy.
PO Box 3244
PUTNEY NSW 2112
Ph: 02 9809 5260
Fax: 02 9809 5638
Web: www.wsnsw.org.au/

Riding for the Disabled Association (NSW)

RDA New South Wales is a voluntary, non-profit organisation dedicated to providing horse riding and associated activities to people with disabilities.
7 Underwood Rd
HOMEBUSH NSW 2140
Ph: 02 9746 0950
Fax: 02 9674 2301
Email: rdansw@bigpond.net.au
Web: www.rdansw.org.au

VICTORIA

Companion Card
Companion Card promotes the right of people with a disability, who require a companion, to fair ticketing at Victorian events and venues.
Ph: 1800 650 611(Companion Card Information Line)
Web: www.companioncard.org.au/cc/index.htm

Disabled Winter sport Victoria (DWV)
DWV is a voluntary organisation based in Victoria, Australia, that seeks to encourage disabled people to participate in all aspects of snow sports.
PO Box 28
MALVERN VIC 3144
Ph: 0408 030 124
Email: gosnow@hotmail.com
Web: www.dwv.org.au

Eastern Recreation & Leisure Services Inc. (ERLS)
ERLS increases the participation of people of all abilities in community sport and recreation through facilitating the development of accessible and inclusive sport and recreation environments.
Rear of 699 Doncaster Road
DONCASTER VIC 3108
Ph: (03) 9855 9977
Fax: (03) 9840 2515
Email: erls@infoxchange.net.au

Riding for the Disabled Association (Victoria)
RDA Victoria is a voluntary, non-profit organisation dedicated to providing horse riding and associated activities to people with disabilities.
457 South Road
MOORABBIN VIC 3189
Ph: (03) 9532 0411
Fax: (03) 9532 2808
Email: admin@rdav.asn.au
Web: www.rdav.asn.au

Victorian Disabled Sports Advisory Committee (VDASC)
The VDSAC is the peak organisation servicing sport for people with disabilities in Victoria, Australia. It acts as the umbrella organisation for sporting bodies responsible for helping people and athletes with disabilities. It aims to promote the development of sport for athletes with disabilities.
699 Doncaster Road
DONCASTER VIC 3108
Ph: (03) 9840 0123
Fax: (03) 9840 0123
Email: vdsac@alphalink.com.au
Web: http://home.vicnet.net.au/~vdsac

Victorian Network on Recreation and Disability (VICNORD)
The Victorian Network on Recreation and Disability (VICNORD) is funded by Sport and Recreation Victoria and is a statewide information and advocacy network of people with disabilities, their carers and advocacy groups in relation to recreation, sport, physical activity, tourism and the arts.
179 High Street
NORTHCOTE VIC 3070
Ph: 03 9489 2999
TTY: 03 9489 1179
Fax: 03 9489 2988
Email: vicnord@advocacyhouse.org
Web: www.advocacyhouse.org/vicnord/about.html

Victorian Sport & Recreation Association of People with an Intellectual Disability Inc (VICSRAPID)
VICSRAPID is a statewide, non-profit, community-based organisation formed to enhance the lifestyle of people with disabilities through opportunities in community sport and recreation.
Ground Floor, 120 Jolimont Road
JOLIMONT VIC 3002
Ph: (03)9639 3399
Fax: (03)9639 3057
Email: vicsrap@tpg.com.au
Web: www.vicsrapid.websyte.com.au

Wheelchair Sports Victoria (WSV)
Wheelchair Sports Victoria (WSV) is a sports club for people in wheelchairs who share a love of sport.
PO Box 207
ABBOTSFORD, VIC 3067
Ph: (03) 9473 0133
Fax: (03) 9473 0134
Web: www.wsv.org.au

TASMANIA

Cosmos Recreation Services
A community organisation which assists people with an intellectual disability to participate in recreation and leisure activities. Cosmos aims to promote self-determination by supporting informed choice.
52 New Town Road
NEW TOWN TAS 7008
Ph: (03) 62286394
Fax: (03) 62281782
Email: info@cosmos.org.au
Web: www.cosmos.org.au

New Horizons Club
The New Horizons Club provides interaction, sporting and social benefits for people who have a disability.
PO Box 49
MOWBRAY TAS 7248
Ph: 03 6326 3344
Fax: 03 6326 3344
Email: horizons@tas.quik.com.au

Riding for the Disabled Association
Riding for the Disabled Association is a voluntary, not for profit, organisation which provides riding instruction and other activities associated with riding and harness driving for people with disabilities.
PO Box 99
BATTERY POINT TAS 7004

Ph: 03 6224 9497
Email: peter-brown@bigpond.com
Web: www.rdav.asn.au

Lord's Taverners Tasmania
GPO Box 185
Hobart, Tasmania 7001
www.lordstavernerstas.org/whowehelp.shtml

This organisation desires to give disadvantaged and/or young people with a disability a sporting chance and have a variety of activities available.

Tasmanian Sport and Recreation Association for People with a Disability (TASRAD)
TASRAD is the peak body in Tasmania for people with disabilities in sport and recreation. TASRAD aims to promote the inclusion of people with disabilities in sport and recreation from the grass roots through to elite competition. They are also the Tasmanian coordinators of the Australian Sports Commission's Disability Education Program.
PO Box 324
PROSPECT TAS 7250
Ph: 03 6336 2012
Fax: 03 6336 2014
Email: tasrad@tassie.net.au
Web: www.tasrad.com.au

WESTERN AUSTRALIA

Recreation Network
Recreation Network is a small dynamic and creative organisation, which responds to the individual needs of people with a disability who wish to become involved in community recreation.
391 Oxford Street
MOUNT HAWTHORN WA 6016
Ph: (08) 9443 8788
Fax: (08) 9443 8799
TTY: (08) 9443 8788

Email: info@rec.net.au
Web: www.rec.net.au

Riding for the Disabled Association

Riding for the Disabled Association is a voluntary, not for profit, organisation which provides riding instruction and other activities associated with riding and harness driving for people with disabilities.
SEC, Cathedral Avenue
BRIGADOON WA 6069
Ph: 08 9296 4655
Fax: 08 9296 4655
Email: rdawa@iinet.net.au
Web: www.rda.org.au

AUSTRALIAN CAPITAL TERRITORY

Athletes With Dreams Squad

Its mission is to provide a safe and enjoyable environment in which to encourage participation in the sport of track and field. We seek to integrate both ambulants with a disability and able-bodied persons. Participants are encouraged to excel towards their personal goals.
35 Rubicon St
KALEEN ACT 2617
Ph: 02 6255 7191
Email: awdsquad@goplay.com

Independent Disabled Tenpin Bowlers of the ACT Inc.

Independent Disabled Tenpin Bowlers of the ACT Inc. (IDTBACT Inc) is a group established to assist disabled persons within Tuggeranong and the ACT region participate in the sport of tenpin bowling.
PO Box 1738
TUGGERANONG ACT 2901
Ph: 0262922426
Fax: 0262922280
Email: mecooke@austarmetro.com.au

RAID

RAID provides recreational activities for children and adults with and intellectual disability.
YMCA London Circuit
CANBERRA CITY ACT 2601
Ph: 02 62498733
Fax: 02 62471258
Email: raid@ymca.org.au
Web: www.ymcacanberra.org.au

Riding for the Disabled Association

Riding for the Disabled Association is a voluntary, not for profit, organisation which provides riding instruction and other activities associated with riding and harness driving for people with disabilities.
119 Drake Brockman Drive
HOLT ACT 2615
Ph/Fax: 02 6254 9190
Email: prda@bigpond.com
Web: www.rda.org.au

QUEENSLAND

Access Recreation Inc

Access Recreation hosts recreational avenues for people with disabilities 5yrs and above. They seek to create an atmosphere where people feel valued and respected.
PO Box 1146
ROCKHAMPTON 4700
Ph: (07) 4922 7151
Fax: (07) 4922 5412
Email: enquiries@accessrec.org.au
Web: www.accessrec.org.au

Life Stream Foundation

Life Stream assists state sporting organizations and offers a wide range of programs directly to people with an intellectual disability to enable them to participate in the community.

PO Box 1512
COORPAROO DC QLD 4151
Ph: 07 3891 5466
Fax: 07 3891 5706
Email: info@lifestream.org.au
Web: www.qrapid.org

Riding for the Disabled Association (Queensland)

Riding for the Disabled Association is a voluntary, not for profit, organisation which provides riding instruction and other activities associated with riding and harness driving for people with disabilities.
PO Box 904
KENMORE QLD 4069
Ph: 07 3720 2345
Fax: 07 37201457
Email: rdaq@bigpond.com

Sporting Wheelies

Sporting Wheelies opens the world to over 20 different sports for people with disabilities across Queensland. Their head office resides in Brisbane however, they can be found at Bundaberg, Cairns, Rockhampton, Mackay, Maroochydore, Toowoomba and Townsville, so contact them to find out more.
Ph: (07) 3253 3333
Web: www.sportingwheelies.org.au/

SOUTH AUSTRALIA

Riding for the Disabled Association

Riding for the Disabled Association is a voluntary, not for profit, organisation which provides riding instruction and other activities associated with riding and harness driving for people with disabilities.
1A Gladstone Street
FULLARTON SA 5063
Ph: 08 8338 6100
Fax: 08 8338 6155
Email: admin@rdasa.org.au
Web: www.rda.org.au

South Australian Sport and Recreation Association for People with Integration Difficulties (SASRAPID)

The South Australian Sport and Recreation Association for People with Integration Difficulties Incorporated (SASRAPID) assists people with integration difficulties get involved in community activities, sport, recreation and leisure activities.

Level 2, Station Arcade
52-54 Hindley Street
ADELAIDE SA 5000
Ph: 08 8410 6999
Fax: 08 8212 8666
Email: admin@sasrapid.com.au
Web: www.sasrapid.com.au

Wheelchair Sports Association of South Australia

Our mission is to ensure that members of the public of South Australia with a spinal impairment, amputation or classifiable disability, are provided with the maximum opportunity to participate in sport and recreation.

PO BOX 144
GREENACRES SA 5086
Ph: (08) 8349 6366
Fax: (08) 8349 6223
Email: wheelcs@senet.com.au
Web: www.wheelchairsports-sa.org.au

NORTHERN TERRITORY

Riding for the Disabled Association

Riding for the Disabled Association is a voluntary, not for profit, organisation which provides riding instruction and other activities associated with riding and harness driving for people with disabilities.

PO Box 1727
PALMESTON NT 0830
Ph: 08 8931 0093
Email: rdanorth@octa4.net.au
Web: www.rda.org.au

Total Recreation NT
Provides sport and recreation programs for people with a disability in the Northern Territory.
PO Box 3217
DARWIN NT 0801
Ph: 08 8981 3686
Fax: 08 8981 3616
Email: totalrecreation@bigpond.com

So now that you have all of this information, what are you going to do about it? (smiles)

Enjoy, Violet Valentine.

Chapter two

Travelling with metal

bit one – metal can't flatten dreams

When my mum and dad moved into town from their farm, there was just one lady who was my mum's best friend. And so it was only natural that the little girl of that lady became my best friend too. This lovely lady loves her sugar and all things sweet, so if I were to picture her as a type of coffee, it would be a Vienna. So, I shall call her Mrs Vienna in this story.

So Mrs Vienna and I spent almost every waking hour together in the primary school years, we were inseparable – like two peas in a pod, like fish n chips, like Jack n Jill. And on one of the many days we played, we day-dreamed about what we wanted to do when we were all grown-up.

Mrs Vienna dreamed and yearned to have a house filled with children and laughter, while my mind was firmly set on exploring the world and everything in it. At the time when we made this decision, I was seven years old while Mrs Vienna was only six.

Mrs Vienna's dream started to become a reality for her in 1998 when she gave birth to one of the most gorgeous little girls that I have ever laid eyes on, and yes, I am totally the biased and adoring 'Aunty'. Since then she has made a homely nest, still in the town that we grew up in, with her serenading husband, one gorgeous girl and four very dashing boys. Meanwhile, my dreams come true every couple of years when I venture off again, to another part of this wonderful world we live in.

Pre-accident I had not travelled nearly as much as I had dreamed of doing, touching bits and pieces really - Bangkok, England, Japan, New Zealand, France, Scotland, Canada and America. Later, as I lay in the hospital bed at the Spinal Unit for six agonizing and boring long weeks, I just assumed that travelling to Paris or Prague would be something that I could only do via television shows from then on.

But, as I worked out how to do all the day-to-day necessities, I was able to turn my attention to bigger and bigger things (technical term for tasks), week by week, month by month. Feeling more comfortable with my new situation and more confident in what I could do. Then one day I thought, 'I want to go travelling again.'

It didn't take me long before I made my first travels again over the oceans. My first official overseas holiday was to the USA in August, 2000 (one whole year post-accident). Patience is not one of my strengths, being an Aries........

Actually, I think by doing something so much bigger than anything else I had done, by physically making it happen and actually doing it, I learnt so much more about myself and saw just how little difference being in a chair really makes to the big picture of my new life. For me, being able to get on a plane by myself again was an exhilarating moment and gave me an acute insight. It meant that I didn't necessarily have to be dependent on anyone, not really. Sure, I find it a challenge to change light bulbs, vacuum, clean the bathtub and such, but come on – who really wants to do those things anyway???

I was able to grasp my (new) life from a whole new viewpoint. Suddenly, I saw myself as one of those horses that had 'blinkers' on their eyes. Blinkers are used on horses so that they can only look directly in front of them, thereby making it easier for the farmer to direct them and to focus on the job at hand. The horses physically cannot look anywhere except straight ahead. But my blinkers had now been removed by stepping outside of my comfort zone, stretching myself. As a result of this experience, I learnt that I was still the person that I was pre-accident, sitting down a lot of the time, but still 'me'.

Come hell or high water, I was not going to let a bit of metal stop me from living the sort of life that I wanted. After all, a wheelchair is an inanimate, emotion-less piece of metal - it has no magic powers or super capabilities! This piece of machinery cannot tell the future, nor can it take it away, this wheelchair cannot tell you what you can and cannot do, nor can it stop you from travelling. The only thing a wheelchair is capable of is doing is moving people from point A to point B, and we (the owners) are in complete control of it - not the other way around.

The point that I have just made above, is so integral to the Part Two of your life that I am going to talk about it a little more here. So I need you to stop right now and think about a newly born baby.

When a baby comes into this world, the event is neither 'good' nor 'bad', right? The emotions that you and I attach to the event can make it a 'good' or 'bad' experience.

Let us take a twenty-two year old girl who was just having some fun with a boy she met on the summer break from university. This girl was in the middle of her degree, she's at the beginning of her life, she was not in a relationship, was not thinking about starting a family and was looking forward to finishing university and getting out into the world. She was in no way ready or wanting a baby at this point in time. So, when she was informed that she was pregnant, naturally, she would be viewing this event from a negative point of view.

On the flip side of this scenario is a woman and man, a married couple, who have been trying to conceive for more than two years. Finally, they discover they are pregnant. The emotions that this couple will be feeling probably will be pure joy and gratitude for this gift of life. So for them, the event will have a completely positive meaning and outcome. As we can see, the event itself is neither positive nor negative; it is all about the emotions that we attach to each event or thing or person or behaviour in our life. The angle from which we view life will colour the person, event or experience. Now, the fantastic fact of all of this is that we have the power to choose how we colour things. This is also true when it comes to a wheelchair and the sort of life you can have with it. Yes, wheelchairs have limitations and so do our different disabilities, yet I believe it is our mind and attitude that limits us the most.

bit two – Travel agent

When we travel within Australia, we have no need for a travel agent, yet when we desire to go further abroad (such as across the oceans), we will indeed require the services of one such professional to help our dreams become a reality.

Now, I would be so bold as to wager that the majority of people who work as travel agents don't get a whole lot of experience in the task of organising travel for people with a disability, lest we forget that we are a minority in this big wide world. As some people (no matter the profession) are not agreeable with doing anything outside of their black and white outlined duties, others will not make you feel like anything you ask is a bother at all. I would recommend that you source an agent that you believe you can trust to do what they say they will do. In my experience, I have found that it is best if I source and book accommodation that is suitable for my needs, contacting the hotel directly to be certain of what they claim as wheelchair friendly accommodation – this way, I have no worries or concerns about something that should be pure enjoyment. The agent is left only to book the flights, travel insurance (including my wheelchair) and the necessary airport arrangements (outlined later in this chapter) that will make my holiday straightforward. While it is easy to blame others for what happens or should have happened, we all know that ultimately, we are solely responsible (like it or not, that is the truth). Which is why, I will persist until I know for certain that all arrangements have been confirmed.

FLASHBACK

A friend and I had organised a stop-over for two nights in Zurich, Switzerland. Even after confirming all of the details with my agent again and again about accessible rooms, we still had a mix-up with the hotel in Zurich. Fortunately, the hotel was able to relocate the person (who did not have a disability and was assigned the wheelchair-accessible room into another room so that we could use it instead. The moral to this story is that you need to be very clear about your needs and confirm your requests until you are certain - there needs to be no doubt in your mind.

Oh, yes, I forgot to mention that it might be wise to consider choosing a country to visit that has previously held the Paralympics. It makes sense that if they have held this auspicious event; the city will have needed to have installed certain strategies to allow it to be seemingly wheelchair friendly.

TIDBITS

- There are a lot of blogs on the internet written by people with a disability and their various experiences they have had in different countries around the world.

- Also, looking up the countries' organisations for people with a disability will give you quick facts about access and various concerns.

- You just might also find a book (on the internet) written specifically about travel within a country for people with a disability, such as *Easy Access Australia* written by Bruce M Cameron in 2000.

- I also find the 'Eyewitness Travel Guides' – A Dorling Kindersley Book, helpful in terms of information about access to points of interest and such. They really do cram pack their books and are great for those of us who get a lot out of photos and all things visual.

Of course our primary concerns are with getting around, bathrooms and accommodation.

There is one thing that might take a tonne of stress out of your travelling, and that is a leg-bag (indwelling catheter). It will mean that you won't need to worry about hydration and finding a bathroom, you won't need to count the clock all day long which will mean that you can literally just sit back and enjoy your holiday. And for those of us who could not stand to use a leg-bag, I would suggest that you never, ever go past any sort of bathroom at all.

I just want to thank all of my friends and family who have helped make it possible for me to access inaccessible events, experiences and locations, thank you for being You and seeing possibilities, not problems.

bit three - Packing

Ok, let's start with the job of packing our suitcase. It always pays to include extras, both medication and toileting supplies. After all, you never know when you might have to stay extra days due to flight changes or delays. I usually allow enough extras for approximately one week. That way, I know that I will have time to make contact with an organisation (in that country) to get me some more supplies, should there be need.

Sometimes in life, with anything, we become so familiar with something that we often miss the signs. Learn from my mistakes.

FLASHBACK

In January 2008 I was in England for a few days and discovered that I had contracted a Urinary Tract Infection. I could have picked this up sooner had I been more observant of my body and the things that were happening. Just a note on symptoms while we're on the subject, at first when an infection is a new experience the symptoms are like resounding church bells in your kitchen – very loud and alarmingly clear. Over the years though I have noticed that the symptoms become more subtle and less obvious, making it easier to miss or ignore them. But, let's get back to the story. Fortunately, I had some very beautiful and dear friends in England who drove me to the outpatients section of a local hospital where we waited for about two hours before being seen by a doctor and finally getting a prescription for the necessary antibiotics. Not the way to spend your holiday. But you still need to survive the next three to four days with the infection, because that is how long it takes for the medication to kick in. So, until the time when my body went back to normal, I went through catheters like some girls go through chocolate (Myself included). I was using twice the amount of catheters I usually did in a day as I was going to the bathroom almost every single hour. My poor hands were as dry as sandpaper from the frequency of bathroom visits. Moral to the story, pack extra!

Please allow me to take a moment here to acknowledge two very caring and generous people in my life – Mr and Mrs Cappuccino; to whom nothing is ever too much trouble. I lost my boyfriend, but they lost a son. I could not wish more for any two people in this world than I do for them.

But, back to the point – catheters.

Let me tell you about a little gem that I choose to use when I travel. It is called the SpeediCath Compact. Now, I believe this little pocket-rocket came to town, in Australia, in around 2004, but I don't know if many people know about it. It is about the same size as a lipstick, thereby taking up about half the space of a normal catheter in our chair bag or suitcase. It comes pre-lubricated and is fuss-free. It is not cheap, yet it has a couple of good pluses, so you weigh up the options for yourself (Heehee).

www.coloplast.com/products/urologyandcontinencecare/speedicath/productandaccesories/speedicathcompactcatheter

In my Carry-On luggage:

All medication (keep in original bottle) + letter
Catheters (as many as I can fit)
Gel
Gloves (fill a zip lock bag)
Suppositories (remove from box + put into zip lock bag)
Wipes (enough for a few days)
Change of skirt/trousers/underpants

Since getting sand in my castors on my holiday in Mauritius, I will not be caught out without a set of spares and tools again, ever! On the second last day in Mauritius I found that one of my castors was physically seizing up, so I was forced to ask my friend to help move the chair as it was impossible for me to do it myself. If you are anything like me, this will be a very challenging thing for you to do – ask for help that is. It was frustrating as all hell, but hilarious too. So now I make sure that I throw a few tools into the main suitcase (so I don't get in trouble with Customs) to keep me out of any 'sticky' situations, hee hee.

<u>Items I carry in the main suitcase:</u>

A spare inner tube
Allen keys for the castors and brakes,
Some spare nuts for the castors,
A tool that allows me to remove the castor stem from its casing and,
A few spare rings to repair the back rest lever, (I have found that these stretch over time and will tend to break at the most inopportune moment).

Anything that comes in a box (like gloves, suppositories) I remove and put them into zip-lock bags so that I can spread them around the case in amongst my clothes – I have found this method the best in terms of space-saving.

bit four – the Check-in

When I check-in for a flight, there are a few points that will need to be re-confirmed to ensure that all goes as planned. Of course, when things don't go as expected it is natural and easy to become flustered or frustrated, however, that usually does not benefit the situation.

If you experience hiccups, let me say this. A lot of things can be sorted by respecting the staff member in front of you, respecting their responsibilities, and focusing on the desired outcome.

<u>TIDBITS</u>

- For flights that are under 6 hours I was informed by a stewardess that *most planes do not have* wheelchair-accessible bathrooms, *nor do they* keep an aisle chair on board.

- The last thing I do before boarding the plane is access a bathroom one last time. Personally, I also avoid drinking fluids for about one or two hours prior to arriving at the airport so that I know there is very little liquid in my bladder before I step onto a plane.

- Request a seat near the window (for domestic flights) as it is easier for the other customers to climb over people who can move their legs out of the way.

- Request a seat on the aisle (for international flights) so that you can access the bathroom with minimal interference to other passengers.

- Confirm that all *wheelchair assistance* has been requested at all airport stops on your journey.

- Enquire when and where *your wheelchair will get its own luggage tag?* Put it somewhere you won't misplace this tag!

- Confirm that an aisle chair has been requested on all aircrafts *for accessing on-board bathrooms.*

- Confirm that you will be transferring into the aisle *chair at the door of the aircraft.*

- When you arrive at the gate, *make yourself known* to the staff and ensure that you are transferring at the door of the plane again. I know it feels like you're repeating yourself, but in my experience, it is necessary.

- It is only at the door of the plane that *I ask about putting my chair in to their overhead luggage compartments,* because they can see how compact the chair is. Of course this option is only possible if there is indeed space and it will depend upon *how* you are asking and *who* you are asking. The only person who can make that decision is the head of the flight crew. I remind them that this chair is my legs and that if the chair is damaged, then I might as well turn-around and fly straight home. Most of them understand.

- Confirm that when you arrive at the destination, your own wheelchair will be brought to the door of the plane so that you can transfer into it directly. This means that there is less chance of damage to your metal legs (wheelchair).

bit five – the Aisle chair

Next, I want to tell you a bit about the aisle chair onboard the aircraft.

I want to warn you that aisle chairs are not always kept on board planes – you must request it (I know I have said this before).

You need to be aware that the aisle chair that is used for us to board the plane DOES NOT stay on the plane – it belongs with the airport and stays at the airport for other customers to use. The airline uses a separate aisle chair, which is why it is vital to ensure that the airline has one on board.

Once you are fully strapped down, the staff will usually get you on the plane by going forward, lifting your wheels in the front onto the plane (like how you would lift a pram) and then spin around so that they can reverse you down the aisle and stop right next to your seat – so the transfer will be a sideways movement. This is also how they take you off the plane, but the only difference is that you will leave the plane last. In my experience though, at least one crew member will stay with you until your chair arrives.

There has been one occasion though when the staff members manoeuvring the aisle chair had started to turn the chair around and reverse up to the plane when I quickly suggested that if they did it that way, I might be on the floor before they knew it. I recommend that you are always alert to what is happening. After all, you are the expert when it comes to the public sector.

So, with that in mind, the very *first thing* I do when I board and am seated, is ask a steward/ess to tell me when they have located the on-board aisle chair and have seen it for themselves. *This is so important, I cannot stress it enough!*

I cannot accept an answer like "I think so" or "I'm sure it is", because those statements make me feel scared that the staff have not actually seen the aisle chair. I need to feel 100% satisfied that the person telling me that it is on board has actually seen it with their own two eyes. Now, I understand that this is the busiest time for them because they are trying to get everyone on board, sorted and seated. I appreciate that they don't want to stop what they are doing to find a silly little aisle chair. That is why it is necessary for you to help them understand why finding the aisle chair is necessary. Help them understand that you will need to access the bathroom at least twice during the flight, and that should no aisle chair available, that you cannot be held responsible for what might happen. Now that I have said that, I want to tell you that I have never had a problem at all, however you know what happens when you're not prepared – things go wrong just because they can.

As soon as I know the aisle chair is onboard, I inform them that I will need to access the bathroom during the flight. I usually try to give them an idea of how many times that will be and then ask them for their assistance in order to make that happen. You may need to tell them about your disability to explain the circumstances. Be very clear that they understand it is the only way you can reach the bathroom. Any decent human will respect your rights to access a bathroom and willingly assist you. It is part of their job, yet don't get them in a bad mood as it will affect your flight. I also want to inform you that regardless of whether I am flying with a friend or not, I always ask the staff to assist me with the aisle chair.

The aisle chair itself is very, very small with a seat that is about 30cm x 30cm. It cannot be self-propelled. It has foldable foot plates and armrests that fold up. It has two belts that cross over your body and click in place to make very sure you are going nowhere in a hurry. Actually, I feel like I am going to fly into outer space, the way they strap me down.

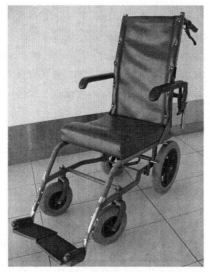

The aisle chair

Wheelchair lift at an airport

bit six – Sitting on the plane

I thought I would talk about sitting on the plane while we were at it. Some people take their chair cushion and get the staff to put it on their seat and then they transfer onto it from the aisle seat. You can choose to do this or not. When I was first in a chair, I was told this is what I had to do, yet I have since found that so long as I move from side to side in the chair and/or do some pressure relief (by lifting myself up off the chair) my skin seems to be just 'fine and dandy'. But your skin may be different to mine, so this is something you need to work out for yourself.

bit seven - Transferring

Let me talk to you about transferring for a second.

You will need to make a 90 degree transfer from the aisle chair to your seat on the plane. Be sure the staff get the aisle chair as close as possible as it will make the transfer easier. Most seats in economy have arm rests that will lift, making the whole transfer process a little easier. In Business Class you will have enough room to get the chair right next to it. So there is only a 45 degree angle.

Regarding transfers into plane bathrooms, I touch on that subject later in this chapter when I talk about 'bathrooms'.

bit eight - Airplanes

Airplanes themselves really don't have to be so scary. There are a lot of points to talk about here so let's jump on in.

First thing is first, the only real difference between all the different airlines in the world, are the people who staff them. The way you get onto the plane is basically the same, for smaller airports there will be a manually operated lift on the tarmac for us. Really small planes won't have a lift at all, you will need a person to lift you onto the plane, (Fingers crossed they brushed their teeth and use deodorant).

I have tried and tested all of the 'big name' airlines and a stack of the smaller ones, and below is a list of the ones that I can thoroughly recommend to people with a disability –

Thai airways,
JAL,
Singapore Air,
Emirates,
Air New Zealand and
Virgin Airlines.

Economy is economy, regardless which airline you are travelling, but when you put your hand even deeper into your pocket for business class there are things that stand out. I have had the pleasure of trying business class on a few different airlines, and the pick of the litter for me is Air New Zealand for so many reasons!

I cannot go past the friendliness of the staff, the fact that they are so keen and willing to serve. Add a great lounge and last, however most importantly, the bedding and you have a winning package! Air New Zealand is one of the few airlines that offer an absolutely 100 per cent lie-flat bed, complete with mini mattress, duvet and a truly decent pillow that won't give you a stiff neck by the end of your flight. I have noticed that if you can put your feet up during your flight, you will not have to worry about swelling, back aches or fatigue and you will almost walk off that plane as fresh as you walked on. Worth every dollar, I say. Bottom line – if I had my choice of any airline, I would only travel with Air New Zealand.

Oh, and a huge benefit of travelling business class is that your chair can be stored in the overhead luggage compartment, instead of the underbelly of the plane. This puts my mind to rest because I know it is not going to be thrown around or pass through the hands of people who don't recognize the importance of this piece of metal. I should probably point out here that I do not have a collapsing wheelchair but a rigid-frame, titanium chair with a folding back and removable wheels. This means that my chair will fit in a lot of small spaces.

bit nine – Domestic flights

Each airline is individual and has its own policies and procedures in regard to people with a disability. I prefer to fly with Virgin Australia when flying domestically for two reasons, (1) they do bring my chair to the plane door and (2) I have never had any damage to my chair to date (touch wood). They do have a policy of flying no more than three passengers with a disability on the same plane, so you may need to be flexible with your flight dates and times. Unlike Virgin Australia, other domestic airlines in Australia have taken longer to get my chair, gave me headaches with my chair, caused unnecessary problems and basically made travelling with them an unenjoyable process in general, and this is why I am a Virgin Australia girl through and through.

I don't know who has trained or provided information/training to both the main airlines in Australia regarding people with a disability, but it is obvious to me that all of the airlines other than Virgin Australia need to review their policies and procedures again. People with disabilities will travel more if they know they can be certain of what is going to happen and that they will be treated with respect and human decency. Bottom-line, if companies don't address and make changes to improve services – they will lose customers and money.

Of course your chair will require some form of 'tagging' in order to assure that the chair does accompany you on to the same plane somewhere. This is usually done at check-in (on international flights) and at the gate (on domestic flights). But always confirm when this will happen to ensure that it actually does occur.

When you reach your gate, you will need to make yourself known as you will be one of the first to enter the plane. The staff at the gate will not approach you; they have a lot of things on their mind. You will need to be assertive and make yourself known because the staff will need to ensure they get the aisle chair for you. When you are travelling with someone, that person will usually accompany you at the same time. The airline staff will invite people with a disability, the elderly, and children to board the flight first, and when you reach your destination, people with a disability will be left to exit the plane last.

So, after I transfer into the aisle chair, yet before I board the plane, I ask for a couple of minutes to set up my wheelchair prior to storage.

<u>This is what I do to my chair before storage -</u>

1. I apply my brakes into a locked position on my own chair,

2. I remove the cushion (to take on board with me),

3. I fold down the back rest, and

4. Secure a strap around the body seat and back rest to ensure the chair stays safely in that same position. You could use a strap with Velcro or Occy strap (Bungee cord). I do this because of some damage that previously happened to my back rest.

5. I remind them that this chair is my legs and ask them to be as careful as possible with it; so that I can still use it when I land.

Now I prefer to be safe than sorry. I have heard some tragic stories about damage to chairs during flights and that is precisely why I speak to the people taking my chair - I endeavour always to speak to others with respect and kindness, because sour lemons get you nowhere quickly.

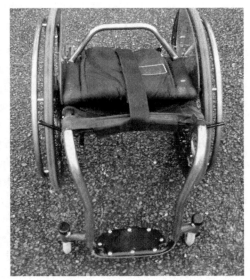

My chair wrapped ready for storage on an airplane.

bit ten - International Flights

For me, there is nothing more exciting than going to a country where everything is different – the trees and flowers, the architecture and its influences, the culture, the food, everything! Like in Europe, Asia, South America and the East in general. But, there are also times when you still want to be somewhere different, but without the whole communication struggle, like England, Canada or the USA. Whenever you find yourself sitting on the plane for more than six hours – that is when you know you are going on a real, fair dinkum, u-beaut holiday! (Don't know if I put quite enough Australian slang in that sentence, I'll look over it later).

So when I consider the differences between flying overseas to flying locally, there are only a few differences really, and they are :

1. Packing the luggage
2. Accessing bathrooms on the planes, and
2. The time difference.

bit eleven – Bathrooms on-board planes

Talking about airplanes, it is probably time we had a chat about bathrooms onboard planes. Toilets are mostly the same, but there is one thing that will make a huge amount of difference and that is – attitude. Your attitude will infect the flight staff, and that will make the difference between a comfortable flight and one that is less comfortable.

As with anything, honey will get you much farther than sour lemons. Personally, I like to acknowledge the staffs' roles and try to work with them and their responsibilities. Respecting others seems to result in positive relationships and outcomes. In my experience, attendants have opted to take me to the bathroom in the business class section, even when I hold an economy ticket. The bathrooms (in business class) are slightly larger than the ones in economy, making the transfer that bit less challenging.

Now, when you are transferring from the aisle chair to the bathroom seat, it is just a matter of getting the aisle chair as close as humanly possible to the toilet seat. In my experience, it has always worked best when there are two people involved, because – one person is in front lifting the small wheels over the ridge at the bathroom door and the second person is pushing and guiding the chair forward from behind. Of course the lid on the toilet will need to be up before you transfer and now it is all up to us. Due to the lack of space and just the design of the bathroom, it will not be possible for anyone to assist you with the transfer, but don't let that turn you off. The transfer will need to be a 180 degree transfer and there is not a lot to hold on to either. There is a handle on the wall opposite the basin and you might be able to hold onto the bench. Please don't let this put you off flying though, it is very do-able and when we put it into perspective, it is but a very small part of the holiday itself. This is what is important.

It is necessary for you to keep hydrated, however keeping it to a minimum will mean that you only require access the bathroom every four – five hours. While you're on the plane, you will still need to be conscious of your intake of fluids and the time. Obviously, it will not be convenient for flight attendants to assist you to the bathroom during particular times of the flight such as serving times, take-off and landing. For this reason it is smart for you to think about this in advance so that you are aware of how much you are consuming and when you might require assistance. It will make your life and the staffs' life a lot easier if you work together.

When you are out of your comfort zone and basically outside of your own country I have a 'back-up' plan.

One of my "back-up" plans when I am flying is Imodium, and can be bought without a prescription (in Australia). This pill causes constipation. I only do this if I will be flying at the exact same time as I should be performing my morning routine (if you know what I mean?). When you are flying to various locations within a short period of time, you might find that things start to clog up down there anyway. While I am flying I don't take the medication that I usually do in order to cause a 'result' either. I keep my watch at Australian times though, so that I can stick to my 'routines' while overseas – which minimizes 'accidents' and keeps regularity. I know, I know.... this can be awkward, like when I was in New York and had to be back in the room at 2pm for 1.5 hours. But on the other hand, it does give your travel partner freedom and space to themselves, while you needn't be worried all the time about 'accidents'.

You may choose to insert a leg bag for the entire trip and just get the flight attendants to empty it. Of course with this option, you will be able to keep hydrated and you will not need to ask attendants for assistance. But you will be stuck in the chair and it might be necessary to do some lifting so that your touché gets some relief. I have used indwelling catheters a couple of times and have had some UTIs (Urinary Tract Infection) but that doesn't mean that it will necessarily happen to you.

bit twelve – World clock

It will be necessary for you to look at a world clock (when you are planning your itinerary) to work out (1) if you will be in the air at the exact time when you would need to do your routine, and also to (2) find out what time it will be at your destination when you need to do your toilet routine. Why??? Well, because if you usually go to the bathroom in the morning at say six o'clock and if you also try to do that in say New York, then there will be an eight hour difference and your body will be out of whack! (technical term meaning disorientated and/or confused). You may very well find that your chances of experiencing an accident will be increased because you are not doing things when they are usually done. I don't want you to be in that position when you are in a strange country, so I am telling you this now in advance so that you can think about what you want to do.

bit thirteen - Hotels

In my experience a four star hotel in Australia is miles apart from a four star hotel in Paris, USA, and the UK for that matter. The one thing a friend of mine has taught me (Mrs Black Eye) is that, No expectations = No disappointments.

For one-night stays I will put up with a lot of things, but if I am staying longer, I try to get a place that is going to cater for my needs, as frustration can affect the enjoyment of the holiday.

I remember one time I booked into a YHA (in Germany) that claimed it offered disabled facilities, and it actually did. I was booked into a room that had the wheelchair-friendly bathroom directly opposite. As it was not a busy time of the year, the hostel was happy to block it off for everyone else. Yet I believe I was just very fortunate at this moment.

Also, when you travel, the rooms will never be the same, standards even vary within our great country from state to state and city to city. In a chair I have visited Adelaide, Arizona, the Barossa Valley, Blue Mountains, Brisbane, Canberra, Cape Town, Casino, Colorado, Frankfurt, Gold Coast, Hobart, Hong Kong, London, Mauritius, Melbourne, New York, North Carolina, Paris, Port Macquarie, Singapore, Sydney, Toowoomba, a safari game park, and Zurich. Please don't take me wrong here, I am not bragging, merely giving you an idea of my knowledge and experience when it comes to wheelchairs and accommodation.

Sometimes, even if the wheelchair-friendly room is not available, it doesn't necessarily mean that you won't be able to stay there. I have found that sometimes I just have to work with what I've got. For instance, I had an accessible room in a hotel I visited and at first sight it was just perfect. That was until the friend I was travelling with took a shower. The floor was completely flat, and that meant that the water did not drain well, but in fact, leaked out of the bathroom and on to the carpet in the main room area. Yes, there was a squeegee-type tool, however I can't squeegee when I am having the shower, which gives the water plenty of time to run out onto the carpet. When the water is all over the bathroom, it makes it particularly tricky to transfer into your chair when it is slipping and moving very easily. If you're not careful, you might end up on the floor too. So, instead of staying in that room for the next three nights, I transferred into a 'normal' room with a shower in the bath tub. It was very do-able and was just fine. The bathroom in that room was just as convenient and the rest of the room was perfectly fine too.

I generally do not give the responsibility of booking accommodation to my travel agent, because my needs may not be as important to them as they are to me. When I source the hotels myself, I can be assured of the type of facilities they offer, and I will not have any lingering questions so that I can really relax, right from the get-go and enjoy the holiday.

FLASHBACK

A friend and I found ourselves in Paris for a few days back in 2005. It was a last minute decision and the person who booked the hotel knew my circumstances and needs. The hotel advertised that it provided facilities for people with a disability, but I know now that it is sometimes necessary to go to the hotels website to confirm these details and even call them to double check these facilities.

The hotel that was booked, via the internet, claimed to have 'disabled' facilities, yet, after we got out of the taxi, checked-in and made our way up the lift to our room it became blatantly obvious that the only facilities this hotel offered people with a disability was the lift that we crammed into. I started laughing uncontrollably and could not stop; to be honest, that is all that I could do. We went downstairs to the desk to ensure that the room we were allocated was the correct room (that being one with wheelchair access), and the man standing behind the desk looked at us as if to say "I don't make mistakes" and simply said "bien sur" (of course). It was getting late and I didn't know where an internet cafe was, so we just stayed in the hotel and made do.

It was absolutely hilarious though, because the only way I could make it into the bathroom was in the arms of my friend, as the chair could physically not fit unless we disassembled it outside and re-assembled it inside - which took too long and was just plain silly.

The size of the room was a challenge as there was not any space either side of the double bed they gave us, so I just parked at the end of the bed, jumped on and scooted up the bed to the top. I fear most hotel rooms are like this (in Paris) unless you step up to a Five Star or higher.

The moral to this story is that some times what hotels claim and what is reality can be two very different things. Be prepared for anything, be open and see the funny side in everything and there will never be a problem you can't solve. It would have done me no good to go downstairs and yell and scream, it is not their fault that the hotel's advertisement is incorrect. However, feedback that helps them and people with a disability serves everyone.

When you arrive at your room there are some things to check while someone walking is in your room, so don't let that bellboy escape just yet. One of the first things you might like to do is locate the tea and coffee facilities to ensure they are within reach. It might be an idea to find out what else is stored out of your reach, like the towels, extra pillows, rugs, and not forgetting the shower head. Scan the room in case you require any furniture to be relocated and ask your case to be put on a chair or something that will put it at waist/chair level.

While a lot of hotels in Australia have a walk-in shower (in wheelchair accessible rooms), they aren't so easy to come by when you are travelling overseas. In both England and the USA, you will find that they tend to have their showers in or over their bathtubs. But there are pros and cons to both. Let us take a closer look.

With the walk-in showers in hotels, more often than not, you will end up mopping up the excess water that spills over the miniscule lip they have designed. I have found that they also have ridiculously small, painted wooden slat seats in them that fold down from the wall. I have a pretty small derrière (size 10), and I feel unsafe and vulnerable perched on them. They barely give me enough space to sit on it, and I would definitely suggest you hold on to anything while you are sitting, because they usually have an enamelled surface, and when mixed with water and suds, can become particularly slippery. More than once friends have heard me squeal from the bathroom because I have been slipping off the seat.

(By the way)........ if anyone is reading this that has any power in regard to building standards for people with a disability, I beg you to review these pint-sized, slippery when wet, poor excuse of a shower for a person with a disability.

I have three issues regarding hotel showers and they are –

- They are barely wide enough for a person to sit on.

- We do not have the ability to keep our bodies in place, like able-bodied people can with their feet on the ground; by using their feet, they can prevent themselves from slipping and sliding around.

- Because these seats have zero padding and force the person using it to sit straight upright against the cold, tile wall. I just want to know did anyone actually try this when it was originally created. I really have to wonder.

The fact is that there is such a wide spectrum of people with a disability, stretching from bone fractures to quadriplegia, and it is my opinion that it is near impossible for hotels to cater to one and all. It would be ideal, but impossible.

TIDBITS

- I know that I don't want to come home from a holiday and have to waste my time on bed-rest. So, because the shower chairs have zero padding - I fold up a spare towel to cushion my skin.

- My suggestions would be to get your shower items and put them within reach of your tub, lower the shower hose into the tub, get a towel for the bath tub rim and one for your chair and fold up another to sit underneath you in the tub. Again, you don't want to go home with any damaged skin.

- Now if you find yourself in a room that only has a bath tub, don't go thinking it is the end of the world. I guess you could have a make-do wash in your chair, surrounding yourself with towels, or you could give it a go and you might be surprised.

bit fourteen – Getting around

I believe the next thing to talk about is how you are going to get around when you are abroad or just escaping to somewhere different within your own country. Now, you know that I am all about independence and freedom, so one of the first things that comes to my mind is 'how can I get around?'

In our own country, getting around is fairly easy, as most of us will have our own car or at least be aware of how to get to where we want to go and who to contact to organise transport. Of course, knowing what is where and how long it should take us to get to our destination helps as well. Whereas, when we are overseas we are literally on unknown territory and at the mercy of whoever is driving the taxi at that moment. If only we could take our hand-controls with us....

Actually, I know for a fact that in America its citizens can purchase removable hand-controls that can be removed and affixed to most cars, without the expense of needing a technician to do it; I know this because I lived in Arizona and played basketball with a very cool group of guys in chairs so I got it straight from the horse's mouth, so to speak. Now, because the laws are very different even between various states in the USA, I would advise you to do some research into the area you intend visiting.

Much to my disappointment in Australia, we apparently do not deem removable hand-controls safe enough to approve their use. Our hand-controls must be fitted by an authorised organisation and you must receive certification of this to show the Department of Transport in Australia when registering your car. I want to warn you here because I am about to bitch, so if you don't want to hear it, skip to the next paragraph now. I just changed cars, that is I sold my old one and bought another used car, and the bill for removal and refitting of the hand-controls was $645........ just for the labour! Because they could re-use the equipment I was previously using in the last car, so this fee was just for the removal and fitting!!!!!! You have probably guessed already that my mouth almost fell on the floor. And when I checked to make certain that they had used my old equipment, the staff just said that prices have gone up. I thought, "gone up, that's not inflation, that's discrimination". Because I am certain that the last time I had the change over, it cost around the four hundred dollar mark.....

Yet, moving on - from sources that I have in the UK, apparently they also agree that hand-controls must be professionally installed and fixed into place in order to be road worthy. So, naturally, when travelling overseas, the next best choice is car hire. As I have not attempted to hire a car with hand-controls within either the USA or UK, I am not aware of the ease or difficulty, but what I can tell you is what I have experienced in my own country.

Now let me tell you about a little holiday I took in 2008. I was planning a holiday for a friend and I to the Barossa Valley (South Australia) followed by Hobart (Tasmania). After I organised the flights and wheelchair assistance, I decided I wanted to hire a car. So I started doing some research for hire cars with hand-controls on google. com.au and found nothing much except the run-of-the-mill car hire companies here in Australia.

So, I started making calls and enquiring about (1) if they offer cars with hand-controls, (2) where they offered these cars and lastly, (3) the cost of hire. This is what I found. Yes, some car hire companies do offer cars with hand-controls, I think I used Hertz and it was great, a breeze. No problems whatsoever. Next, I found it easier to get a car at the airport than in the CBD (central business district) for some reason, no reason given. And lastly, the only cars that offer hand-controls are a gigantic boat of a car, something like a Ford Fairlane, which of course would swallow my tiny, little red Mini in one gulp. As you can imagine, I felt a little bit out of my depth. The only other thing I will tell you is that the car that was available didn't have the same controls that I usually have in my Mini, it was the other type; in Australia there are only two types (a) the push and pull or (b) the push and pat. But, this was another aspect that made me feel uncomfortable about driving the car. But we adapt quickly us humans, don't we? I just had to think all the time about what I was doing while I was driving – but I guess that is a good thing, right!

Oh, I also want to let you know that when booking something like this you need to give them about two weeks notice, more if possible and particularly during popular holiday times like school breaks or Christmas. Actually, I even look up information regarding accessible buses too, as another option. It is quite common now to find buses providing wheelchair access in a lot of major cities, both in Australia, the UK and the USA. Remember I told you that I lived in Arizona for a while, well one of the guys that I played wheelchair basketball with didn't have a car at all and relied solely on buses; some states (in the USA) offer wheelchair access on all public transport, while in other states it appears almost non-existent. But that is another story altogether, for another book.

If I am just planning to stay in the midst of the city that I am visiting, then I won't bother with hiring a car at all. Instead, I would prefer to choose a hotel smack-bang in the middle of things so that I can just walk everywhere and save my money for fun things, like ice cream, tickets or a new pair of shoes. That way I can also walk off that ridiculously super-sized breakfast I just enjoyed too.

FLASHBACK

And, I recall a time when a friend and I went to Paris and we were walking around the streets when my worst fear became a reality. My chair felt lop-sided and I thought, "oh dear, that's not feeling right", so I felt both tyres and it all became horribly clear - I was pushing around on one full tyre and one steel rim.

So, we found ourselves in the middle of city in a country that refuses to speak English, and there we were trying to find a bicycle shop. It was an interesting experience, but not one of the best that I have had. Needless to say my high-school French didn't serve me very well, so we made our way back to our hotel and by the grace of God, managed to get it repaired.

The moral here is to get some solid tyres before you travelling overseas, especially to countries where English is not the first language and/or you are going off the beaten track. Let my stories be your lessons.

Now, don't be afraid to use trains either – just call them to find out about the stations that are wheelchair-friendly.

FLASHBACK

Now, I am going to bring up the time I went to Frankfurt, Germany with my dear friend Miss White Choc Mocha again, as I want to talk to you about my experience with getting around in Germany.

The first day there Miss White Choc Mocha and I decided to do some sightseeing outside of Frankfurt and so headed toward the train station. We ended up getting a ticket to a very old town about two hours southwest of Frankfurt. As we were attempting to board the train we saw staff hastily trying to get to us. They proceeded to tell us that we should have organised this trip two days in advance in order to warn/prepare them so that they could cater to my needs. But we were both new to Germany and we didn't know that. And to be honest, I thought our trip had abruptly ended there. I guess my face must have dropped big time because the staff changed their attitude from disciplinarian to resourceful – as they began to sort out how they could help us and make it possible.

The kind staff working on that day rang ahead to get assistance at the numerous stations where we would need to change trains and then started to help me onto the train in Frankfurt. I will never forget it and I don't think Miss White Choc Mocha will either. The kind man who was on staff on the train started pulling me onto the train from behind me while I was facing Miss White Choc Mocha. At this point I didn't really know what his intention was and when I realised it was merely to pull me from behind, I began to worry. Yet I just assumed that he had experience doing this sort of thing and trusted him. As I started sliding off the seat and getting closer and closer to Miss White Choc Mocha, I couldn't stop myself from laughing – yes, I was falling forward off my cushion towards my friend who was standing in front of me. Yet, I could not stop laughing.

Moral to this story - perhaps it is better to plan ahead so that you don't miss out on anything you want to and remember that you are the expert when it comes to chairs, don't let anyone tell you otherwise. The staff at the station informed me that they had equipment they could use, had they knew that I was coming, to board me on and off the stations.

Oh, I wanted to mention, the train from Frankfurt had wheelchair accessible bathrooms on board and were pristinely clean too, as is most of Frankfurt. Congratulations Frankfurt.

Other forms of transport such as ferries are usually accessible, as I have tried them too. In my experience, a plank or ramp is used to provide wheelchair access which is decent enough, yet don't expect an accessible bathroom too! So, locate a bathroom before boarding or go afterward – depending of course on the length of trip. Factor that into your day and work out when you need to use a bathroom again.

bit fifteen – the Snow season

When you find yourself in the middle of the snow season, as I did in Colorado a year ago, mobility can often provide more challenges than normal. While you are in your car it is easy, but when you are in your chair, the goal to get from A to B can seem near impossible.

Thankfully, in America, the towns have those snow ploughs and machines that move the snow out of the way for pedestrians and vehicles. But the people who work those snow-moving machines may not know that there is a person in a chair around, unless you make them aware. I would recommend this because most able-bodied people can just walk on top of the snow, yet we can't because our chair just sinks into it and then we get bogged down! So, perhaps these machines need to make some more pathways that connect and make getting to where we want to go achievable.

But there is more than one way to skin a cat. With snow about 2 feet deep, my friend and I thought the only way to move around was by piggy-back. That was until we saw another patron pulling their daughter along on a bob sled. We immediately looked at each other and wondered if the sled was theirs or if the resort offered it to its guests. We asked the obvious question and we were very happy to hear that they do provide them to hotel guests. All of a sudden life was a bit easier. Again, the point here is to think outside the square.

bit sixteen - Taxis

In England you have the quaint black cabs (also known as a Hackney), in America it is mostly a yellow cab, in Germany your taxi will be a Mercedes, in Japan taxis have automatic doors and drivers who wear white gloves, in South Africa there is no public form of transport, and it is generally suggested to hire a car, while in New York there are literally thousands of taxis, thus making it often faster and cheaper to walk...... but no matter what it looks like, its condition, expense or efficiency, a taxi is just another way that a person can move from place to place.

In Australia, we have taxis that are sedans, station wagons, people movers, and those very special vehicles specially designed for us people who use wheelchairs. You know, from the first time I used one of those special vehicles (built for us) I felt the love from the community..... (Bad girl Violet! Sorry, I apologise for my sarcasm. I know it is the lowest form of wit, I just couldn't help myself).

Firstly, I want to say loud and clear – *if* you can transfer independently, you don't need one of those special taxis. The taxi driver might kindly hold your chair steady but that is where his knowledge, experience and responsibility stops. It is not my intention to attack taxi drivers, I just don't want you to be disappointed and have unrealistic expectations. So, if it is not part of their job description, they won't be doing it. I guess what I just said was a bit of a generalisation, and unfortunately, I have found it to be true a lot of the time; especially when it comes to the big cities like New York, London, Sydney and Melbourne. I have even met some taxi drivers who won't even get out of their car to get your luggage for you, but, on the flip side of the coin, I have also met some taxi drivers who could not be any more patient, kind and understanding – usually you will find these types of taxi drivers in the smaller, regional places or the outer suburbs of big cities.

A taxi driver in Santa Monica let me in on some information that I thought I need to pass on to everyone else in chairs, so here it is.

After landing at LAX (Los Angeles Airport) my friend and I lined up to get a taxi to make our way to Santa Monica for a two night stopover, on the way back to Australia. You probably know by now that I am Miss have-a-chat and so I started gasbagging to our taxi driver. And it was during this conversation I was informed that it is not uncommon for taxi drivers in the area (Los Angeles/Santa Monica) to avoid taking people in chairs as passengers. Apparently it has to do with a lot of bad experiences by a number of taxi drivers, mine included. According to this taxi driver it is not uncommon for people with a disability to soil the seats and/or leave an unpleasant aroma due to their lack of hygiene. My taxi driver went on to tell me how he had to spend an hour one day scrubbing the back seat of his car because of this very experience. I have to say that I was gob-smacked when I heard this and insulted that I could experience discrimination because of what someone else had done. But, if that has happened more than once, then I can see their point.

Moral to the story - I would recommend (a) not mentioning that you are in a chair when you book the taxi and/or (b) be well groomed to show others that you care for yourself. Hopefully that will put their mind at ease. I love talking to people and it is so interesting what you can learn.

When I was in London a couple of years ago a friend and I did most of our sight-seeing and shopping on foot, as we stayed pretty central to most things. Yet sometimes we might need the service of a cab/taxi to get us where we want to go, and I want to tell you that you can access black cabs if you have a friend with you. I say that you will need a friend, as mostly, the drivers won't want to get out of the cab and sometimes you only have a couple of minutes to get into the cab because of where it has stopped. But let me tell you how you can get into a black cab.

The doors on black cabs have the capability to open to a full ninety-degree position – the driver can release the strap in the door which allows this. With your friend positioned behind you, get your castor wheels up onto the floor of the taxi. Yes, this is incredibly high and yes, you will need your friend to help with this manoeuvre. However, once your castor wheels are up there (on the floor of the cab), it is a simple matter of getting your friend to lift and move you and the chair into the cab. Obviously, you will need to leave your brakes off, duck your head and lean forward during the pushing motion. You can also hold the sides of the cab to help with getting the chair inside. After you have done this a couple of times, it will literally be a breeze for both of you and the taxi driver will be amazed! And when you are sitting inside the cab, you may or may not wish to transfer into the seat next to your friend. Be mindful that when you are in your chair in the black cab, there are no restraints so I always put my brakes on, grab onto to the cab and have my friend hold the chair as well. No, this is probably not something your occupational therapist will tell you to do, but in a perfect world our needs would be catered for, which is why we sometimes have to work with what is right in front of us.

Personally, when I need the services of a cab/taxi, I do not ask for one of those specially-designed vehicles for a person in a wheelchair. And the only time I would suggest you get one is if you cannot easily transfer out of your chair and into a car seat. "Why not?"

Well, let me give you a few reasons.......

Firstly, because you are requesting a specific type of vehicle, it can take ages for this vehicle to become available, as there are not a lot of them on the road. Secondly, the whole process of getting into the taxi, getting the chair locked down and then doing the reverse at the destination can seem to take forever. I know that the drivers have to ensure they do everything correctly in order to make us safe, but gees ... it is a slow process – especially if the driver is inexperienced with this equipment. Thirdly, there is the fact that we (the people in chairs) are separated from the rest of the passengers who are most probably our family/friends. And lastly, I won't even mention how it might impact a person psychologically; sticking out like a sore thumb, isolated and different to everyone else!

I have found that the quickest and easiest taxi to use is a station wagon; the taxi driver can just throw the chair in the back still intact, which minimises time and hiccups. With a station wagon I just transfer into it, take the cushion with me, ensure my brakes are locked into place, fold down the backrest and Bob's your aunty! (Grins).

If the taxi that turns up is a sedan, it is not too much more difficult. It is the same process as the above but you just need to pull off the wheels too and then get the taxi driver to throw it all in the boot. Let's remember that not a lot of people, let alone taxi drivers, have had experience with a wheelchair; so don't go getting all frustrated because they don't know what to do with the chair or how to put it together. If you are travelling with a friend, after the first few times the whole break-down routine can be pretty quick.

After all, it really is not rocket science!

TIDBITS

- This is only a personal opinion but I think brands like TiLite and RGK are more compact than a lot of other wheelchairs, thereby making them easier to travel with.

- There are moments when we all need a helping hand, when you reject a person's offer of assistance, do it nicely so that they offer again.

- Consider the terrain of the country/place you are visiting. When I went to South Africa I chose to fit BMX tyres as I had planned going on safari.

- Consider how you will carry your personal items when on foot, so to speak, eg: to keep your passport, money and such secure. I do not keep money or important documents in a backpack, that is just inviting trouble if you ask me.

- Do they speak English in the country you are visiting and how can you get repairs done to your chair should something go wrong? Remember Murphy's Law?

- I always ask the taxi driver if they mind if I sit in the front seat, as it is awkward and harder for me to transfer into the back seat. They usually don't have a problem at all.

- Before I actually choose a destination, I really do a stack of research which later allows me to relax and really enjoy the whole experience.

- When I purchased travel insurance, I was able to increase my luggage item limit to cover my wheelchair. Of course I had to provide paperwork that verified the monetary value of my chair. How much it will cost will depend directly on the value of your chair, it cost me an extra $180 to cover my wheelchair that is valued at $AUS4500. I have heard some really shocking stories, so I don't travel without it, but that is my choice. Your chair is like a pair of shoes that you don't want to replace too often.

- Learn from my mistakes and take some tools for your chair. I talk more about this in the section on 'packing'.

- Some cushions require special treatment when flying eg: the egg-shell cushion. Talk to a professional at a seating clinic or your local disability organisation. They will know. Otherwise you would have received instructions/information with your cushion when you purchased it in the beginning.

- I have never used solid tyres, yet they sound like a practical solution when travelling – it is one less thing to worry about when we are in a foreign country! I know I am going to consider them next time I travel overseas!

- If you really plan in advance, you will probably be able to get a local disabled parking permit in the country you are visiting.

- Part of your identity now is educator as the general public have no training or knowledge of wheelchairs or their users, only what they see, hear and experience; we can teach and influence others – positively and negatively. Just like when we see or hear about football players behaving badly.....

bit seventeen – travel websites

Unfortunately I don't have enough space in this book to list all of the websites that contain any sort of information/advice on travel (for pwad) but below is a list of websites that I have found and are useful.

Name a location anywhere in the world (specify handicap access) and this site will not only list all of the bathrooms, but will tell you if it is clean, its condition, and the opening hours to boot – www.thebathroomdiaries.com/search.html

Your one stop travel source – www.wheelchairtravel.com

This site helps with everything to do with travelling to Australia, around it and finally going home - www.amazingaustralia.com.au/disabled_wheelchair_friendly_travel.htm

Here is another website that will give overviews from people who have travelled within the major cities of Australia – www.accessibility.com.au/city

e-Bility.com is a one-stop accessible website for people with a disability - www.e-bility.com/aboutebility.php

Loads of helpful links and stories of people who have travelled – www.able-travel.com/links/travel.htm

Specialising in wheelchair friendly and accessible tours, safaris and travel within Africa – www.access2africasafaris.co.za

Need an accessible cab in London? Look no further – www.cabguide.com

This site has most of the world covered when it comes to accessible travelling - www.disabledaccessholidays.com

Wheelchair Accessible Holidays in Thailand - www.members.ams.chello.nl/danblokker/index.html

Accessible France, Italy & Spain – www.yourfrenchconnexion.com

Thailand Holidays – Jai Dee Holidays – www.jaideeholidays.com

Accommodation in Tuscany
www.agriturismo.net/accessible-holidays
www.tuscany.net

This site would love to plan your wedding in Italy, or just a holiday to Italy - www.accessibleitaly.com

Imagine a wheelchair accessible motor home (South East England) that is purpose built – www.nirvanarv.com

This site solves the private transport needs of residents and visitors to the United Kingdom - www.wheelchair-travel.co.uk

Wheelchair accessible motor home for travel within New Zealand – www.mobilitymotorhomes.co.nz

Accessible Auto Rentals - Self drive wheelchair accessible transport in Australia www.wheelabout.com

Learn how to access Sydney. Headed up by another wheelie, so you know the knowledge & information is spot on – www.globalaccess.com.au

I hope you get out there and have a tonne of fun travelling!

Violet

Chapter three

A place to call home

bit one – it won't happen overnight, but it will happen

There are two important factors that will determine your length inside those white walls (the hospital) and these are (a) the availability of wheelchair-friendly accommodation, and (b) proficiently managing your personal care (ie: bladder and bowels).

Those who only need superficial changes to their present home end up leaving sooner than those needing to apply for a completely new place to live. From personal experience (and stories from friends) I know it will be quicker to find something for yourself through the rental market rather than waiting for accommodation provided by the state housing authorities, regardless of which country you reside in. If you are dependent on the government, accommodation is allocated on a priority basis and it will take at least one year before you have your own place to live.

After completing the rehabilitation process I chose to discharge myself from the Stoke Mandeville Spinal Unit in Aylesbury, UK and return to Australia to a tiny hostel (YWCA) in a small town northwest of Brisbane, called Toowoomba. The staff at the hostel were most kind and accommodating in every aspect, and the hostel itself was very wheelchair friendly, allowing me my independence and giving me a way to leave the hospital and start my life again without endless waiting and anxiety. Of course, it is better if you can move into a place or area where you have support (emotional and physical), but it is possible to survive without it, as I did. I want you to really comprehend that you already have all the resources that you need, inside you right now! You are enough, right now!

I want to tell you right now that all you need to do is take things step by step by step, and know that you will get where you want to be in the end. Pantene says it oh so well, 'It won't happen overnight, but it will happen'!

bit two – Buy or Rent?

When considering to buy or rent, there are only three (3) aspects that will make or break the deal, these are the entrance, toilet and the shower. Later in this chapter I will be going through these points in much more detail.

Of course you could 'nitpick' about a lot more areas in a house if you really want to, but that will only sabotage your objective. And if that is the case, then you will recognise that perhaps you are in fact not ready for this step. As far as I'm concerned most structures within a house can be managed, except for the toilet, shower, and entrance; these facilities need to be suitable to fulfil their purpose.

If you think that because of your disability you can't live in a house, and thereby you are destined forever to live in an apartment/unit then you are playing small. By playing small, your mind is closed to ideas, alternatives and options. You are pilling more restrictions and more limits on yourself. Whether you want to go back-packing in India or buy a penthouse in Hawaii, there is always a way when there is a desire. Open your mind and you will find that anything is possible, it just depends on how badly you want it! In truth, that is always the bottom line.

As for me, post injury, I have resided in a few different types of residences. In the beginning I was renting a room in a YWCA (a women's hostel). While it was not the homeliest of places, it did provide for my physical needs, if nothing else. The board and meals were included in the one price, it was very reasonable and simplified my life. Linen was provided, and the sheets changed weekly. The hostel had laundry facilities on site, a common room with books, piano, pool table and television. Both bathrooms had wheelchair access and were enormously roomy. The management even allowed me to hire a shower chair and keep it in one of the bathrooms on an ongoing basis, and my room was right next door to the bathroom, which was perfect. All in all, it was pretty darn good.

Now I want to talk about our other option, renting.

Next, I rented a single bedroom unit in a high rise that was right on the beach. It was nice to have a space that was completely my own and meant that I could run the washing machine any time of the day or night, which is sometimes necessary if you happen to have an 'accident' in the wee hours. It did mean that I needed to get a cleaner to do minor housekeeping duties every week, particularly the vacuuming. But who wants to be doing those boring jobs anyway. I liked the fact that it had secured parking and entry, and that I could also carry my groceries from the car to my room completely undercover. There weren't really any bad points, except that I could not get a pet at that time.

Since then, I have lived in two very different houses. The first house had steps at the front and a couple here and there throughout the house; the second, has ramps on the exterior, but is completely and utterly flat inside. I have to say that I definitely prefer the latter. Yes, it is tricky getting the groceries or anything that is larger than my lap inside the house (up the ramp), but it is not impossible. Especially if you can co-ordinate your grocery shopping on the same days that your cleaner visits. Yes, you will have to work out a way to get your garbage from inside the house to the wheely bin (outside), and then work out how to move the wheely bin from near the house to your roadside and back inside, but it is all very workable. Maybe there are some teens or a retired neighbour in your area that could do this job on a weekly basis for a few dollars?

You will also have to pay someone to do your lawns, clean the gutters and windows, general cleaning, but it is worth it. Maybe you could organise something with your neighbour, or perhaps you are fortunate enough to have people who care for you that live nearby. There might even be something that you could do in return for them. It is amazing what you can come up with when you start thinking 'big', or thinking about possibilities rather than obstacles/ problems.

The feeling of pride, self-worth and respect that you will get from being independent far outweighs all other factors.

As anyone that knows me will tell you, I am a person that will talk to just about anyone, a 'gas bagger' I guess. I genuinely love meeting new people and care about others. So I have no shortage of people who offer their assistance, should I need it at any time. But, if you are not as outgoing as I may be, I would suggest start by smiling at neighbours when you see them and build to speaking to them, stepping outside of your comfort zone sometimes brings wonderful surprises.

It is also handy if you happen to get phone numbers of one or two of your neighbours, should they go on holiday and need someone to water the plants or hold their mail or whatever. There might also be moments when you might need their legs to change a light bulb or reboot the power to the house. After this happened to me a few times I decided that I had to find out if I could organise for an electrician to install a safety switch inside the house, at my level. And it was possible, so I did. This is one less thing I need to worry about now should something like that happen again.

It is always smart to be prepared with a torch, some candles or lanterns in the house. Oh, and have something in the pantry that you can eat without cooking or defrosting. We lost power to our house one night and we didn't have anything to eat, but then we remembered that we had one of those gas mini-grills in the pantry. So we fired it up and cooked on that. Think outside the square. (Heehee).

Now, I want to get back to the topic and discuss one of the three aspects of a house that need to be appropriate and accessible.

bit three – the Entrance

Even if there is a whopping big step at the entrance of your residence, you have a couple of alternatives to look for.

- Look in the garage, the step in there might be smaller or it might be possible to put a wooden ramp that can permit access.

- One of my friends lives in a house with a gigantic step at the front door and when I visited her I wondered how the heck she got into and out of her house? But after a demo and practice, I got inside too. It is the same skill that you will learn in rehabilitation – get in front of the door, lift your castor wheels up onto the step, reach forward and use the door frame to pull yourself up. Sure, the first few times are going to stretch you, but if you give up that easily then you may as well just throw yourself over a balcony somewhere right now (please laugh now).

When you are considering a house or unit, whatever, I want you to take a moment to stop and think about the environment and what it might be like day-in, day-out, week in, week out. Only then can you decide if the house is appropriate for you. Consider the practicality of the house, and decide if that is something you are prepared to live with day-in and day-out. I want to tell you about one house that I lived in to show you what I mean. I lived in this gorgeous Balinese-styled house and going from my bedroom into the en-suite there were two small steps. They were very small and accessible. When considering this house I did not think about those moments in the middle of the night when you need to go to the bathroom. There were a couple of chances when I could have gone head over feet out of my chair because I was not completely awake. Don't make your life harder than it has to be inside your own home, you will get enough challenges outside in the world.

bit four – the Bathroom

Regardless of the size or lack of size in the bathroom, there are a number of ways you can get onto the lavatory seat. The easiest way will be positioning yourself (by this I mean you are your chair and you) right up close, at a 45 degree angle. However the seat is still approachable at a 90 degree angle too. The hardest of course is at 180 degrees, yet with practice even this is possible and I will say now, this will be necessary if you want to fly in a plane at any time.

Putting rails onto the walls will make the transfer easier, and taking away any doors will also create more space. In my experience, sliding doors are the most convenient. They are a huge space saver and are easier to close than regular doors. So to me they are my first choice.

My favourite transfer is from my left side, even though I am right-handed. After putting the chair into a 45 degree angle, I hold onto the push rim and lift myself to the end of my cushion, put my feet flat on the ground, place my left hand onto the seat of where I want to go to (so that when I transfer it will be next to my left leg) and put my right hand firmly under my right cheek. I lean toward the seat and complete the transfer. Be confident when you do a transfer, none of this half-hearted business or else you will most surely end up on the floor.

In the transfer back from the toilet to my chair I place my left hand onto the seat near my left cheek and my right hand firmly on the far side of my cushion so that I have enough room to land on the cushion and make the transfer. You will need to be leaning towards your chair prior to the manoeuvre.

On occasion I will use the cistern to help with a transfer. It can be utilised in both transfers on and off. Give it a go, see if you like it, beware old toilets though – they might not be that sturdy anymore.

When transferring onto any toilet seat be sure to completely clean the seat beforehand. You could use antibacterial hand wipes or get a handful of toilet paper and add water and liquid soap as an alternative.

Any physiotherapist will advise you the importance of the position of both your feet and your head and I want to back up this claim. I find it especially true in the water – if my head is back in the water, my feet will be up towards the surface and vice versa. Yet don't take my word for it, try it yourself and see.

Most public toilets will not provide soap and may even be without toilet paper, in this instance, I will use the items I keep in my car.

Following is a list of <u>items I keep in my glove box</u> or inside the car -

Anti-bacterial hand wipes
Face cloth (as a mini hand towel to use only in bathrooms)
Face cloth (use when raining, to clean tyres before putting then into your car).
Garbage bags x 2 or 3
Gloves (in a zip lock bag)
KY Gel (small)
A sanitising liquid for your hands in bathroom
Spare change of bottoms (skirt/ trousers)
Towel (to sit on if necessary)

As for your home bathroom, you could go the whole hog, so to speak, or you could live life pretty 'normally' – for lack of a better word. As I have probably mentioned before, I didn't want to live in a fully handicap-adapted home, so I have done the minimal alterations that still allow me to live comfortably, physically and psychologically.

My toilet

I had a long stainless steel rail installed on one side of the toilet wall and it doubles as a place for towels and such. Then I had my renovator remove the shower screen door and install a rod for a shower curtain and that is it. (Photo in coming pages) If my shower had a really big old lip on it then of course I would need to rethink the whole shower scenario. Finito. That's all folks. Have a look at the photo on the left.

The wash basin in my bathroom is not really wheelchair-friendly, but it is low enough for me to reach over, and I position myself side-on and for now, it is just fine and dandy!

If your sink is completely inappropriate, I would suggest you look at a pedestal basin. They are old school (1940ish I think), but absolutely lush and our chairs can push right underneath them so they are perfect. Check that the taps are easy to reach. Make sure you can see yourself in the mirror. Mine comes right down to the sink anyway, so that might be one idea for you. Especially if you have other people to consider that use the same mirror. The towel racks here are great, it looks like a fan and they have individual spokes. Next to the toilet I put two big weaved baskets to store all of my personal management items. So, it really can be that simple.

bit five – the Shower

I have probably mentioned this in another chapter so I will not go into a lot of detail here. It is possible to access most showers, regardless of how they come. I have tried my fair share of different showers, here in Australia and across the world, and I have seen some doozies. When travelling, either inside or outside of Australia, the most common form of shower is the one that is found on the wall above a bathtub.

So, let me spend a couple of minutes talking about this kind of shower and how best to attack it. I know that I have said this before, yet it is so true, "Everything is difficult in the beginning". Then after the first attempt, while still in rehabilitation, I came to the conclusion that getting into a bathtub was not nearly as daunting at it first seemed.

When dealing with showers above bathtubs, there are only really two courses of attack, one I would do and another I would never do in a million years - (1) transfer directly onto the teeny-weeny, almost non-existent rim of the bathtub or (2) transfer onto a tiled area at one end of the tub and then lower yourself down into the tub. Let me clarify the reasoning behind why I would never attempt to do a transfer onto one of those free-standing, old English bath tubs – (a) it is not stabilized or secured into position by anything - meaning there is a possibility it could tip, (b) this type of bath tub usually provides nothing to grip or hold onto for security or balance, (c) because the rim is so miniscule we would be playing a balancing act on it, (d) what if the bath moved? It would be a different story if someone was to lift you in and out of this type of bathtub, but this is definitely not the type of bathtub I would have in my house. I also doubt that any occupational therapist would suggest this as a safe option either.

I know the topic here is 'showers', but while we have touched on the subject of bathtubs I thought I might as well finish off this sub-topic, what do you think? So, just quickly....

When I transfer directly onto the rim of a bathtub, I always place a towel over the rim of the bath to prevent any possible damage. I don't know if you've noticed (heehee) but these days our derrieres don't have a huge amount of padding on them, so they need all the help they can get. In the beginning, it would be smart to have someone with you while you perform the transfer until you feel confident in your skills. I've never wanted my house to look 'disabled' so I have never been a big fan of 'rails' or the like, yet nowadays, I do have one in the bathroom near the toilet. Perhaps as we age, their presence and aesthetics can be overlooked as they ease our day-to-day activities and enhance our lives in general.

Obviously, transferring into a bath tub is made easier if there is a seating area at the end of the tub, which is usually the case in hotels. Again, I would put a towel or two down in order to provide some cushioning for the derrière. The lift down into the tub and out of it is relatively simple in comparison.

Before we finish on 'tubs', I also want to mention that because I am top heavy (no, not a double D), I tend to slip n' slide all over the place when I am in a bath tub – which can be fun at times (depends if you are alone or with someone) and you probably will too. Usually, I just make certain that I am holding onto to something or someone, whichever is available (cheeky grin). Perhaps you might want one of those non-slip mats on the bottom of the tub to see if that makes any difference. I haven't tried this option yet, but you could and let me know if it works....

Ok, so let us get back to 'showers' -

Before we make our transfer into the shower/bathtub we need to ensure that everything we need, including the shower hose is within reach. After all, it would be a pain in the neck if we had to get out again.

Reminder: Two towels are best = 1x to sit on the chair & 1x dry us with.

As for me, at home, I just use a standard shower. It is located in the corner of the bathroom with one glass wall, a glass door and two tiled walls. I have had the glass door removed and replaced with a shower curtain. The shower frame has a very minute rim that is effortless to get over. I don't tend to splash water all over the place, so this is a sufficient solution for me. See the picture below:

My shower

Inside my shower I place an everyday, run of the mill plastic outdoor chair to sit on. After using a varied list of products made especially for 'disabled' people, I have found that this cheap and easy option suits me down to the ground –

- The height is similar to my chair and unlike other products I do not feel uncomfortably high,
- Because it does not have wheels I am not scared it will move when I don't want it to,
- Because it has armrests I feel safe, and
- It is easy to buy, it is not going to break the budget and usually available at most hotels when I'm travelling – just give it a clean before use.

Side track

When I first left hospital I hired one of those shower chairs and the staff at the YWCA were kind enough to let me leave it permanently in one of the female showers. I think I used it three times before I started looking at alternatives. I felt completely unsafe because I was up much higher than my own wheelchair, so I could not reach the brakes to put them on, but even when the brakes were on, I didn't completely trust it. When water is added to rubber, there is not a whole lot to feel safe about, and I definitely didn't feel safe enough to bring my legs up so I could shave them. So something had to be done about that quick smart.

But, getting back to the chair I use in the shower.

I have recently started using those outdoor chairs that are made of a plastic/metal with mesh inserts in the seat and the backrest of the chair. I thought they might be softer on the back and they are..... they are fabulous, yet they take up more space in the shower and make it awkward to turn. I am conscious about the mesh wearing and tearing over time from the day-to-day use with water. Now, if you were really worried about the chair moving around inside the shower, I guess you could get a couple of those rubber mats that have suction cups on the underside that help them stick to the tiles on the floor.

To get into the shower, I lift my castors over the rim of the shower and push in as close as my rear wheels allow me, then I apply the brakes and bring the shower chair as close as possible to my chair. Next, I lift myself up and move to the front of the cushion on my chair. Put one hand on the shower chair (my right) and one hand on my chair (my left), I should probably mention that I am right-handed. This particular transfer is made safer if I place my right hand on the shower chair and is focused on pulling the chair towards me while I transfer.

If you are still using the sliding board you were given in hospital to get from point A to point B, that is good and fine, and a great way to start. However I want to encourage you to start using it less and less before it starts to become your safety blanket. I know these transfers can seem very daunting at first, but I want to assure you that I am not a risk-taker, or a thrill seeker, and I do these transfers every single day.

I want to tell you that the sooner you transfer without a board, the sooner you take control of your life again, the more you will be able to do, the less limits you will have, and how you see and feel about yourself will lift as well. You will gain confidence, you will be able to trust yourself and you will start to feel more like yourself again! So, come on – dump that silly old board.

Now, I am going to inform you of another method that I have used to get into a shower.

This particular shower was built in the 70s, I think, because the rim on the ground was about 15 centimetres wide and at least 20 centimetres high, meaning that I could not just pop my casters over the rim because it would not fit between my castor and my rear wheel. This manoeuvre I call the Jane because replicates a Jane/Tarzan like swinging method. Now this is probably not something that a physiotherapist would recommend or even suggest, and I am only telling you about what I did as I was travelling, it was late and we had tried a number of hotels that didn't even give me access to the bathrooms. This is something I did because I was forced, there were no other options, so I had to work with what was in front of me – which is often the case because the world we live in is nowhere near 'perfect'.

Ok, so basically this is it.

Hopefully, you would have previously placed all of your cleansing products into the shower, and also taken a towel with you on your lap to the cubicle. Because a staff member would have put a clean plastic chair into the shower cubicle, all you have to do now is get in it. So you need to get your wheelchair as close as humanly possible to the shower chair, facing it. Thrust your towel over the rail and pull the short length even, so that you can hold onto both when you swing. Now that everything is in place, you need to move your feet into position and then lift and move your body towards the front of your cushion and check your feet are in the best position for your transfer. Finally, grab the two towel ends tight with one hand, and with the other hand (the one that is closest the shower chair) place it on to the shower chair where you are going and complete your transfer. And you're in.

If you attempt this type of transfer, I would advise you have someone nearby, or perhaps this is just outside your comfort zone, and that is just fine. In no way do I want to put you in any sort of danger or harm at all, just look at the situation, look at your options, take help from people, or ask for help if you are unsure, weigh up your choices, don't take unnecessary risks, and consider the risks carefully before you do anything. In the end, this is simply another option.

I cannot explain why or how, but when I try a new move or transfer, if I am alone I am more likely to succeed than if I have support around me. It could be something psychological, but maybe I don't try as hard when there is someone there waiting in the wings – I honestly don't know. This might not be the case for you, or perhaps you could tell me a story or two of your own wild transfers, either way, we will get there in the end!

Before I leave this topic I think it would be remiss of me not to talk to you about our skin. Now I know that this topic, during your rehabilitation, would have been drummed into you because it was definitely drummed into me. We were shown a lot of really horrifying and horrible pictures of real life sores and accidents, I think in an attempt to scare us into proactive behaviour. Then we left hospital and thought, 'but that won't happen to me, I'm not that stupid'. I want to add that it is actually a little scary how a little thing like a scratch can turn into weeks on bed rest if not caught immediately.

The fact is that our skin (below the level of injury) is now far more fragile than it was before, and will incur damage far more easily than it did beforehand. I liken my skin now to that of a senior community member, because the slightest thing can and does turn into something horrible sometimes, which is why we need to be more proactive than before so that we don't end up having to spend week upon week upon week on bed-rest. Having to spend time on bed-rest is limiting, a time waster, and just frustrating as all heck.

It could be as simple as buying shoes half a size too small and not noticing a mark on your heel because you're busy doing this and doing that, until one day you see a horrible looking sore. That's what happened to me, and then the doctor tells me that I can't wear shoes on that foot for 2-3 weeks; actually it was more like 4-5 weeks in the end because we heal slower nowadays. Anyway, it was embarrassing and I felt stupid. Be smart - check your skin regularly.

bit six - Handrails

I know they are not aesthetically pleasing and might make your house feel more like a hospital than a home, yet I understand the difference they can make to your everyday life. If you want handrails, why not think outside the square and see if they can't add to your décor. If you have a white shower, why not try to find a white handrail that will blend-in. Why not consider using wall-paper on your hand rail or painting it? I only have one rail inside my entire house, and it is in the bathroom right next to my toilet - I disguise it by hanging towels on it. Think outside of the box on this one, but don't let a handrail define the beautiful woman that you are, ok!!!!

bit seven - Mats

Mats in the bathroom look great, yet can really get in the way sometimes. I have one in front of the toilet and shower and I am endlessly flattening them out or jumping over them because they have scrunched up. I prefer to keep a cloth under the sink that I use to wipe the floor after I leave the shower. Yes, I am a bit of a neat freak, but I guess it also has to do with water and safety too.

When you stay in a hotel, overseas or domestically, no two bathrooms will ever be the same. I don't know why there is not a national standard that can be instigated, but the fact is, there isn't and probably never will be. There will be all sorts of differences come your way. I have learned to expect nothing and keep my mind open, not to be afraid of those things that are different, and to have faith in my capabilities!

Obviously, when you add water to rubber, there is not a lot of grip. If you are travelling with someone, ask if you can take your shower first before the floor gets way too slippery and unsafe. If you can't, dry the floor of the bathroom to prevent unnecessary slips or falls. Use an old face cloth to dry your wheels outside of the shower.

Oh, if you carry water on your wheels when you leave the bathroom, know that it will mark the carpet in your bedroom and that will be more and more visible as time goes on. These are just some things to be aware of. I personally love wooden flooring and therefore have a lot of it in my house. It hides a lot of floor marks and is very forgiving.

bit eight - Kitchens

When it comes to kitchens I have had the best and worst of both extremes. I have had ones that were totally designed for people in chairs, but had absolutely zero storage space (designed by an occupational therapist), and I have had kitchens that have had zero adaptations. When it comes to kitchens, the only two areas, in my opinion, that demand alteration are the stove and the sink. I hear you questioning why just the stove and the sink? Well, we don't want you to have to spend thousands of dollars unnecessarily, and in my experience, we can get by using the rest of the kitchen just the way that it is.

Let us consider the cupboards in a kitchen. One option is to have the cupboards extracted from under the sink, but keep the doors and have the space designed so that the builder can create a way for the doors to slide back in underneath the sink itself on either side of your legs. I saw this idea in a hotel room in North Carolina, fantastic concept. So the kitchen still looks 'normal' (I detest this word) most of the time, but is practical when I need it to be. If you are anything like me you do not want to live in a place that screams 'disabled'.

The same strategy can be used for the stove, but the storage space for pots and pans will need to be found somewhere else.... Be sure to explain to the electrician that any wires or pipes will need to be covered somehow to safeguard your legs and feet. I have seen people who did not realise that they were leaning up next to something hot, and let's just say that they were out of action for a very long time, and it definitely was not pretty.

When it comes to storage in the kitchen, I have found that drawers are the most practical for me, you will need to allow the space necessary to pull out the drawer before you actually do. One of the kitchens I have was filled with doors so I asked the builder remove them, and I found some fabric I liked, and had my dressmaker create some curtains that I hung from wire to cover the naked nooks and crannies (sounds like I'm talking about something naughty, doesn't it). You could also use this option to cover the space under the sink and stove too. This idea is very cheap and cheerful.

Obviously, if there are high cupboards in your kitchen, you won't be able to reach them. I still use them though for the items that guests use. They can get their own items down, and hopefully replace them to the same spot themselves, which saves me space for everything else down low where I can reach them.

My kitchen curtains

It is common sense anyway, but, I will point out that in the pantry and fridge the things you use the most will need to be toward the front of each shelf, as it will be (quite literally) a pain in the neck if you always have to put your chair in the exact, right position in order to reach everything you want. I like the two-door fridge/freezers the most as I find them the most convenient.

Moving heavy equipment from any location will be a pain in the neck and back (literally), so why not store it in a spot that you can reach without having to move the item too much. If I was to design a kitchen from scratch I guess I would have most of the heavy equipment eg: toaster, blender, juicer stored on top of the bench, but away from eyes behind one of those pull down or slide across shutter doors. My pantry would consist of those tall, pull out shelves. I had them once and I found them very practical.

If you have assistance with the cleaning, you will need to check that all switches (the ones you can't reach) are 'on' before your assistance leaves the house. I spent about ten minutes one day trying to turn on the switch to the kettle that I had forgotten to check before they left. It was a giggle, but you better believe I have remembered every time since.

I shouldn't have to, but I still need to remind myself to use gloves when washing up in the kitchen sink. Due the to fact that we need to wash our hands before and after every trip to the toilet, I don't have to tell you how easily and quickly our hands will dry out – particularly during the winter months. When I say that our hands will dry out, I want to tell you about what has happened to me, this is not at all unusual. Because I am always moving, always doing things and rarely sitting still, I find it time consuming and a pain in the butt to apply hand cream (mental note: must do it this year!) at all. During the winter months my hands have been so bad that it hurts me to perform a transfer. It is possible for the cracks to get so bad that they open up and sting when I finally apply the hand cream. Because the cracks are so deep, it takes days before they cease to cause me pain. So please, please, please do not be a silly girl like me, drink your water, use moisturiser on your hands, and care for your hands in the winter months, if not all year long. But, I probably don't need to tell you this because I am sure all of you put gloves on when you are washing up anyway, right? (Wink, wink).

Most Occupational Therapists will kill me for what I am about to tell you next, but for me, it works. *So, this is the official warning. Please be aware that what I am about to tell you could be dangerous and I do not advise or endorse this behaviour in any way, shape or form.*

There is no easy way for me to say this, so I am just going to say it. So here goes.

The benches are too high and I can't see directly over what I am chopping, so, I chop things like fruit and vegetables on a chopping board which sits on a tray that rests on my lap. There I've said it. Difficult items like pumpkin, sweet potatoes and such, I do actually choose to chop on the bench, but otherwise, I use a paring knife to chop on my lap. Watch out for spillage from juicy fruits, like oranges and watermelons, if your lap is not completely flat.

It is possible to lower the benches, but that might cost a little, but the only difficulty you will experience in regards to the height is when you are cooking something in the pot. You might also want to consider your partner's height, because if they are about 6 Feet tall and you are a shortie, then they will undoubtedly get a sore neck and back from bending down so much. So, I simply take it off the stove, down to a height I can see, and then return it to the heat. Fiddley, I know, but do-able. When you find yourself pouring a coffee or anything hot, pour at your side not over your lap please.

Next, I am sharing with you a very funny story that is a perfect example of the need to check things are as they should be, before they leave your house.

FLASHBACK

I usually get up at six o'clock in the morning, and when I get up out of bed, I let my babies (puppies) out for a wee wee and play. I had not noticed that the lawn mower guy had forgotten to close the gate to my backyard until I heard my dogs barking at this little old lady that was on a peaceful morning saunter pass my house. Poor lady. I felt horrible that this had happened. But, before I went out to physically remove the dogs from in front of this lady I had to put the fence and security back in place so that they could not escape again. This was a huge headache and took what seemed like forever. I had to climb over the rock-like gravel to get into my backyard, move across the grass to the gate. Manoeuvre the wide wooden plank to a point where I could reach and grasp it, close the gate and then gradually position the plank. When things like this happen, we could think that people do not care, but it could be as simple as their mind being elsewhere at the time. People are people, and mistakes will happen from time to time, and we are not perfect all the time either.

I know it is easy to get so excited about having your own space that you can lose all sense of reality, however, we really need to think about every aspect of the house/ unit before we make such an enormous and financial decision. I know how exciting and liberating it is to even contemplate finally having a place that is all yours, which is why I am going to repeat myself and ask you to come back down to reality and think about the practicalities of the home you are considering.

Perhaps considering these different scenarios might help you see through your rose-coloured glasses –

- Think about what it might be like entering and leaving the house in different weather conditions, eg: the rain, snow.

- Ponder what living there completely alone might require?

- Imagine you have just had surgery, would it still be practical?

- When you are more mature and perhaps need to change to an electric chair, would it still be practical?

- Imagine the block loses power, can you still get out of your property?

- Consider if you can close the entire house by yourself, should you be alone when it storms.

- Is there sufficient security?

- Could you physically carry your shopping from the car to inside the house by yourself?

- Can you reach the power box attached to your house?

I mention these various situations because I just want you to look at it from all angles so there are no surprises and no regrets.

bit nine - Steps

I never noticed before all the Steps are out there in the community, but now I see them everywhere! Sometimes there will be ways around them and sometimes there won't - which is why I want to spend some time with you now on this subject.

When you are new to this situation (being in a chair), all of a sudden it will feel like you've just been born again – like a baby in a whole new world. You will notice things you never ever saw before, the smallest things like a pebble can make your chair stop in its tracks and almost throw you out. Now the smallest of things, like a grate in the concrete, a change in the level of the concrete paving, a pot hole in the road, or the severity of a curb can be the difference between going out or staying in your chair.

But this is when I will tell you that it will only be as difficult or as fun as you make it! In my experience, this is the only deciding factor – how we view the world, our perspective and attitude will make the difference between misery and a full life. Steps will be a big part of our lives now, but they don't have to be the Grand Canyon of our lives. Let's take a look at them now as I share with you my various strategies and stories.

While in hospital your physiotherapist is your greatest ally, because he/she is the one who can give you the set of skills you will need for the rest of your life. It is best to make them your new best friend, pick their brain, try out as many different scenarios as possible and push the limits inside the safety of those white walls.

Well now, I will tell you that one of the skills you will acquire is the ability to climb steps.

Of course, during your rehabilitation your teachers will start you slowly, on steps that are made from wood so you can do it in the physiotherapy room. The step you will learn on is only about fifteen centimetres high, the more you do it, the more competent you will get, and the steps out in the real world won't seem so daunting.

One thing I want to tell you is that the quicker you can master this skill – the less limits you will have!

One of the houses I have lived in had one enormous step at the front. But, because I didn't like being dictated to, told where I can live and where I can't, I was determined to find a solution. I will tell you that I got around that nasty step by getting a builder to make a series of shorter steps graduating up to the top one. I asked the builder to make them deep and wide enough for my wheelchair to climb, land and climb the next step. The builder was impressed with my solution and so were various people who visited the house. Of course for this concept to work, you would need sufficient space.

My dressmaker works from her house and also has one whopping step (approx. 40-50 centimetres), at her main door. I get inside by lifting my castors up onto the house level, leaning all the way forward onto my lap, using my hands to get a sound grip of the doorframe on both sides, I literally pull myself up from a stand still position. The first few times I want you to have someone around you for support. No, 'it won't happen overnight but it will happen'.

Just like when we were younger and learnt how to ride a bike, things are always uncomfortable and awkward in the beginning. Of course, there will always be the expected crash or two, but with perseverance and practice, it all comes together in the end. This is the same for anything new in life that we are trying to conquer, whether it be learning something on a computer, a new language, how to sew, or learning to play something. Just remember the two Ps - Perseverance and Practice.

Because the world is not perfect (in terms of access), and I don't know if it will ever be, you have to know that there will be some stores, businesses and services that you will want to access, yet will not be physically able to due to three little steps. Regardless the reason, it doesn't matter, the fact is that there is zero access. The fact that there are steps is a whole other matter, and perhaps that can be fought on a local council level. Perhaps the building has been heritage listed, it might have been built before the right to access was acknowledged and advocated, or maybe it simply slipped through the system. We don't know, and to a point, it is inconsequential.

Right now, I want you to know that I have been in this predicament myself on more than one occasion, so you are not alone. I am not telling you what to do, however, you will need to consider your options, because undoubtedly, you too will find yourself in this situation at some point.

I don't know what is running through your head right now as you consider this challenge, but I have to tell you that we only have two choices here, the first is to feel defeated by the situation, walk away feeling sorry for ourselves and continue to spiral down and down each time something like this happens. If we did choose to react like this, we would work ourselves up into such a state that pretty soon we end up miserable, spiralling in a downwards motion. Frankly, this choice doesn't really do anyone any good - it doesn't make the shop owners think about access, it doesn't get people who walk by think about our right to access. There is no positive impact and this kind of thinking isn't in any way healthy for us either. Now our other option is to try to get the attention of someone inside the store or a person about to go inside, so that we too have access to customer service. Our aim is to get service, so put your focus there. Hold your head up high and you can get your desired outcome. Then go home and make a decision that this will not happen to anyone else in a chair and do something about it! Feeling pity for ourselves, we are giving our power away, but by doing something about it, we are holding on to our power.

Make contact with the store owner, council or a local member of parliament to inform them that you, as a paying member of the community, were not permitted access to this service. Try to stick only to the facts (emotions don't belong here), as you will get better results using this approach.

Step-by-step guide to complaining about access (AUST)
www.humanrights.gov.au/disability_rights/index.html

Step-by-step guide to complaining about access (UK)
www.direct.gov.uk/en/DisabledPeople/index.htm

Step-by-step guide to complaining about access (USA)- www.ada.gov

You know how I said that I had been in this same situation myself, well I want to tell you a brief story about one of these times. I was out doing grocery shopping at my favourite fruit and veg store (Yuen's) with a friend when I noticed it was lunch time. So we decided it was more convenient just to grab something while we were there. We made our way to the pie store (Dad's Pies) on the corner, only to notice that there was a big step that would be impossible for me to get up by myself. I mentioned to the staff that if I was by myself they would have lost my custom as there was no way I would have made it into the store. I knew that they had just taken over ownership of this store and renovated it somewhat, so I reminded them about the Act that came in 1980 about people with disabilities requiring access to all buildings built after that date.

To my surprise, I was driving past their store about a month or two later and I noticed that they had changed the concrete step entrance so that there were no steps, just a gradual incline. Some things in life are easily changed, while others need a lot of time and effort to get things done. Anyway, I was impressed. Congratulations Dad's Pies – you've won me over.

With the help of someone, man or woman, we can climb more than 1 step (2-10 or maybe more) if there is a rail nearby. My girlfriend from the UK taught me this one, let's call her Miss Lady Grey. I know that my friend would want me to share this tactic with you too because she loves to help people.

So, this is the process - start at the base of the steps, get onto your back wheels and have your partner (in crime), who is standing behind you, grab a hold of your bar/ handles on your chair. Together, while your helper is pulling you backwards you will need to be holding the rail with one hand and pulling your other wheel in a backwards motion with your other hand. This takes some practice but it is do-able. I will admit that I will try other options before attempting this skill, but I have used it and am thankful to have it up my sleeve. Another form of this that I was forced to use was having the helper in the front rather than in the rear. In the front they hold the frame on either side of your legs and push your chair like crazy while you are doing the exact same process as mentioned above.

FLASHBACK

I spent six or seven months between 2007-2008 house-hunting for somewhere to call home. I inspected house after house, after house without any success. Then my agent informed me she had one more up her sleeve. After pulling into the drive way and getting out of my car I noticed that there was a set of steps at the rear of the house, so I asked if there were steps at the other end of the house too? The agent reluctantly said 'yes', after she returned from her inspection. But she added that she believed we would be better off at the other end of the house and she said that she was more than willing to help me, however she could.

Now, you know that I don't take 'no' for an answer, and I'll be darned if I was going to let a few pieces of wood stop me from getting where I wanted to go. Fortunately for me, the real estate agent that showed me the house, had the same amount of determination and gumption as I have. That day, together, the agent and I single-handedly beat those measly steps and made it inside that house. And because of that moment, I wake up grateful every day for the beauty and tranquillity that this quaint little home on a hill provides.

But let us keep going - more on steps.

Some of the guys that I used to play wheelchair basketball with would go down a stack of steps (say 10) by balancing on their back wheels - forwards. Now, if I am honest, I will say that I am completely jealous of their lack of fear and 'can-do' attitude. Some people might look at them and say it is utter stupidity because something as tiny as a pebble could put them off balance and see them kissing the concrete, but if you do want to do the step-thing, just make sure you have the attitude – because that will make the difference in our lives.

I'd like to take a second to give credit to the girls that I played wheelchair basketball with because of their can-do attitude! They're chicks in chairs, but wow, what gumption! I have seen a lot of them go down a hill forward, solely on their back wheels. Meanwhile my stomach is in my mouth just watching them do it, ugggh. (Which, really makes me wonder how I ended up in a chair because I am not a big risk-taker at all). Regardless, you are awesome chicks!!

If you do worry about falling out of your chair and losing all of your teeth, you do have another option. You can always go down steps backwards. Now I started doing this with someone behind me and now I can do it alone, if needed, but if I am with someone I always ask them to stand behind me just in case. You will need one hand on the rail and your other hand on your tire so that you can control the speed and guide your direction. Start by lining up parallel to the rail and lean completely forward onto your lap and start to wheel backwards. Get your aide to hold your bar or handles, and take it easy in the beginning. It's pretty straight forward or backward (heehee).

bit ten - Doors

I want to take a second here to talk with you briefly about Doors.

Ah doors, before they would probably not have even entered our minds; just another thing that, without much effort, we would have literally breezed through. However nowadays, in the Part Two of our lives we can still make our way through, it just looks a lot more like a storm, than a breeze. What I am trying to say, somewhat clumsily, is that nowadays it takes a tad more huff 'n' puff to get through them, depending on the type of door and their location.

Some doors you will find on flat, even ground while others are at the top of a mole hill, and yet others can be at the top of a Mount Everest-type of incline.

FLASHBACK

A girlfriend, who also uses a chair, and I used to have a competition in trying to trump each other with the worst ever door scenario for a person in a chair. It was one way of making light of our situations and challenges, and also just having fun. It was hilarious and very entertaining. The worst scenario we came up with, was one of those heavy glass doors that opened outwards, towards us at the top of a ramp that is lined with tiles and it is raining. Could you imagine? Geez. (Smiles).

But what can I tell you that will be of help, let me think?

I find myself struggling with trying to give you a general guideline regarding doors as there are so many different situations and types of doors. Let me think out loud for a second here, there are the wooden doors that are in hospitals that are heavy, but in offices they can be somewhat effortless, but then the ones in bathrooms at shopping centres require a great deal of effort too, but not the wooden doors in public bathrooms in parks. I recall one of the worst ever doors I have encountered though, was a glass door at the entrance to a business, and I have a fair amount of strength in my arms for a woman. A lot of times when I have had to get through doors, there has usually been someone who is either inside that can see you or a passerby that is more than willing to hold it open for you. And I have had just as many women open doors for me as men, actually, maybe more now I come to think about it. Poor men, their roles and responsibilities have become so confused nowadays, on one hand they don't want to offend anyone but on the other hand they don't want to take our power away by opening the door for us.…

So what do I suggest in most cases. Hmm, I would give the door a test push first and as you do, look up to see if it has one of those arms attached– I find those ones the most challenging.

Now, when it comes to the place that is your 'castle', I do have some definite guidance for you. In my experience, there are only two kinds of doors I choose to have and they are, (1) Sliding and (2) French. I have found that both of these types are not only aesthetically pleasing, yet very wheelchair friendly because they cause me the least amount of headaches. Closing a door can be a pain in the butt because you have to position yourself a number of times but let me assure you that in time, you get to know what works best and where is the best position for each sort of door. I love sliding doors because I don't have to re-position myself a thousand times to close them, I don't have to strain to reach them, they won't fly back to where I can't reach them, they don't take up unnecessary space and they are extremely neat and tidy. There are a lot of pluses that add up to a big fat A+ for me, but I want you to decide for yourself.

Oh, I have almost forgotten to mention those glass sliding doors that are all too often found in the home. In the current place I am living, there are four of them that separate the inside from the outside world, which gives me plenty of experience. They really aren't a bother actually, it is as easy as just giving your castors a little lift over the track and then pushing your rear wheels over as well. It is a different story though when you are carrying a cuppa or a plate.

We have two options in this scenario.

- If there is a table close to the door (and you think you can reach it from the other side of the door), put your cup down, get over the tracks, then pick up the cup again and you are on your merry way.

- If there is no table near the door, I place the cup on the ground on the other side of the door (out of my way), lift my castors over the tracks and then push the rest of the chair over the tracks, and pick up my cup again.

Not rocket science really (Heehee).

bit eleven – the Ramp

A few years ago I was a board member for a not-for-profit organisation that advocated for people with a disability and their rights. The ramp at the front of the building that housed this company was absolutely preposterous! And yes, that is Preposterous with a Capital P (I love that word and I'm glad I could squeeze it in somewhere). For people who utilise an electric wheelchair, it is very negotiable, however, for us manual wheelchair users, it is a whole other story.

The building was obviously built pre-1980 and pre the right of access for people with a disability and the severity of the ramps incline meant there was no way that one could negotiate it head on in a manual chair. If you did attempt it head on, you could be sure to end up on your back on the concrete, probably sliding backwards down the ramp stopping at the bottom. So every month when I needed to access this building, I had to face it but as I had faced something similar before it really wasn't much of a challenge. I've got two words for you – zig and zag.

What made it a tricky ramp was the fact that it was no more than 3 meters wide, meaning that the movements will be smaller and the climb slower. Going down the ramp, even in a side-to-side movement, I was somewhat apprehensive as I found it difficult to stop the wheels at the end of the zigzag motion on each side. So I decided to adapt the method so that I felt a tad safer. Instead of going from one side of the ramp in a diagonal motion downwards to the other side, I did the same motion yet only moving one push in each direction.

See if you can picture this – I zigged forward diagonally downwards only one push, then zagged back and diagonally down one push, then zigged forward diagonally down one push and zagged back diagonally down one push, and repeated this motion until I reached flat ground. This movement could be likened to a zigzag from a sewing machine, I guess (smiles). I know, I know, I am probably not doing the best job at attempting to explain this, so just take a look at the picture I've drawn below.

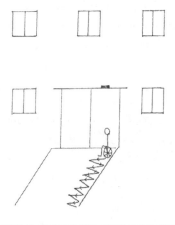

I don't know how much experience you have with ramps, so I will just assume zero knowledge and go from there, if that is ok with you?

By the time you would have read this book, I'm sure you have pushed up and down more than your fair share of ramps, and undoubtedly, you would have worked out that when pushing up ramps, leaning forward will make it all the more easier.

Another point to remember is that when you are going up ramps alone, you will not be able to carry everything you want on your lap because when you are moving in an upward motion, leaning forward limits how much space you have on your lap. For example, I have two beautiful little children (my puppies), that I sometimes have sit on my lap, ok probably more often than sometimes (Heehee). But regardless, as light and as small as they are, I can only fit one on my lap and they also need to lay down or else there is no way I can lean forward enough for me to be physically able to push. You would be surprised how the slightest movement of your head can also mean the difference between moving forward or falling backward, when pushing up a ramp.

Another point we should chat about is going up ramps when it is raining, as rubber and water really does not mix too well; especially if your tyres are really bald and in need of replacing – like mine are right now. You know how cars can slip 'n' slide on roads? Well so too does a wheelchair. I've also noticed in the rain that water gets onto my push rims and thereby, my hands too – making it all the more challenging to control my rims, not impossible, just tricky. This is also the same when you find yourself in snow too.

Side track

In January 2008 I was on a wonderful adventure in Colorado Springs in the USA, and boy it was just magical place. I don't think I would be exaggerating when I tell you it was absolutely picturesque.

Up until that date I had not experienced a lot of snow, not that much and not to that degree. And being in a chair in snow was a whole new experience for me. In the movies snow looks so romantic and dreamy, it evokes images of fireplaces, eggnog and cosy nights that completely ignores the very reality of snow. While I was excited about the opportunity to experience snow, I didn't stop to think about the practicality of living with snow and how it would impact on my day-to-day activities until I was in the middle of it. Still, it was exciting to learn about it too.

TIDBITS

- I discovered that it is not possible to roll over mounds of snow, like we would mounds of grass.

- Because there are puddles of water or moisture everywhere, it is a challenge to get up ramps that would normally be a piece of cake; just like when it's raining.

- Of course gloves are needed because our push rims get stupidly cold and wet, making it difficult to be in complete control of our piece of machinery.

- Then there was the whole de-icing the vehicle before being able to drive, which is more time and effort.

- Finally, I discovered the easiest way for me to get around on the snow was via a toboggan. Just make sure you hold on tight on both sides because you are basically sitting on a plank and with our lack of balance we are sure to fall over if we hit a bump – luckily, the ground is pretty soft and not that far away (big grin).

- Gloves with a tread on the inside provides added friction/grip and thereby increased control; just like a big tread on a pair of shoes.

- BMX treads on your wheels would be the most helpful.

So, as for snow, I still love it. Just make sure you have the appropriate clothing, probably, be prepared to be carried a lot and see if you can access a toboggan, and don't forget to enjoy it.

But getting back to ramps....

If you find yourself heading up an exceptionally long and steep hill/ramp, you might find that if you grab onto your tyres instead of the rims, it might be less frustrating and a tad easier and quicker. I don't know the science behind this, but it works. Yes, your hands will be disgusting, but you can wash them when you get to a bathroom, this will save your hands and your body in general.

And finally, if we are going up a ramp and there is something on it that we need to step over, we can do so by just giving our castor wheels a ever-so tiny bump over. Remember we need to ensure we are leaning forward as well. In this predicament we would need to make the movement as controlled as possible. Throughout the process, ensure we keep our head in a forward direction as we attempt this.

Some people have found it easier to travel down ramps on their rear wheels only, if you want to try this I would be sure to get someone behind you the first couple of times, but I do know a lot of people who do this (mostly men) so it must be a good method.

Oh, I just looked outside at my yard and wondered if I had told you about using wood for ramps? It is not a major point, but it makes a big difference to me every day, especially in the rain. The builder that made the ramps for this house turned the wood over when he was nailing the planks onto the ramp part as the topside was smooth and flat, however, the other side had grooves in it, meaning that it would hold my wheels a bit more in wet weather. I thought this was a great idea and I thanked him immensely for his thoughtfulness concerning my wheelchair and what would help make my life a little easier. And, never in my wildest dreams would I ever consider having a ramp made of tiles, they are far too smooth and virtually dangerous in wet weather.

Ideally, if I was getting ramps built for a new house, I would try my hardest to make certain I could have them covered because of the amount of time it takes for us to get our chair out of the car and then push up the ramp and open the door or gate – if it was raining, it would be more than uncomfortable.

Ok, I think that about covers it for ramps but I still get frustrated when I want to go somewhere and I can't because it does not allow me, I mean prams have been around for donkeys years, so, to be honest I am disappointed that women did not make a stand a long time ago about access for them and their families. Then again, perhaps it really does take a long time for changes to occur.

bit twelve - In Your Wardrobe

For a girl/woman this is one of the most important parts of the house and our life, because, let's be honest here, a lot of us girls have been dressing up since we have been able to walk. Dressing up for me has been mostly exciting, yet I understand that for others, it is more like a chore that they abhor (Heehee, I'm a poet). Please pardon my weird sense of humour.

There are many ways to store our garments - some like to fold, some like to hang, some like to categorize by color, some sort by description, some like to roll their items, some have to iron absolutely everything and some just really don't care. What we do and how we store our clothes, much like the pieces themselves, is individual and very personal which is why I am not going to tell you how to organize your wardrobe. What I will tell you is what I have seen, what works and what does not for me as a woman in a wheelchair.

TIDBITS

- I adore the old style wardrobes that were made from wood and stood freely off the ground in the bedroom, unfortunately the clothing rail inside of these were made far too high for me to reach now.

- This is usually the case also with modern day built-in wardrobes, but sometimes the rail seems to be lower and do-able. I don't know if there are standard heights for these rails. I have found, in order for me to get a good hold of the coat hanger, I need to get right inside the cupboard and under the clothes.

- Those free-standing aluminium simple clothes racks that are traditionally used for holding your ironing are extremely practical and appealing, depending on your decor style as the height is often adjustable.

- Get a builder/carpenter to professionally lower the rail in your cupboards or just add another one, at your exact height. Perhaps your partner can use the top rail and you can use the bottom one.

- Perhaps you and a friend could hang a lower rail inside the cupboard. Just be certain it is really sturdy before they leave.

- I have seen specially made 'disabled' rails that have a handle attached so the rail can be pulled down to our height.

- Drawers are better than doors for us chicks in chairs.

- I use a tallboy in my bedroom and I have found this particularly useful.

- For shelves that are above my level of sight, I use clear lightweight wire baskets that are transparent and help me see what I have put inside. Just make sure that what you put inside is lightweight because it is up high.

- Folding jumpers or towels and storing them on high shelves has not worked for me, for example: what if I want the pullover in the middle of the pile? Due to my height and limited movement, I would have to pull every one down to get the right one and then do the reverse to put them back in place. This consumes too much time.

- Dresses are the only awkward item to hang on the bottom shelf, due to their length. To solve this, I had a rail installed half way between the top and bottom rails – it is long enough for my dresses yet not ridiculously high.

- Cupboard doors will start to get frustrating after a while, especially when you're in a rush, what about curtains or sliding mirrors?

If you are not happy with your wardrobe the way it is, do something about it, or organise a handyman to help you. There is always a solution out there. Now let us move onto the area that cares for our garments – the laundry.

bit thirteen - Laundry set-up

Every year, us women spend thousands of dollars on clothing, we know this because we've been doing it for a long time now. Sometimes there are mistakes and items we would like to return, but other times we get it right. When we get it right we do everything to keep that garment looking like new for as long as possible. And, that is where our laundry comes in. Keeping our clothes looking good, in their original shape and condition also plays a big part of our lives. In fact it plays so much importance that statistics claim we will spend 23,214hrs of our lives just washing our clothes.....

In most laundries there will be a laundry sink, washing machine, dryer, and if you're lucky, a cupboard or two, and a bench. Let us take a look at these pieces in more detail.

Some people use their laundry sink for soaking items, others for dying clothing a new colour, some people use it to hand wash items, and others for washing their dogs, like I do. When I am washing my dogs I usually secure one of those temporary hoses to make it easier for myself, but when I am hand washing things I prefer to just use the permanent neck that is always in place. Because I am using my hands to scrub the garment I don't have a spare hand to hold the tap too. Consider the main purpose you will use your laundry sink, before changing it. Funnily enough, when I was living in the unit especially designed for people in chairs, the sink was so wide that it made it really difficult for me to reach the taps on the wall. Perhaps you could get a handyman to change the position of the taps so that you can actually use it. Lastly, while it would be highly beneficial to be able to get your legs under the laundry sink, you want to be sure that there are no pipes touching any part of your body. I have seen people who were damaged from this exact scenario and it was not pretty, and resulted in permanent damage.

Remember too, if you have a cut-out area under the sink, you will need to replace that cupboard space somehow for your detergent, wool wash, pegs and the like.

At the moment my washing machine is a top-loader and sits on the ground next to the laundry sink. Personally I have only had top-loading machines to date, but I lived in a share residence that had a front-loader; it was so annoying because it took over an hour to do one wash cycle. I easily reach the bottom of the barrel of the top-loader, and have no dilemma getting all of the washing out. Yes, I have scrapes and damage to the paintwork on the bottom of the machine, and I probably could have prevented that had I given it a second thoughts. For example, I could have gone to a hardware place like Bunning's and purchased some flexible transparent plastic, and then screwed or glued it onto the bottom of the machine. But, it is not like I am going to sell the machine, I guess I could always paint it, and then do the plastic idea I mentioned. What do you think? (winks).

However, when this one eventually dies, I would like to take another look at a front-loading washing machine, I think they have improved a lot in the last few years. It would be a lot easier to get the items in and out, and of course, more water efficient, and therefore planet friendly.

If you have a front-loading washing machine there are a lot of options for you. Don't forget, if you have a dryer you will need sufficient wall space for both of these machines. Either dryer or washing machine would work well sitting on the floor, so it's up to you and what you prefer. In a previous residence I had the dryer on the wall a bit above my eye level and it wasn't great. I always had to feel around inside the machine to ensure I didn't leave anything behind. So, in hindsight, I wished I had the dryer at eye level. Because we don't tend to put a tonne of garments into the dryer, like we do the washing machine, which is why I would suggest the dryer goes on the wall, but think about it, and look at all your options before you make your choice.

Next to the washing machine and under the dryer I store a clothes basket and the washing trolley. My clothes line is on the verandah, under cover, which means that I can hang out the washing any time of the day or night, which I love. With the washing basket in one of those trolleys – it is much easier for me to hang out the washing. I also use the clothes trolley to help me bring in the groceries too. After I move the bags from the car to the veranda, I put them into the trolley and wheel them into the house to empty. This has come in very handy in deed.

Another item that comes in handy is one of those clothes stands that you hang small items onto. You know the lightweight ones that are easy to move. As it is lightweight, it is easy for me to move from the shade to the sun and back. A lot of them are flimsy, mostly the cheap ones, so spend a bit more and you won't regret it. These stands can come with wheels too, so do some research and think about what is important and what is not. If you don't like these, I also have a smaller 5 rung portable clothes rail that sits on the balcony railing. It is great for undies, towels and small things. And, this item is even easier for me to relocate should it start to drizzle.

What I want most for you is that after reading this chapter, you can see that you are not really that limited to how and where you can live. I want you to see possibilities and opportunities, rather than barriers and limitations. I want the experiences, stories and knowledge that I have shared with you to really make a difference in your life, and be useful for you and your family.

A home is somewhere you feel safe, comfortable and relaxed! Make your home everything you want, and nothing you don't!

Violet

Chapter four

See your own diamond!

I won't assume that you have seen the widely-acclaimed movie, *Bridget Jones's Diary*, but if you haven't, you really ought to – and yes, you have to watch both the first and the sequel.

Why? I hear you ask me. Well, apart from the fact that the films are well written, have actually cast actors that are believable, and the story is deliciously romantic - there is also the fact that they depict a very real and current version of the time-old favourite fairytale of almost every woman - Cinderella. The distinct difference being that, in the Bridget Jones's version, Cinderella does not look like a Barbie doll! (Which in itself, is already a huge injection of reality).

Yes, the *Bridget Jones* film gives heart to every woman that dreams of love, marriage, and happiness, because despite her age, hair colour, lack of social skills, or the size of her undergarments, an intelligent, accomplished, sincere gentleman (Darcy) reveals that notwithstanding her shortcomings, *he really, really likes her, just the way that she is.* I don't know how many times I have watched this film, but I always feel my heart skip a beat with this scene.... isn't it every girls dream to hear a man proclaim unconditional love? (Even if you can't say it out loud, I know you agree). And, even though the experts claim that women come from Venus and men from Mars, I have a sneaking suspicion that it is every man's dream too. Every creature on this planet just wants to be loved, accepted, and have some sort of 'family' or place to belong.

However, as much as I am elated that the directors and producers of this movie have corrected a very idealistic fairytale, I don't want to linger..... as I would not be able to stop myself from climbing up onto my soap box again to talk about how fairytales have damaged and distorted the relationships and lives of millions of women. So, let me climb back down from my soap box, and we can get on with my next point – self-love.

bit one – Love yourself
- warts, wheels and all!

There is a scene, in *Bridget Jones's Diary*, post Darcy's declaration of love to Bridget, where she (like most women) replays the moment word for word to her group of friends. Up until Darcy's declaration, Darcy and Bridget's interactions had been both frosty and tart, which, is why her friends were dumbfounded, and sat open-mouthed, in awe of what Bridget was recounting. What struck me though, as I sat there considering this scene – is how we, mainly women, find it so incredibly impossible to believe that anyone outside of our family or close friends could actually love us – warts, wheels and all!

I recall from a very young age, being taught (subliminally), to care about what other people thought of almost every aspect of my life – what I wore, my school grades, how I walked, what I said and how I spoke to and treated others. While I can comprehend the important lesson that this teaching gives a child, and how thinking about others makes us better adults, it was in this scene that I identified the flip side of this lesson; that another's opinion of us holds more weight and value than our own! And depending on the personality involved, and how well this lesson is learnt, the outcome could be a very dependent, insecure and sensitive individual who is afraid of *'doing something wrong',* and out of fear, never does anything. As I have said before in this book, there will be storms in life that we need to weather, and if we depend on a lot of external assurance, we may not be able to pick ourselves up, brush the dust off, and get ourselves back on track! I know that I am not a psychologist, but this just seems commonsense to me and I guess I should put my hand up in the air and admit, 'yep, I have done this too and got the t-shirt'.

My last point to come out of *Bridget Jones's Diary* is this - why is it so unbelievable that we are unattractive to the opposite sex if we are anything less than a Barbie Doll lookalike? By the way, a huge round of applause should go to 'Mattel' for creating a buxom blonde with a zero waist as the centre of the universe that has influenced thousands upon thousands of little girls, generations over. Apart from negatively impacting every girl who wasn't caucasian, or blonde for that matter, Mattel has naively constructed unreasonable concepts of what girls think they need to look like in order to be considered 'pretty' and deserving of love. And, why do so many of us (notice, I said us) yearn, hunger and even hold our breath until the day someone else tells us that we are worth loving? Does it have any less meaning when we tell ourselves we are lovable and worthwhile?

At birth, we know nothing of our strengths or imperfections, the status of our family or their associated bank balance to which we are connected. We are not aware of our gender, talents, intellect or culture. But slowly as we grow, in age, knowledge and experience, we gain an awareness of the world that is around us and where we seem to fit in. Somewhere along the line we collect a whole truck load of ways to categorise every single thing that exists in this world, which can be useful at times, but more often than not - is not! Then we spend the rest of our lives trying to un-learn those very same things. Categorising people puts them into boxes, and I don't know anybody that likes being put into a box, do you?

There are the infomercials that endorse the ab-cruncher that will give us 'that stomach we've always apparently wanted', *because you need a six pack to be attractive right?* Then there are the television shows with all of those gorgeous women who all have one thing in common – a size 'zero' waist, loosely translated into *'skinny people are desirable and popular'.* The magazines tell us that if we buy the latest pair of Sevens jeans, we too can look as delicious as those Hollywood celebrities who flaunt around in them and we too *will get everything we want and be happy* just like they are! However, unfortunately our worst enemies are ourselves! With a tonne of negative self-talk that goes on in our head every day, about our hair, our bust or lack of, how fat or short our legs are, the bump on our nose, our crooked teeth and.... well, you get the picture. We are by far our worst critics, not really needing any assistance from other people to make ourselves feel more "ordinary" than we already do!!

Ok, now let me tell you a little story......

FLASHBACK

When I was on bed rest, I had not even considered how my body had changed, or even that my body would be any different to what it was like just six weeks earlier when I was still walking. The comprehension of the changes to my body (and life, for that matter) did not yet fully crystallize in one big moment rather it was something that unravelled on a day-to-day basis throughout the rehabilitation process, and even into the first couple of years of my new life.

It felt like forever, but finally my consultant granted me a day-pass, and boy was I dying for that day. I was dying to escape the white walls of the institution, dying to just have a day with my girlfriend, and dying to do some shopping too. I had told my girlfriend the great news and asked if she would indulge me and wander with me through the shops in town. I was hoping to replace some of the clothing that I could no longer wear and had begrudgingly bequeathed to those around me. My girlfriend, let's call her Miss Earl Grey, was not a huge fan of shopping at the best of times, but I think this time it was even exciting for her too. For as much as I had missed just doing normal things (like shopping) with my friends, I felt that they had missed me also. So, after she arrived at the hospital, we called for a taxi and waited very impatiently in the front foyer of the Spinal Unit.

The taxi came and I jumped into the front seat (this door opens the widest), while my friend and the driver sorted where and how to store the piece of metal that was now my legs. The disassembling didn't take long. At our destination the taxi took the pieces out the car, looked at the wheelchair and said to me, 'How does this go together?' I started to panic a bit because that was one thing they hadn't taught us yet. But together the three of us worked it out after a couple of minutes – definitely not rocket science. Miss Earl Grey and I were off.

First stop was an ATM so I could get some cash out, but my friend had to help me with this as there were a few steps up to the machine and no ramp in sight. But that was ok – I got the money in the end, next, the shops.

Before I started wandering around, I stopped to take in my surroundings and get my bearings. As I did I noticed it was a typical tiny English village – too adorable for words. In the middle of it was a round small grassy patch with a statue in honour of somebody who did something worth remembering apparently (Heehee). There was the odd new shop here and there, sprinkled amongst the majority that have stood the test of time, just like the country itself. On this particular day the common drizzle that hangs around was nowhere to be seen as sky shone with a summer sky. And as I quickly noticed from my wobbling disposition, the streets covered in cobblestone – cute, but ridiculously painful for people in chairs, but I loved it, all of it!

My girlfriend and I were having a ball wandering in and out of shop after shop, after shop. In the beginning I guess I was too focused on shopping to notice all the mirrors around the place, until it happened. They don't really have mirrors in hospital. I caught a glimpse of something out of the corner of my eye as I walked past a full-length mirror and I was stopped in my tracks. I wheeled myself backwards to the mirror and there it was. That thing that I saw out of the corner of my eye was 'me'. And, I don't know what made me do this, but I positioned myself face on, right in front of the mirror and I just sat there, literally frozen!

This was the first time I saw the complete picture, me and the chair together, and so, this was another step that I had to take. It was kind of like someone had taken out my spirit and literally put it in to someone else's body.

I was dumbfounded, because, I could not physically smile, move, or say anything (even inside my head I did not utter a word). I did not recognise that person in the mirror, nor did I want to. 'Yuck', I thought. I continued to sit there and look at it in wonderment, disgust and shame. (No, I have to correct that – wonderment and disgust was what I felt initially, the shame came afterwards when I had to acknowledge that *thing* in the mirror as me). 'How did I get like this?' came into my mind, and this one thought kept on playing like a broken record (for my generation) or a CD jumping (for younger ones).

'I'm in a wheelchair, I'm in a wheelchair, *I'm* in a wheelchair, I am in a wheelchair, *I am* in a wheelchair, *I am* in a *wheelchair*' (Note the intonation changes). It was as though each time I said this sentence out loud, the words and their significance sank down through the particles in the air onto my skin, through my pores and into my being shouting 'this is my new reality'.

Then I heard something in my head say, 'that is you now, you better get used to it', and as much as I wanted to just run away from the mirror and scream – my feet remained planted (or rather my wheels).

I took some time to study her, because, I had no idea who this person in the mirror was - her body was so different because of the paraplegia. Then I corrected myself and said 'No, my body is so different now'. In my previous life, I had a much smaller waist than that woman in the mirror and held myself more upright from years of dance lessons. I looked at how her feet sat on the foot plate, sitting however they were placed, bumped or knocked. She was wearing a pair of joggers with zippers in them, as well as a pair of those white opaque stockings that people in nursing homes wear. The legs were no longer the toned and womanly limbs that she could be proud of, but rather, now those limbs lay limp and dare-I-say, lifeless, however they were placed.

It was as if her hands had now become her feet. I could already see the damage done from using a wheelchair every day, dry hands, with blisters and cuts all over them. Gloves were a new fashion accessory that she neither wanted nor liked. In no way did this woman resemble the sassy and vibrant woman whom I had known for twenty nine years of my life. As I sat there I wanted to scream –

'This is not me!
This is NOT me!
THIS IS NOT ME!

I am not one of those people in wheelchairs. This is not who I am. I wanted to tell everyone that passed me in the street, that day and for a while, that I am not just what you see in front of you today. I was so much more, I am so much more! I did not want to be put in the 'disabled' box, however, it was very plain and clear that I simply had no choice in the matter. I was no longer the person that I had known, and I was no longer a part of the life that I had before either – these were the facts.

Side track

(Words on paper are one dimensional right? Then there are two and three dimensional which is commonsense, but, I propose humans are four dimensional, as not only do we have a body and mind, we also have a spirit/soul or whatever name you wish to use).

So since we are four dimensional creatures, and the most intelligent life form on this planet, why is it such an obstacle for us to grasp and hold onto the concept that we are so much more than what we can see in front of us? (Myself included!) I'll be the first person to put up my hand and say that I didn't look past what I saw, and up until my accident, I will admit (due to my ignorance and small-mindedness), that I did not stop to ponder the other dimensions of people who used Wheelchairs.

Yet, I have learnt and grown. I have learnt that regardless of what people have or don't have (physically, psychologically or financially) I can learn something from every single person on this planet. And secondly, I have learnt that every single person has a story worth listening to. Whether these people have served our country in WWI or been a single mother of 7 children who left an abusive relationship, they could have been one of the first women in the secret service, or perhaps a father who lost his entire family in a car crash. Regardless of the story that comes with the person, all human beings deserve kindness and respect. Ok, ok, I'll climb down off my soapbox now.

....Back to the point.

Ironically, I understand that before the accident, I was just looking at the exterior parts of people in chairs and putting them into the 'disabled' box. I was misguided to think that what I saw in front of me was the total of who they were! I had not taken the time to see or think past their exterior circumstances. (Shame on me). Because I was doing the exact thing that I do not want people doing to me now! What I do believe is, that until we have a personal experience or event (with someone close or ourselves), it is difficult (but not impossible) to put ourselves into the shoes of another. Some people empathise with others easily, some of us don't have the time and some of us don't until we are forced into a predicament. No matter what happens, being able to see life from another's perspective gives us the opportunity to learn and grow as a human being.

What we have just chatted about is something that I believe is important to keep in mind when we go outside of our homes and interact with the community, as we were once in the same boat. So, I would ask you to remember what you were like, and give people a little slack.

From my observations, it is only human for us to equate who we are with our job title, how we look, where we live, what car we drive, and what labels we have in our wardrobe. Actually, permit me to clarify the point I am trying to make here. It is not wrong in any way to have or like having the best of everything like a convertible Mercedes, a holiday house in Florida, a wardrobe full of Dior, but, I do believe it becomes dangerous when we begin to identify with these 'things' so strongly that we see them as part of who we are, our core, or as Eckhart Tolle would say, 'our ego'. And, I fear that when we identify so personally with the external pieces of our lives, there is the risk that if we were to lose them, we would consider our life to be worthless and without meaning! We have all read at least one story of a person who loses what they consider to be everything and then commits suicide. This doesn't have to happen, and I don't want it to happen to You!!

Recently I was reading Dr Phil McGraw's new book, Real Life, when I came across the following statement - 'whether we like it or not, our body image and self-image are inextricably intertwined. If your body image is compromised by disease or injury, your self-image is likely to take a serious hit'. When I read this, I felt an enormous sense of relief and justification too, because this is exactly what I had to fight inside of me in the beginning of my new life. But, up until now, I did not have the proof or knowledge to support what I had discovered during my change of life. Here was a credible source with decades of training, knowledge and experience, confirming exactly what I felt, saw and believed to be true.

Self-image is a fundamental aspect of all human beings, and is something that needs to be acknowledged and addressed for any survivor (of any trauma), so that they are able to move forward from their experience or event.

bit two – Take your mind back

I need you to take your mind back (for a couple of minutes), to a time before the incident that altered your body and life, and try to recall if you had any issues around self-esteem, image or self-worth. This only works if you are honest here. Now, don't you think that if we had challenges around self-image before, then it is going to be exacerbated 100% when our life is changed? When our body is different? I will be the first to admit that pre-accident, I didn't like going for a jog because I was nervous about what others would think about what I was wearing, how I looked, or how I jogged. And, if I had those issues beforehand, of course they were magnified when all of a sudden I ended up standing out of the crowd all of the time, had specific needs that were not 'normal', and looked nothing like I did before. However, I could look at this from two different perspectives – one way was seeing that I now stood out like a sore thumb (where on earth did that phrase come from?), and the other way to see it, was to accept that I am even more unique and rare now!

But it took an accident to wake me up! That was one of the most significant lessons to come out of this experience for me – I am so much more than what looks back at me from the mirror; that is the physical package that houses the true 'me' inside.

TOOL – THE TRUE YOU

Are you just your face? Are you just your legs? Are you a woman only if you have breasts? Are you only beautiful if you are a size 8? Are you only worthy of love if you are prettier than your friends? Or are you only worthy of love if your legs work?

I want you to close your eyes and picture yourself with a man you love, then, picture yourself pregnant to that man, now picture your new born baby. Now, years later when that baby is about 8 years old, see a doctor informing you that your little boy or girl has developed a disability and needs a wheelchair. Finally, I want you to hear your little boy or girl asking you a question – 'Mummy, do you love me, how I am?'.... I doubt you would hesitate with your response, and it would be something along the lines of, 'I love you to the moon and back'.

What I want to know is, why do we give ourselves a different answer?? Why are we any less deserving of love? Because, the time old question of, 'how can you love another when you can't give love to yourself?,' is proven and true. Before another can see our beauty – we have to be able to see it ladies! Getting external validation, from our partner, is not as empowering as when it comes from ourselves, and can put us at the mercy of others.

From now on, each time you get out of the shower, or before you leave your house, you need to stand in front of your mirror (full length) and say one thing that you love about yourself – out loud, so that you really hear it!

We tell other people all the time, why not tell ourselves? .... just one thing that you love about the person standing in front of you.

I have now been in a chair for thirteen years (2012) and I will admit that in the beginning I hated how I looked for many reasons; I looked 'different' in every sense of the word, because, I could no longer walk, no longer wear high heels, or short skirts, I was no longer the Size 8 (in Australia) I previously was, I no longer felt sexy or even like a female, and I also discovered the meaning of 'flaccid', that is limp, flabby and drooping. And I stood out like a sore thumb now.

How we see ourselves influences how we feel about ourselves, yet, just as important, is how we think and talk about ourselves too. Because, if we are only working on how we look to the outside world, it will only impact on one dimension. The thoughts inside our head and the words that come out of our mouths (about ourselves) need to agree with each other. If one aspect, words, thoughts or feelings are not in agreement, then positive change won't happen. What good is it to work on one dimension when we are multi-dimensional creatures? For example, say you want to learn how to drive a car, if you only learn how to use the accelerator and brake, how can you pass your driving test? Operating a car is more than merely using the accelerator and brake – we also need to learn about steering, road rules, parking, reading and responding to other road users... the list goes on.

Unfortunately, there is no magic wand or miracle pill, and I will tell you now that it takes time, effort and practice to change your outlook, your self-image or how you feel about yourself. Of course, you can get what you want, if you want it badly enough! P.S. Look up my reading list at the end of this book.

I have used a lot of **methods and tools** and below are some of these -

- Start a journal

- Source a psychologist in your area

- Literally re-train your mind (by choosing a CD that is positive and uplifting) and listen to it over and over and over and over and over....

- Listen to the thoughts that go around in your head and write them down to become more conscious of them (because we become what we listen to or focus on)

- Determine if there are any thoughts that you can or should discard

- Set yourself some daily actions that align with your desires and wants

- Look at your diet, perhaps with a professional, to assess how many carbs, proteins and such you need in your weekly intake

- Consider various sports or exercise that interests you

- Get an exercise 'buddy'

- While you are doing the form of exercise you choose, use that time to yourself to tell yourself that every day you are getting fitter, stronger, leaner, healthier and happier.

- Source a mentor or organisation that contains resources of relevance.

- Get a piece of A3 paper, draw you in the centre of it and list all the reasons around you why you want/need to do 'this'

- On another piece of paper, put your name in the centre and around you list all of the wonderful facets of You

- When you are feeling 'down' sit as upright as possible, put your shoulders back, with your head up towards the ceiling and try to bitch and moan about yourself and your life – I dare you!! It is not the easiest thing to do.

- Ask your closest friends to do something for you. Ask if they would make a list of the physical, emotional and psychological facets that they admire, love and respect about You. I am certain you will be surprised.

- Ask them to give it to you when they finish, then you stick it on your bathroom mirror and finally, ensure you read it every single day for 3 months!

- Whenever you leave the house, put a smile on your face, sit up straight, hold your head high and tell yourself that you are a beautiful, intelligent and worthwhile human being AND that you can do anything that you can dream! Say this over and over until you forget that you are saying it.

I don't know if these ideas will be something that you actually try or just a giggle, yet regardless, just know that you are not alone. According to the facts, there are at least another 38,999 women in the USA alone with a physical disability. Please here me when I say that the most important part of you cannot be taken away, injured or disappear.

So you need to remember that the external parts of us can be improved by physical effort, conscious choices or (if needed) some sort of surgery.

bit three – Diamonds and Rubies

Our lives may not have followed the path that we predicted, promised or planned, yet perhaps, if we let it, we will come to see that from the challenges we face, there are diamonds, Diamonds and Rubies that we might not have discovered, except for the change to our course.

At this point in time, I would love to recommend a very small but insightful book by Dr Russell H. Conwell, *Acres of Diamonds*. I am not going to give away the plot, however, this book is an all-time classic that has profoundly touched the lives of millions of people around the world. You can find it at this link, www.classicbooks.com.au

What has happened has happened, the cards have been dealt, and now we must play our hand. Let the past be where it is meant to be – behind us and open your eyes and heart to really see what is right in front of you! A diamond in the rough.

Finally, you need to know that the general public won't even see your wheelchair, if it is not at the forefront of your mind! This reminds me of a friend I will call Miss Flat Black.

Now, I have to take a minute or two here to tell you about one of my girlfriends, Miss Flat Black, who is really great about the whole image thing! Regardless of how many kilos her frame carries, whether it is 45 or 80 kilos, I can say without a hint of doubt, she truly loves herself the way that she is. Regardless of how her hair looks, regardless if she is wearing a suit or board-shorts and a tee – she totally accepts and values herself inside and out. Now, I can hear that some of you would be saying in your head that a lot of women love themselves, but I would like to argue that most of that is just 'hot air'. Why? Because when they stand alone in front of their mirror (without anyone around), I wonder what words are going around and around in their head? I know for Miss Flat Black, it is no different to what she would be thinking about herself if I was there, and that is the difference I am trying to point out here! That is complete love of the self.

But Miss Flat Black does not go around telling everyone that she loves herself or making sure that other people can see that she loves herself, because it is not about anyone else. It just 'is' for her, it is utterly natural and just imbedded within her. She is totally comfortable in her own skin and if she isn't, she does something about it. I believe this to be rare, because in today's world there is so much emphasis placed on how much fat we are carrying, what we wear, the colour of our teeth, the colour of our skin, how big our boobs are, how many wrinkles we have, how tall we are, bla, bla, bla...........

There is an ever-increasing amount of pressure being thrown at us from all angles ... messages on the television, in the magazines, the internet pop-ups and newspaper stories. Then it drifts into our office or school because someone is going to fall for all the hype at some point. It does not matter which stage of your life you are in either – whether you are ten, twenty or sixty six years old. It's wonderful marketing, but it makes it really difficult for us to not be influenced.

Unfortunately, Miss Flat Black promised me that there was no secret behind her positive self-image, and trust me, I probed, dug and prodded her for years. The only thing she came up with is the following story.

When she was 13 years old she contracted a bout of Glandular Fever which meant that she skipped Year 9 altogether. Miss Flat Black was confined to her home and it was impossible for friends or teachers to visit her, this is why it was not possible for her to keep up-to-date with homework. She had the whole of Year 9 off school, which meant, that when she went back in Year 10, she had to do double the study to catch up with the work and keep her grades average – which she did! Girl power. I still can't believe this, but, Miss Flat Black told me that she spent most of her time stuck at home (remember she was only thirteen), reading a stack of self-development books her mother borrowed from the local library, and Miss Flat Black says that this is what shaped her mind into what it is today.

What I have gained from spending time with Miss Flat Black, and watching her, over the years, is that (1) she places little importance on what other people think about her, and (2) she believes in herself utterly! I mean, totally, like 1000 per cent, if that was possible (Heehee).

I want to tell you something about that woman in the mirror I saw that day in the shops at Aylesbury. It took time for me to connect with her, and acknowledge that she was in fact me, and yes, it took still more time for me to really love her again; caring about how she looked, about her future and her life in general. When I look at myself in the mirror nowadays, I see me, not the metal. And, the woman who looks back at me from the mirror, is happy and self-confident, strong yet feminine, and makes me feel proud of the kind of person she has turned into, what she has accomplished, and the kind of life she has created for herself, despite challenges.

I say, 'find a way to love who you are' – warts, wheels and all, then and only then will genuine happiness be possible. Worry less about what others might be thinking, and instead, be thankful for what you have, remain steadfast to your goals and hold your head high. Every single day, you are a Winner!

Look at the big picture of life, while remembering that the car we drive, where we live, our place of employment, and our diamond rings can all disappear in a natural disaster!, something that seems to be happening more and more frequently these days.

Then answer this question, 'what is it that you truly value in this thing called life?'

Put a great big smile on your face and keep others guessing why?

Violet

P.S. When my man, Marty, was editing this chapter, he thought of Jack Johnson's song, 'Gone', that talks about the subject we have just been considering....

> Cars and phones and diamond rings
> Bling, Bling!
> Those are only removable things,
> What about your mind,
> Does it shine?
> Are there things that concern you more than your time...?

Chapter five

Female things

bit one - Moon-Time.

It is quite obvious to me now - God must be a Male!

I have had the thought several hundreds of times that we most certainly deserve and warrant some sort of reprieve from this menace to our lives. Well, that's my viewpoint due to the pain and discomfort I feel. I demand reprieve, because we now have lots of other reasons to be in pain, like the constant sitting, and the 16 hours we spend in the one position all day long (if you get up at 6am and retire at 10pm, like I do), and for the number of times that we will catch our knuckles squeezing through small spaces, not to forget the shoulder and neck aches we will get from throwing our chairs (not literally) into and out of our cars day in, day out, all year long.

Regardless of what and how many limbs/muscles may be functioning or frozen, responding or response-less, I must report, that I unfortunately have not come across one woman with a spinal injury who has a "get-out-of-gaol-free" card for their 'moon-time', 'the red river', 'monthlies', or whatever pet name you may have for that womanly time of the month. It confuses and baffles me, that while I am unable to feel my toes or my calf muscles, I can still feel the pain of my moon-time.

I had high hopes there for a while, but they were quickly shattered. During hospitalisation, four months had passed and I was completely oblivious to the fact that I had not yet had a menstrual cycle. There seemed to be other pressing things on my mind (smiles). When I realised that it had been four months, I went to my nurse to get some answers. Nurse Café Mocha (who also happened to be from Australia) was my nurse, and she informed me ever so delicately that my body was just in a state of shock from the trauma, and that it would most probably regulate itself within the next few months. As you could imagine, I was jumping for joy - not. As nurse Café Mocha finished her sentence, I can't be certain, but I thought that I saw something that looked like a smirk coming from the corner of her mouth. 'I didn't think that I was asking for too much – to get a pardon from this one aspect of womanhood', I said. Then the smirk quickly surfaced as a full-blown grin, from ear to ear like a Cheshire cat.

But joking aside for a moment, I want to thank nurse Café Mocha for her honesty and her compassion which I could sense under the guise of her humour. You, nurse Café Mocha, are where you are meant to be, and even though you probably deserve to be in a management position, it would mean a great loss for the people you care for. They need you and what you bring to the nursing role.

Pardon the pun, but it took just one more week for it all to come flooding back – my womanhood, quite literally actually.

Ok, now that I have given you the worst news I might as well tell you the rest.

Now, I don't know what 'it' was like for you pre-accident, nor do I know the measure of pain that accompanied this wonderful moment of the month. Some women get it so bad that they need time off work, others take a hot-water bottle to bed and dose up on Panadol Forte, while my girlfriend only gets them every three months – lucky girl you are, Miss Earl Grey!

I don't know quite how God wires it all up inside us, but I will be mentioning this point when I am in front of him, because, even though I can't feel if I'm hungry or not, can't feel if my shoes are too tight, and am unable to feel if the heater is burning my leg, yet I can still enjoy the back ache and stomach cramps that accompany the 'red river' every month.

This is just not right. But, for right now, all I can say is try out all of the old tricks you used to use in part one of your life and see if any of it gives you any relief. For me, I swap between a hot water bottle, chocolate and Neuro fen. I prefer not to load my body up with medication though, because I believe that medication only masks what our body is desperately trying to tell us. Yet, each to their own.

Next on my list of topics are the trusty tools that we use during this time of the month – the Tampon.

bit two – the Tampon

As I was thinking about this topic the other day, I thought about the ways I could remind myself that I still have a tampon in that needs to come out before I forget about it and leave it in overnight and get something horrid like Toxic Shock Syndrome - uggh!

Then I guess because the subject was on my mind, it came up in conversation with a girlfriend. And she informed me that sometimes she forgets about having one in too, and I have to say that this surprised me. As we were talking about the topic she went on to explain that she can't feel whether a tampon is inside her either.

I could not believe that I had forgotten this part of my life, and every now and then I catch myself falling into the whole 'disabled' mindset – which is very easy to do considering. Let me explain.

Because I am now living a life in a wheelchair 24/7, my mind now naturally will consider life from that perspective first, as I am sure you will find yourself doing too. Let me give you an example of what I am talking about so that it all fits into place. I was complaining to one of my friends about how those bubble-like things on the ground near the intersections annoyed the heck out of me. You know the ones that I am talking about, the ones for visually challenged people. Well, they asked me this question 'Would this have been so important if you were still walking?' And quite frankly, I decided that it would not be an issue at all. For me now, it is an issue, but for the greater population it is not even within their realm of problems. Yet, it is highly vital to those people who have difficulty seeing our world. This question put it all into perspective for me. It is necessary to remind myself of my prior attitudes and opinions in order to see things from a balanced perspective – rather than being completely lop-sided, and perhaps, somewhat biased.

Let's get back to the problem-solving.

<u>TIDBITS</u>

- On a calendar/diary write 'In' and write 'out' after removal of the tampon. That way you have a calendar to check for a reminder.

- Set the alarm clock on your mobile for the time you want to remove the tampon, or set a reminder on the calendar application on your mobile.

- Put a sticky note on the fridge, reminding you when to take it out.

- Put a tampon in your purse, if you are out you will be reminded each time you open the purse.

- Primitive but effective - write it on your hand!

Now, if you are on the 'pill' your period will be almost precise which is great, because you will know when to expect it. Mine used to be like clock-work, I mean that I could time my moon-time down to the day and even the hour. Can you believe that? Chemicals are wonderful sometimes, aren't they? Nowadays, I have made a decision to live as chemical-free as possible, and so, have stopped taking the pill, which means that my moon-time is not as predictable as before, in turn, meaning that I have to be more prepared for what might happen. Thus, now I am a born-again girl scout – always prepared for the worst. I won't lie, it took time to adjust, and every now and then I am caught out, but it is never the end of the world. It is a trait that I have had to acquire since injury. For the purpose of emphasising just how unorganised or spontaneous I am naturally, I will regrettably tell you a story that will probably haunt me for life.

My girlfriend (let's call her Miss Chamomile Tea) and I, were probably the least organized people on the planet. I'm so embarrassed to tell you this story, but we are both big enough girls to have a laugh at ourselves, so here goes.

At the time we were on a Working-Holiday Visa in grand, old England. We wanted to get away for Christmas, and if possible enjoy a snow white Christmas, so we booked a trip up to Edinburgh, Scotland. We went with a couple of other people and met some nice girls that were from our part of Australia, the Gold Coast, as well as a load of good value people on the tour. The tour ended so quickly, and we still had some time off before work commenced for the New Year, so, I called her up and I went over to her town, and we went out for a coffee. While sitting in the coffee shop we were talking about how much fun it was and I said, 'We still have some time off, so why don't we do something else?' Miss Chamomile Tea grabbed a paper while we were sitting there, we saw an advertisement and called up about it. Before we had finished our cuppa we had booked ourselves on a 3 day tour for Paris, leaving tomorrow. She said come over to my place and we'll get up at 4am and catch the express train into London to meet the bus. So we did.

Now, be kind to us here. We did not require a passport to go to Scotland so it didn't even cross our minds to bring our passports for Paris. So needless to say, we couldn't board the tour that day and were majorly disappointed. Not to mention feeling really silly and sorry for ourselves. But do you think we let that stop us? Of course not. We were determined, and caught a bus the next day to meet up with the group at the hotel that night. I have to say that it is one of my fondest memories with Miss Chamomile Tea, we've done some silly things, but that trip was right at the top of the list! I have and always will treasure memories that we share.

I still prefer spontaneity (and so can you), but there are some parts of my life now that require some forethought and planning.

I was never in the Girl Guides or Scouts, yet in Part two of my life I have learnt the benefits of being prepared for all possibilities.

TIDBITS

- If you have your 'moon-time' - a towel underneath you during intercourse will prevent a whole lot of unnecessary washing. And minimising work is always a good thing, right girls? Some days it seems like that is all I ever do. But on the flip side of that - I thank the Universe that I am independent and that I am actually able to do that for myself.

- I don't know if this will be the case for you, but this is what I have discovered – my bladder can't hold the same capacity during my moon-time as it can when it is not my moon-time. Lesson – go to the bathroom more frequently.

- Exercise can ease the pain.

- I have noticed that I still experience bloating at this time of the month and it will be one of the first signs that I can notice, apart from the sugar-cravings! (Heehee).

bit three – Girl Scout

When I talk about being a Girl Scout, I am talking about always being prepared for any situation, regardless of the time of day or the location. As I have previously shared, this is not something that came natural to me, however something that I needed to develop due to situations and experiences. I have learnt that all sorts of 'accidents' can and will happen anytime, anywhere, with a reason or without one. I just want to pass on the knowledge that I have gained from all of the varied experiences I have had in life, so that you might not be in those predicaments.

Suggestions to keep near the bed:

1x old towel that can get dirty
1x small towel for your cushion
1x pad
1x tampon
Some hand wipes in a zip-lock bag
A few disposable bags
Latex gloves
Hand moisturiser
Bedside lamp
Telephone
Mobile phone charger

Suggestions to keep near the toilet:

I store these in pretty boxes and stack them so it doesn't look all medicinal.

1x box of sterile surgical latex gloves
1x bottle of KY Gel
Boxes of suppositories
1x box of hand wipes
Garbage bags (I recycle plastic bags)
1x bag of catheters (50 per bag)
Garbage bin and
Of course some air freshner! Woohoo.

Suggestions to keep in the car:

Latex Gloves
Hand wipes
Hand Steriliser (public bathrooms)
Change of trousers/skirt
Garbage bags (recycled plastic bags)
1x bag of Catheters (50 per bag) in the boot
Face towel (for your hands OR your wheels in wet weather)

Air compressor (pump up tyres)
Replacement rings for wheelchair

Note: I have repeated the list for the car items in the chapter – 'Living in the real World'.

Items for your suitcase (under the plane):

Wheelchair tools
Spare rings for wheelchair folding cable
Spare tyre tube OR patches
Handheld tyre pump

Items for suitcase (overhead luggage):

Gloves	(x8)
KY Gel	(Sml)
Garbage bags (recycled plastic bags)	(x2)
Wipes	(x10)
Spare change of trousers/skirt	
Catheters	(x 4 days' supply)
Any daily medication	(Priority)
Imodium	(Causes constipation)

bit four – storage devices

There are a few different forms of storage devices suitable for chairs. It just depends on your needs.

- You will find that there is a black waterproof, box-shaped bag on the market that can be attached underneath the seat of the chair with a Velcro front that secures closed. I had one of these and found that I would put too much into it, thereby adding to the weight of the chair when I was lifting it into and out of my car.

- There is also a wire-netting option that can be secured under your chair as well, sort of like the net under a high-wire. Some people find it useful for carrying books around university. Whatever you put onto it though will have to be taken off before you lift your chair into your car. Probably handy when shopping.

- You can always hang a backpack over the back of the chair, but depending on the size of it, the arm straps will most likely rub against the wheels, slowing down the pushing process. I had a smaller leather version with smaller straps that worked quite nicely and was appropriate for work. I would not advise keeping your purse in there though. I've never had anything stolen from my chair, but there are all sorts in the world, and you don't want to give them any sort of invitation.

- And then there is the RGK pouch that I use. It is big enough that I can put my mobile along with enough catheters for the day, my medication, some loose change, and of course a lipstick or two! Because it is not enormous, there isn't the risk of adding too many things. Sort of like the psychology of having a small handbag, because you can only put so many things in it.

It is attached by Velcro so it is easy to remove if necessary, and I will swear by this item. It is hidden from predators (because it sits behind my calves) and has the convenience of a handbag without the bulk. It is lightweight, a great size and secured by a zipper so that nothing can fall out while you're throwing your chair around.

The RGK pouch is my all time favourite. Don't just take my word though, think about your needs, wants and situation.

TIDBITS

- Consider the function, its purpose, the practicality of it, what you need to carry, and what you generally do on a day-to-day basis.

- Just on the topic of towels, I have found it useful to have a small towel (about bathmat size) to wrap over my cushion, so that I'm not always washing that every day too. I am all about saving time so I can make use of it doing something more useful.

- I just want to take a moment here while I am mentioning this small towel that I wrap around my cushion to tell you that it also comes in handy when having a shower. While I'm on the toilet, I wrap this small towel around my cushion so that (a) my shower towel doesn't get dirtied and (b) after the shower I can use my bath towel to dry my hair while I'm using the small towel to keep my chair dry and clean. If you prefer to sit on the bath towel, fold it length-wise and drape it over your chair, laying it from the front of the chair, over the cushion and over the backrest, making sure that it's not dragging on the ground anywhere.

bit five – Shaving legs

When I was in hospital, at Stoke Mandeville Spinal Unit, only one of the nursing staff shaved my legs during the eight weeks that I was on bed-rest, and I just want to say – God bless her! This caring and thoughtful female employee, was an assistant in nursing (AIN) as we call them in Australia. And she had a heart of gold and put herself in my position for long enough to go beyond her 'specified' list of duties to care about how I must have felt laying there with my big old hairy leg. Unfortunately, I am unable to recall her name, but let me send a 'shout-out' to all those staff members that go above and beyond their duties and thank them for their kindness!

As I progressed, and was able to start taking showers by myself, for the life of me I could not work out how to shave my legs. Leaning forward into a space that had no safety provisions, like bars or the like, absolutely petrified me – because if I fell, I would have had to ring for assistance to get back into my chair, and that was just not something that I was prepared to do.

The fact that you need to hold your leg in the air, hold your razor and hold onto a bar baffled me for a while as I did not have three arms just yet. But, when I started using the shower chair that I use now, it all became a lot simpler and less frightening. As I have explained in another chapter – the common, plastic outdoor chair is low enough that it is not frightening to lean forward. It has two armrests on it which makes me feel a good deal safer, which frees up both of my arms. So, I simply grab my razor with one hand, put it in my mouth for a bit while I grab the shaving cream and my leg. Then use one hand to hold my leg up and the other to shave. When you are sitting somewhere that you feel comfortable, it really is that simple.

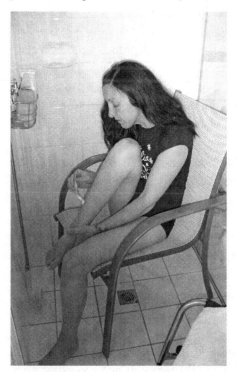

Before the change of life (my accident), I was one of those girls that would bend over at the waist and wrap her head in a towel after washing it, maybe you were too. I don't know, but I can tell you that we can still do this if we want to. However, I have found those really small travel towels (from the chemist) that soak up all the moisture very handy too, yet, not as heavy on the head and neck.

Here you can see me, in my togs, shaving my legs.

Get your chair and wheel backwards, this will put the castors in a forward position – meaning that it will be more difficult to fall out of your chair. Apply your brakes. Have the towel within reach, bend forward till your torso is resting onto your lap and grab the towel and place it over your head. With both hands, twist it and fling it back over your head. You can use one arm to hold the towel in place, while the other hand is helping you get back into an upright position.

See, too easy!

bit six - Diet

Diet – this word can conjure up some interesting images in one's mind!

Pre-accident, I ate what I liked, but in a balanced way so that I wasn't over-indulging or depriving myself. I would enjoy my weekly Copenhagen ice cream, but I would also eat a lot of good stuff, like salads, and combine it with regular exercise and training. Boring, I know.

Post-injury I am still conscious of what I eat and probably more so now, only because our lifestyle is so sedentary. You may even find that you aren't as able to feel your stomach as much as you did before, which can be both a good and bad thing, as we can't feel when we're full or when we're hungry. Maybe for you, it might be a matter of sticking to a time schedule or seeing a professional who can outline a healthy eating plan, I don't know as I'm not a professional nutritionist. What I do know is that keeping to a sensible weight means that pushing the chair isn't too much of a challenge, doing transfers doesn't cause me too much of a bother, and in general, I am not limited by my situation even more than I already am.

Personally, I find though, that if I eat too many refined-carbohydrates things tend to get a bit blocked-up down there, so I am conscious of my intake of white breads, sweets and so on. I am not recommending that you do as I do, your body is not like mine, and your needs are unique and it is not my intention to tell you what to do! I just want you to have a healthy body, mind and lifestyle and you need to work out for yourself what that looks like. Perhaps you need to experiment with different foods, exercise and a whole bunch of things, while recording the outcomes, and pros and cons, to see what works best for you and your body, mind and spirit. I have discovered, over time, that the less changes you make at a time, the easier it is to connect the dots, so to speak, and work out why something is going awry.

Can I share with you a story? I remember being out at the shops one day, picking up a few things in Target, and somehow I was having a conversation with this lady whose daughter is in a chair, and the one thing that I can recall about that conversation to this day was the lady telling me how good I looked and encouraging me to stick to a good weight because her daughter had not. This lady told me about her daughter and the different things she was doing to lose the weight she had amassed, and explaining that it would take a lot longer because she is in a chair. I am telling you this story and encouraging you to care for your health, because I care about the quality of your life, and I care about your self-esteem. It is no different to when I used to walk, as I remember sometimes looking in the mirror and not being over-the-moon with what I saw. So too have there been moments like this since my accident. And now, being in a chair, it is even harder to lose weight. I heard a saying once, 'nothing tastes as good as looking good feels'.... I don't know if I would go to that extreme, however I would say that we need to be conscious about what we are choosing.

I have found a few websites that have information about weight management in regards to people in wheelchairs, so the below website is just one of them. I like most of its content and advice, but the internet is a never-ending resource, so get looking and get informed (Smiles).

www.spinalcord.uab.edu/show.asp?durki=21481

bit seven – Make-up

For people with use of their hands, there is no difference with make-up, except that we can't get as close as we used to, to the mirror. For me it is a double bonus because I can no longer see the blackheads, and if I cannot see them, I will not squeeze them (heehee).

For people who don't have a lot of dexterity, I would suggest purchasing a book titled, *Wheelchair Fashion 101* by Tiffiny Carlson, listed in the reference section of this book. She gives sound tips on fashion and beauty that come from personal experience as a woman living with quadriplegia herself.

TIDBITS

- A hand-held mirror is my saving grace, or a mirror on a door that I can get close to.

- With liquid liner, I need to rest the mirror on something so that I can use both hands for application, eg; lie on the bed, or put the mirror on a desk.

- Carry a lipstick in your pouch under your chair and a few bobby-pins.

TIDBITS for ladies with less nimbleness:

- I have noticed that if I line the lower lip first and press my lips together, the top lip will be virtually done.

- Also if I did not have dexterity, I would use more subtle colours of lip sticks and lip gels/stains are more forgiving.

- When applying mascara – wipe off excess straight away, position your hand and use your blinking to line your lashes instead.

- Apply liquid foundation using a sponge with Velcro glued on the back of it. Have a tape that you can wrap around your hand made of Velcro. Stick the sponge on to the hand wrap. When you purchase a foundation get it poured into a flat plastic container so that you can dab your sponge into the container for application. If you need, dab off the excess foundation onto a tissue before applying.

bit eight – the Bra

Burn the Bra, I say!

Ok, this sub-topic only really relates to those of us who have our point of injury around T6/7/8. Why? Well my dears, it is because this is where the straps of a Bra sit, and it is painful. I know that a bra has a hook 'n' eye sort of clasp and that this is what is causing the pain, but sometimes it honestly feels like someone is digging a knife into my spine! Seriously. And then, I discovered the bras without these clasps that simply had an elastic stretchy panel in the rear, and it was like heaven on my spine. These particular types of bras don't have clasps in any other position and so we put them on over our head, which is not particularly attractive or sexy, but it is totally worth it for the lack of agony enjoyed the entire day. I don't believe they have a specific name, and it is definitely not a sports bra because it doesn't offer any real support, which means that it is probably only suitable for the Audrey Hepburns of the world, like myself, and not the Marilyn Monroes (if you know what I'm talking about).

bit nine – Sex and Self-pleasure

I do not wish to get uncomfortably personal here, and if you are not ready for this topic at this point in time, then just skip forward to the next chapter. And for those of us who are up-for-it, I think it is necessary to at least concede that sex and self-pleasure (masturbation) still exists for us ladies who use chairs.

Upfront, I want to tell you that I won't be going into a lot of detail on this matter, I won't be giving you a lot of dos and don'ts, but what I will do is give you the name of a comprehensive and practical book that has been a reference to me. I will also encourage you to make time to get to know your body again because the only way that another person will know how to please you, is if you know how to please yourself! Makes sense, right? And even though right now this might be the furthest thing from your mind, trust me, there will be a day when it is not, and I don't want to leave you 'high and dry' on this part of our lives.

For me, this didn't really come into my consciousness for some time, about four years I think, and it might be the same for you or not, regardless, sex is a part of every aspect of this world - the bees do it, the fish do it, even the zebras do it and so too can we! There are two points I want to make – (1) we can still enjoy a wonderful sex-life no matter what has happened, and (2) sex can still be lovely for us (and with us).

I don't know if pre-injury you were a once in a week kinda girl or liked it (sex) once a day, but, because we are more than a one dimensional being, we can't deny that we have feelings, desires, yearnings and needs. The act of sex gives more than just a physical pleasure and erogenous sensations, and it is more than just a mere physical feat, since it has the power to make us feel wanted and desirable, beautiful, normal and whole as a human being. Yes, we can absolutely deny that aspect of who we are for some time, but there will be a day when we will be forced to face it – like it or not. And, the reason why I am of the opinion that masturbation is necessary, is because it is a very literal act of loving the body, the self, and that is a wonderful thing. With the type of change to our life and bodies that we have experienced, it often heralds negative self-images, thoughts and feelings, and a powerful way of breaking this down is by physically giving love to ourselves.

Sex may or may not be the same as it was before the change to our lives, but the fact that we are all unique and different in our likes/dislikes, what works for one may not work for another does still stand. Yes, there will be generalisations that can be made about paraplegia and quadraplegia, but unless the injury was done in the precise same way, with the same amount of force and at the exact specific point on the body – there must be some degree of difference. We are, after all, individuals who see, hear and experience things our own way. Like everything else we need to re-learn, for example, dressing and toileting, we also need to start from scratch again when it comes to our bodies and sex.

I want to encourage you not to give up the first time you try it (self-pleasure/sex) if it doesn't feel the same as it did before the accident/disease – the fact is that it won't, and we need to accept that, but it doesn't mean that it can't feel good in a different way either. No, we should not have to do this and yes it is unfair but this is our situation, and for most of us the circumstances won't be changing any time soon. Maybe you prefer to have your self-exploration in private, or perhaps this is something that you and your partner could do together? That is our freedom and choice, but so long as we can be open with our partners it does not have to be awkward.

I recall during sex pre-accident that I had a lot of ideas about what it was supposed to be like, for example: spontaneous, natural, adventurous and exciting and perfect – but since the accident (and growing up) I have realised that this is a truck load of expectations to put on to something that is supposed to be filled with love and pleasure. I want to take a couple of moments here to talk about the expectations you might have in your head, because they may not be helping you.

We see it in the movies, read it in books, and it is even in television commercials – attraction and sex is supposed to be spontaneous. Well, that is the unspoken message that comes through anyway, but I don't know if it works in the real world with real responsibilities, real families and real lives. I'd like you to talk to a woman who is a mother of two children and see how much spontaneous sex she has in her life. I'm guessing it is not regular, and it is not really so 'spontaneous' either. So who are they (the media) trying to kid? And, it is not so different for us either. Maybe we need to go to the bathroom before intimacy is possible. Maybe we need to watch what we are drinking so that love-making is possible within the next couple of hours. And, maybe sex is not an option for us at night time. I don't know what your routine is like, or your body, yet I do know that being up close and personal with that person that you cherish is very special, even if it is not so spontaneous – so that is the first belief we need to get out of our head.

If we have to talk about things before and during, then the sex won't be special – I'm sorry, but that is bull$#?!. If this is another thing that you fear, then we need to straighten this out right now, woman to woman (smiles).

What you need to ensure is that the person you choose to be intimate with is worth it! And when it comes to the actual sex - some people don't like certain positions and other people do – which is no different to us ladies. No, we would not have had to do this before the accident or change to our life, but trust me, it won't make them think any less of you, or desire you less. Yes, there might be some aspects that we might want to talk about, with our partners, before we take the next step into intimacy, and if they have a problem with what you bring up, then, it is clear that they are NOT worth your time or energy!!!

Now, you should know that being in a wheelchair in no way stops you from having adventurous and exciting intimacy – you are only limited by your mind. Experiment with pillows, bed heads, chairs, locations, and whatever else takes your fancy. When you have someone you feel safe with, there are no limits to your love-life.

'Perfect' – this word and 'normal' really should be removed from the dictionary once and for all, as it creates so many problems for so many people. Some people would say that Audrey Hepburn was perfect, yet she herself could not agree with that. For some people, sushi is just perfect, but not every person on this planet would agree. What I am trying to get at here, is that, depending on who you are, where you come from, what your background is, what your preferences are – perfect is going to be different! And sex will be 'perfect' when you find the one that makes your heart sing. Sex is different with different people, and we need to stop comparing ourselves to others in our head, if we are ever going to be happy. Stop comparing how you look to the woman next door, stop comparing what you do with the women in your life and stop comparing how you are now to how you were 10 years ago! Comparing is pointless unless we are trying to improve a recipe or something like that, it does not do us, or anyone else any good.

We don't have to look perfect in order to deserve love, we don't have to be perfect in order to be good enough and love-making will be perfect with the one you love.

In closing, I would like to recommend this book, *The Ultimate Guide to Sex and Disability* by Miriam Kaufman, M.D., Cory Silverberg, and Fran Odette. This book covers sex and disabilities ranging from Cystic Fibrosis to Spinal Cord Injury, and has thirteen chapters of knowledge and information. Pick it up, it is fantastic!

bit ten – If you look good = you feel good!

I want to touch on something I have mentioned before in another chapter, only because it has proven so instrumental to me and might for you too, and that is 'if you look good, you will feel good'. I know this phrase is old and tired, but it exists because it has been proven to be a truth! I know how I felt in the beginning of my new life when I was carrying more weight and couldn't dress that nicely, and I know how I feel about myself today when I make the effort to exercise, eat right and thereby can wear what I want – it feels great. There is a stack of proof that validates the connection between how we look impacting on how we feel about ourselves, and it is confirmed every time we put something nice on and all of a sudden feel more confident or appealing. I have to say that even while I was writing this book I would make myself presentable, do my hair and put some mascara and 'lippy' on – why? Because, if I happened to glance in a mirror, I could be somewhat happy with what I saw. While some people will try to convince you that 'we' dress for others, I know for a fact that I need to make myself feel good before I am ready for anything.

So, I would encourage you to take a second look at your cupboard and really decide if your clothes are a true extension of who you are or not? Next, I would suggest that any items you choose to discard you do so to a charity organisation, think about changing the colour of some items that might improve their usage (eg: dying), and lastly, but actually this should be firstly, pick up some books on fashion and styling or research fashion and wheelchairs on the net.

<u>Here are my top 3 sites for women in chairs & fashion</u> –

www.wheeliechix-chic.com
This site creates fashionable clothing for women in chairs, aged 22-42 yrs old.

www.beautyability.com
Tiffany Carlson created the website, 'Beauty Ability' and writes on topics from disability and SCI stuff, to beauty and fashion tips. Tiffany writes with intelligence and wit, offering a fresh perspective on things and a cheeky perspective on life. Go girl!

www.versaaccesswear.com
Versa Access Wear merges fashion-forward design with construction elements suited for women with limited physical mobility. Check it out girls.

I hope that you look in the mirror and see the beautiful woman that you are, looking back at you!

Violet

Chapter six

Life in the real world

This chapter is all about getting back out and into the world and into Part two of our lives, with our new legs. It is about being aware of the physical challenges we will face in the real world (as it is right now), learning from others who have done things we want to do and basically, re-claiming our life. Part of this process will be learning about our chair, and in this chapter, I hope to highlight not what we can't do, rather, what we can! Because, if someone tells me I can't do something, I like to prove them wrong.... think it has something to do with my aries-ness.

Ultimately, by the end of this chapter, my wish is that us 'chicks in chairs' recognise that we are the ones in the driver's seat of our lives, acknowledge that if we want change it has to start with us, and understand that if more and more of us 'chicks in chairs' get out and get active, then the world has no choice but to change – because numbers and dollars count!

The backbone of this chapter (heehee), will consist of the most basic of human needs, as well as stories and ideas about how to successfully complete our day-to-day activities. I will chat with you about everything from making the bed to shopping for shoes and going to the cinema. You have probably done most of these things I am sure, but sometimes it is just nice to know that how you do something is exactly how another chick in a chair does it too, just knowing that can be enough. It is not always possible or practical to talk about certain things with other people in chairs, yet when it happens, I know from my own experiences it is comforting and reassuring.

Now, as I can't ask you anything about yourself to find out where you are with everything, I will have to just pick a point in time and take it from there. That said, I think the most practical point would be rehabilitation, because then, I won't miss anyone, and even if you are a few years post injury, perhaps you will enjoy the read anyway.

That said, I don't know if the place you are in right now is filled with light and hope or darkness and despair, but I am here to show you and tell you that there is light, hope and everything else that you want –

regardless of what has happened and what your story is. In no way do I mean to undermine what has happened to you at all. What has occurred to you, myself and thousands of women around this big wide world is heart-breaking, challenging, horrible, and profound, yet beyond that, you and I both know that life goes on and not only that, this new life does not have to be void of fun, adventure, excitement, love or anything else that springs to mind!

I have come to realise that 'happiness' is not merely a destination or a goal - it is only a decision. I can't recall when I realised this truth, yet regardless, it just makes sense, because, we could be waiting our whole lives to be happy if we are waiting to get that job, house, car or destination.

It is like going for a drive with your partner from the Gold Coast to Byron Bay, some people are only happy when they reach Byron Bay (me), while others (my Marty) are happy every step along the way. I used to be a 'when I get there, I'll be happy kinda girl and I thank Marty for showing me that about myself. The truth is that happiness is something that anyone can create or suppress at any moment of any day. I am sure you have heard a lot of people say that they will be happy when they get this or do that, yet after they achieve their goals, it still seems to elude them. Another truth about happiness is this, it needs to come from the inside and flow outward, not the reverse. Yes, again, I am saying it is only OUR CHOICE if we are happy or not!

As of this year (2012), I have been living with a wheelchair for thirteen years, and I have tried to pack in as much as possible every year and will continue to live that way, because that is who I am.

I will be honest with you and tell you that in the first twelve months, of this new life, at some point you will probably feel like screaming, tearing-up, punching something out of pure frustration, telling the chair (and the world) to go-to-hell! Or you may not. Regardless of how you handle the situation, this is a learning-curve of Mount Everest proportions and it will test you because it touches every aspect of who we are — our looks, our body, our functions, our capabilities, our home, how we interact in the world, how others see us.... everything! Yet, despite the enormity of what you are going through, I want to stress, that it doesn't have to be 'hard' or 'horrible' - that decision is up to you! Look, from here onwards the only way is up, right? I mean, let's face it, the worst has already happened to us, so it can only get better from here! I think that is the best way to look at it anyway.

I have to say that this is the most exciting part of it all really, because each part of your life that comes together, and each day that goes by, you will feel more and more whole again – and that is the aim. Rediscovering that you are still the same person that you were beforehand might take some time, or it might be something that happens overnight. Personally, it took four years before I felt like the old 'me', or perhaps before I allowed myself to be me again – heck, I don't know, I'm not a psychologist. All I know is that, a light bulb went on at some point, and I realised that I was still me - Violet.

Walking or not walking, blind or seeing, hearing or deaf – we are the women we are today because of the sum of our experiences to date, whether or not they are 'good' or 'bad' experiences. Our background, our family's culture, our race, our gender, our socio-economic status, our sexual preference, our language, our looks, our size, our education, our interactions with others, our circle of friends, where we live, how many women/men we have around us, our work place, our work colleagues, what kind of books were read to us as children, if we had a television as children, the type of television programmes we watch, if we had pets or not as children, the music we had in the house as children, the people our parents chose as friends, our teachers, the cultures in our local community, our neighbours, the kids we played with at school – every single aspect of our world helped shape us into the women we are today! I am sure you have probably heard what I am about to say before, but I am going to say anyway, because it has proven to be true in my life – 'even in the 'bad' moments, there is always something to learn'. Let's take, for an example, when I lost my dad to cancer, in July, 2000. My dad phoned me while I was in rehabilitation to tell me that his cancer had returned, and asked me to come home. My dad offered me accommodation in the town where he lived, but I selfishly said 'no thanks', because, it was a small town and I didn't want to be known as 'that girl in the wheelchair'. So, I stayed in a hostel about 4 hours drive away from where he lived instead. I learnt a couple of points from that experience, one point was that I should have swallowed my pride and taken his offer so that I had more time with him, than what I had, during his last months. Another lesson was that, I wished I had the guts to ask him a trillion questions about him and his life, before it was too late, because today, I could have a memoir of the man I call dad. This is exactly what I mean, when I say that it is both, the 'good' and 'bad' moments that make us into the woman we are today.

The point I am trying ever so hard to make here is that I would not be the person I am today if not for everything that I have been through, seen, heard, felt and learnt– positive and negative – and neither would you!

Do you know that worn phrase about a horse? – 'you can lead a horse to water but you can't make it drink'.... I can sit here and tell you a million times that You are still you – but you won't see that, hear it or believe it, until you are ready for it. And, I know that to be true because as much as other people tried to convince me that I was still beautiful and capable, I just thought they were being nice to me.

Let me tell you something that I found out about myself through the journey that I have been on. In the beginning of my new life I knew I would have to do some positive self-talk before venturing out into the world, for various reasons. I don't recall the very first time it happened, but random strangers would ask me 'the question' (why I was in a chair), and initially, I would tell them honestly what I had been through, usually with tears welling in my eyes. I think those people walked away feeling sorry they asked. That happened a few times, then I had had enough of it, so I came up with a few phrases that I could use as a comeback. Like telling them I ended up in a chair after naked bungy-jumping in New Zealand. I don't care if they believed it or not, the point was to shut them up.

Anyway, about a year later, I decided that I didn't actually like serving up the one-liner as I felt rude. Yet at the same time I felt that these strangers were being incredibly rude for asking me such a personal and private question. It didn't take a heap of soul-searching to realise that I was just protecting myself. And it made perfect sense, because every time I told someone 'the story', it was as if I was experiencing it again and again and again. For the life of me, I could not understand why people that I didn't know from a bar of soap (I love the old funny sayings) would think they have the right to ask me a question about the most horrible thing in my life. I mean, do I go up to pregnant women and ask them 'so why do you want to have a baby?' I don't do this, because, frankly, it is none of my bloody business.

I was talking about this one day with Marty and he saw it as if the strangers think that I am public property and that they have a right to know. Just like some people who think they can go up and touch the belly of any woman that happens to be pregnant – like they are public property. Fortunately, not everyone does this, but it happens.

Having the snappy one-liner stopped me from having to re-tell the story, which in turn meant that I didn't have to re-live all the emotions that re-surfaced every time I told it. This tool (the one-liner) was one method of self-preservation, protection and defence, and it only makes sense that we would want to protect ourselves. Yet, I knew this was not me. I didn't want to be rude yet I needed to protect myself, and let these strangers know that this is personal information. And God-forbid, their question was an attempt at making conversation with me, then perhaps they should try another method. So, for a while I would simply say that 'I had an accident' and left it at that. But still I didn't think that this helped them see the error of their ways. So, after some conversations with Marty we came up a phrase that I felt comfortable with and is what I use these days. The sentence is simply this – 'In order to answer your question I would have to relive a very horrible and painful event and I am sure you don't want that, do you?'

Side track

Just now I raised the fact that the event, our accident, was and may well still be something that stirs up all sorts of emotions and feelings for us – and I want to touch on that just for a couple of minutes, if you don't mind?

By the age of 30 years old, 2000, I had buried my mother, father, only brother and boyfriend too. I don't know if you have lost someone close to you yet, or perhaps you've been through a divorce, had a miscarriage or lost something very valuable to you. In moments like these people are at a loss for 'what to say' to the ones who are suffering - some people will make food and bring it over, some don't say anything, but some want to say something meaningful and/or offer some form of hope which comes from the right place – their heart. Which is why we have all heard things like, 'you'll be alright', 'it will get easier' or 'just give it time'. If you are new to this situation, I know that even though these words are true, you are not in the right space to hear them or believe them. Twelve years on I can candidly say that the pain is not as raw and overwhelming as it was within the first 6 months, I don't burst into tears like I did in the first year, tears don't well in my eyes when I retell the story like they did in the first three years, and the accident is not at the forefront of my mind like it was ten years ago. And while for me the accident will always be surrounded by sadness, I have been able to face the facts, accept what has happened, accept my new legs and make a new life for myself – one that is beautiful.

Ok, let us get down to things then.

When I studied psychology a few years ago, I read about a gentleman who contributed a significant amount to psychology, from his lifelong work he claims that people are motivated by needs that remain unsatisfied. This knowledge and information played a considerable part in what we know about humans today, explaining why his work is still a part of psychology courses in this century. An important factor of his theory is that certain lower factors have to be satisfied before any higher needs can have a chance at being fulfilled. Which is why, when we have just experienced such a dramatic change in our lives (this can vary for each individual), we will want to ensure that our basic needs (such as a home, toilet facilities, food) are met before any ideas of love or romance can come into our realm of consciousness.

It may also be true that you will need a lot more certainty/stability around those basic needs on a day-to-day basis than ever before, because now it can be more challenging to meet and maintain those needs, eg: finding an accessible bathroom when on holidays or out grocery shopping.

Abraham Maslow was this man's name, and this system or model is called the 'hierarchy of needs', outlined below–
1. Physiological needs (oxygen, water, food etc.),
2. Safety needs (roof over their heads, safe area to live, medical services, job security, financial security etc.),
3. Social needs (friendship, support, giving and receiving love),
4. Esteem needs (recognition, attention, accomplishment, self-respect) and
5. Self Actualisation (truth, justice, wisdom, meaning).

So, it makes sense that your team (Occupational Therapist and Physiotherapist) will try their darn-dest to ensure that your basic needs are ticked off before you even consider leaving the hospital. And if there are 'things' (technical term) on your list that they can't achieve for you, they will be able to put you in touch with an organisation that can. However, there are some aspects of our lives that do not fall within their parameters or their colleagues either, like love.

So, if you are still in hospital perhaps your 'to do' list may look something like this:

- A wheelchair
- Accommodation adaptations or a new place
- Service providers for personal care
- Transport adaptations or information on public transport access
- Physical exercise

Within this chapter we will be chatting about most of these points on your list, and those aspects that are not covered in hospital, like love, and wardrobe dilemmas will be covered in other chapters. What I share with you in this chapter is not to replace the professional advice that you get from your team, it is merely lessons and experiences that I am sharing with you in the hope of being of some assistance.

bit one – your Wheelchair

So let us begin with the most pressing need which is, a wheelchair, because let's face it – it is now our legs.

For everyday use there are only two types of chairs in the world – Rigid or Folding, and I would like to talk with you about both because both have pros and cons.

bit two- Rigid chairs

Rigid wheelchairs will give you stability and a guarantee that they will never collapse underneath you, no matter what you do to it, because their framework is welded into place. Most people with paraplegia that I know and have seen around, chose a rigid frame chair. The frame resembles an S-like shape which really is quite easy to work with, when trying to fit them into places like cars, making them easy to throw across the body from outside of the car (not literally, heehee) to the passenger's seat next to you. They fit quite neatly into the boot of most vehicles, except hard-top convertibles and their matchbox-size boot space. Despite what airplane staff will tell you, your rigid-frame chair fits snugly into the overhead compartments on board planes, as I have proven on many international flights. That said, I am talking about the average-size chair.

A lot of rigid frame chairs are very light, ranging from 7 – 10 kilos. This depends of course on the size of the chair, as well as the substance that it is made with. These chairs can be made from titanium, steel or aluminium. Titanium was introduced to the market a few years ago now, and while some users say that they would not choose anything else, some suppliers (that don't sell titanium) claim that other chairs are similar in weight. Having had several chairs myself, it is my own opinion that titanium is a tad lighter than steel and aluminium. My partner tells me that this is also the general consensus of most cyclists too, being one himself. However, don't trust my opinion, test this for yourself.

Now the size of the chair will add to the weight, and the size of your chair depends on one factor and one factor alone – that is, the size of your derrière! If you choose to eat sensibly, exercise, and are conscious about your weight, it can make a difference to your life, for example: it means that you can keep your chair longer (which saves you dosh) and you can squeeze into tight places, like normal size toilet cubicles or ridiculously skinny check-out registers in shops (which saves you time and energy).

The only con I can find with rigid frame chairs is that they are really not adjustable, which means that widening is not an option. Minor adjustments can be made, yet I would talk to the representative and be sure you have all the facts before you make any decisions.

Now, when we are deciding on a chair, one of the most essential questions to ask ourselves is this – do we get a chair off the rack or do we get one custom made? The reason I say this is a key point, is because, there are significant differences of cost and benefits between the two. Buying a chair off the rack is very much like choosing a suit from Coles Myer or Wal-Mart, while opting for a custom made chair is comparable to getting a suit tailor-made to fit your proportions, strengths and personal shape. Both types of chairs are going to fulfil your basic needs, both types of chairs will have similar features and parts, the primary difference will be the difference in quality and design. It may sound insignificant, yet when it comes to something we will spend 16 hours a day using, seven days a week, 365 days a year – it does make a difference. Not only will the design and functionality of your chair make an impact on you physically, but, how you look (physically) and feel in your chair (emotionally) will impact you and your self-esteem on a day-to-day basis, and this is also why the chair you choose, is an integral decision in your life now!

When you place an order for a chair (custom made) it is like Christmas! You will get to choose every single aspect of it from the colour of the frame, to the size and position of your castor wheels, to the type of cushion you sit on, you get to decide if you want side-guards or not, you can even choose the shape of the front of the chair, the kind of big rear wheels you want, down to even the thickness of your push rims. Can you believe that? Of course, you do pay for this privilege yet for me it is worth every cent. Why? Well, like I said above, we are in this chair 365 days a year and it will not only impact our neck, shoulders, and body in general, it is like a piece of clothing or shoes, if you will. The chair can tell others about our personality, about the type of person we are, and to some degree, how we see ourselves. We can personalise the cushion, the backrest, the colour of the wheelchair frame and the wheels too. I have lost count how many times I have been approached by both children and adults because they wanted to tell me how beautiful my wheels are. Who knows if it is the flowers on my wheels (3-spoke carbon fibre), the chair in general, or just me. What I do know, is that when I look in the mirror I am happy with what I see and that makes me feel good about myself. And that to me, is worth a million dollars.

Now that we have chatted about the benefits of a custom-made chair, I also need to tell you about my experience so that you see both sides of the coin.

When I was choosing my first chair, I had no clue at all! None. It was like going on your first ski trip ever and then, someone asking you to buy some new skis for the trip. And like most new spinal injury patients, we relied very heavily on the guidance and opinion of our individual physiotherapists. Of course, us patients talked it out amongst ourselves but we were clueless. I wanted my first chair to look cool and fun, but I was r-e-a-l-l-y scared about tipping backwards and wanted to feel really safe. I remember trying a Kuschall chair in the physiotherapy unit and tipping backwards when I was just sitting there. I knew I would be living mostly by myself and I thought, there is no way I want that to happen when I'm on my own. Even though a couple of years down the track, I asked myself 'what was I thinking?', at the time I still believe I made the best choice.

Like my first chair, yours will probably be more practical than trendy, and that is ok, because in the beginning you will be learning the ropes. Just like when we were beginner drivers learning how to overtake, reverse park and do a clutch start on a hill, our parents didn't buy us a Mercedes or BMW (even though we would have loved it), because, when we are learning, things are going to happen like dents, scratches, dings and collisions with mailboxes. And after we have had our learning phase, we will be better equipped and experienced for the BMW, and probably appreciate it more in the end. That's my take on it though. You might want your first car or chair to be a Subaru WRX. It's your choice.

The wheels on both sorts of chairs, a rigid frame or a folding chair, come off the chair with a simple push of the quick release button found in the centre of the wheel.

Side track

Now, as a cycling enthusiast, my partner told me about this historical tidbit...

the quick release button was actually invented by an Italian cyclist, Mr Tullio Campagnolo, when during a race he had to stop and change a wheel. He decided that day that there had to be an easier way..... and presto, in 1930 the quick release lever was born.

There are three types of wheels to choose between, these include (a) wire spokes, (b) Carbon Fibre or (c) Spinergy wheels. Wire spoke wheels come with most chairs, while carbon fibre and Spinergy wheels are an extra that we can opt for.

The carbon fibre wheels only have 3 spokes and of course, are extremely light in comparison to the wire spoke wheels. Spinergy wheels have fewer spokes than the regular wire wheels, and are made a bunch of really strong, flexible fibres that absorbs impact too. As a bonus, they come in a variety of colours, so that you can show your true colours... heehee.

Below are the websites for both the 3-Spoke wheels and the Spinergy wheels.

www.spinergy.com/Wheelchair/default.aspx
www.4rgk.com/file_library/buttons/101_RGK_Spares.pdf

Some people I mingled with among wheelchair basketball had Spinergy wheels and I didn't really think much of them, as from a distance they still look much the same as regular wire wheels. I guess, the difference is in the ride perhaps. Yet until 2004, I never even knew carbon fibre wheels existed, and now I would never go back to wire spokes. Some people claim these wheels break as easily as looking at them, yet seven years on mine are still going strong – mind you I don't do back flips or go down skate ramps on them either. If you are that sorta person, maybe these wheels are not for you. Heehee.

A very kind lady generously gave me my very first pair of carbon fibre wheels, as she had received them as a gift herself from a company. At the time the wheels was turquoise with yellow tyres, yet I still thought they were gorgeous. I changed the tyres to the standard grey and absolutely adored them, still do today. Thank you for your generosity Lisa.

Carbon fibre wheels come in a variety of colours or you can get them painted yourself, like I did. Remember though, that whatever colour you choose it will need to be suitable for both work and play; don't know how seriously they would take a lawyer turning up to court in a leopard print coloured chair? Hhmmmm. I'd like to see it though (Big grin).

When I received my 3 spokes I went a step further. If you are not familiar with the 3-spoke carbon fibre wheel, it has only 3 spokes which are flat and approximately 10 centimetres wide. I thought my wheels could look really cool with some paintwork on them, so I found something I liked, and found an artist to do it. Why? Why not! I figure I may as well like the look of the piece of equipment that is my legs. I do not seek attention, however, I do feel good when others compliment me on my chair and tell me, 'I have never seen anything like it before'. Perhaps, because of the painted wheels, people see more of the real me instead of just a piece of metal.

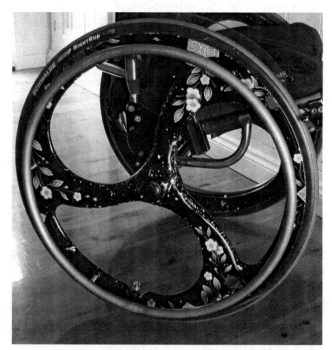

My 3 spoke wheel

But let us get on to Folding chairs.....

bit three - Folding chairs

Now these chairs are chosen mostly by people who can walk or those who have some sort of mobility challenge, rather than a person with paraplegia. Some people might believe that these chairs are lighter than the rigid frame chair, yet I feel they might be mistaken.

When you look at a folding chair, the frame looks to be made using more steel or aluminium, than the rigid frame chair, thereby adding to the weight. The wheels of a folding chair pull off the same as with a rigid chair, while the rest of it stays intact, squashed together. Do your homework first. Folding chairs do not fit in overhead luggage compartments at all. They might fit into some boots of the sedan size vehicle, yet in my opinion they will not have the options a rigid frame chair does.

I ask you to consider that the heavier the chair, the more you or someone else's back and arms will ache at the end of a day – depending on how many times it will be lifted in and out of the car. Remember, when you are going somewhere you will be lifting that chair into your car at your home, out at your destination, back into the car again to leave, and then again at your next location = that is four times you will be lifting that chair just to go to one place. This is why the weight of your chair is so important.

How much your chair weighs can, on occasion, be the difference between deciding to go somewhere or not, depending on how tired you are. Take a moment to consider the worth of your back, shoulders or neck when considering taking the cheapest option. I say this because I care about your wellbeing, and I don't want you stuck at home because your chair is too heavy for you to lift.

Bit four – Let's talk chair bits

When it comes to **tyres** you have the choice between getting (a) normal tyres that are filled with air, (b) tyres that are solid (meaning you will never get a puncture) or (c) normal tyres filled with "gunk" that fills up the hole when you get a puncture. And, don't think you will never get a puncture, because this is life – remember, s*#t happens!

I'm sure I have mentioned the puncture in Paris to you before, as that was a huge lesson for me about my choice of tyres. Life threatening I don't think so, yet at the time I sure felt scared. There I was in the middle of Paris with a flat and high school French, trying to find a bike shop. I am grateful though that I received this lesson in Paris though, and not somewhere like Egypt. I just thank God for tour guides.

Let me just say upfront, that I am in NO WAY a mechanical person and I won't pretend to be, to impress you. I do not spend my time meticulously cleaning the wheels or lubricating the joints of my chair, putting in new bearings or even filling up the air in my tyres. I am in fact, quite the opposite. I will push around on my tyres while they are squeaking and squealing out to me to be filled with air and I will only clean my bearings when I can physically push no longer on them because they are that dirty. Why? Because quite frankly, to me there are better things I can do with my time. And, if I am completely honest.... it is my loving and caring man that does all of these things for me, because I hate it so. (Marty, I want to thank you - my sweet, sweet man for showing your love in this way!)

Now that I've cleared that up, let's talk about the really small wheels at the front of your chair – their technical term is 'castor wheels'. Now, let me tell you that the smaller the castor wheel, the easier it fits into smaller spaces. The negative to this, is that they will also feel every single bump and groove there is in the concrete or wherever it is you roam. Small castors will feel it whether they push over a nut or a drink lid. And, the smaller this wheel is, the easier it will be to get caught in things like grates in the concrete, so consider the pros and cons before you make your decision, and ask others – you could try organisations or forums on the net. Now, I also want to talk to you about the bearings inside of these castors and tell you that they can wear out and need replacing – something that would make sense to most men, yet I never thought about, until the day I needed to. Anyway, long story short.... I needed new castors because of the bearings and through the journey, we discovered that the wheels that fit those new toys called "rip-sticks" also fit my wheelchair. Unfortunately, I could only get the white wheels, however, I am hoping to replace them with red ones when I make the time to find some and order them. I have been surprised how easy and cheap it has been to fix little things that come up with my chair every now and then, take for eg: my castors again. There is aluminium tubing that makes what called 'spacers' between the forks of my castors and the castor wheel itself. Before I met Marty, I would have just called the wheelchair guy to order some more and pay him to come down and put them in. Marty, being my very own Mr Superman just buys some aluminium tubing from Bunnings, measures it and cuts it to fit my wheels. And, I think the tubing cost about $2 for about 1 meter. Give it a go, what have you got to loose? Thanks sweet. Ok, let's keep moving.

Side guards are pieces of plastic that slide down each side of your chair between you and the wheel. I absolutely love them! Why? They protect my clothes from tyre marks, dirt that attaches to the tyres, and wet weather damage. The side guards will fit best if you purchase them with your chair though, not afterward. Some side guards can come out and some don't. I used to think that I could not lift a chair into my car with the side guards still in, yet I have proven that idea wrong, and now I have mine permanently fixed into place. Now, you might find, as I have, that over time the side guards distort in shape. I don't know why exactly, it could be from the way I transfer or it could be putting on weight.... I don't know. I just want to warn you that this is a possibility and that there is a solution! Yay. My beautiful man, Marty, took my guards out, drilled a small hole near the front of the guard, put the guard back in place on my chair, threaded a zip tie through the hole and around the wheelchair frame and pulled it tight. How simple is that? Fantastically easy, isn't it? Obviously my man is not just a pretty face (Big grin).

And as for me and my thighs, I have found my way back to the swimming pool and regular exercise, I will lose those unwanted kilos.

What's next? Ah yes, brakes.

You will have the choice of a few different sorts of **brakes** for your chair. On my first chair I chose the simple standard break that works on a 90 degree angle – it is basic, but easy to use and not fiddley. On my second chair I opted for something a bit different, they are called 'Scissor brakes' and they were great in the beginning, but, in time I just wanted the simple standard brake again. So, when I purchased my third chair I decided on the basic brake again, and I'm happy. It does the job, it is as easy as it can be for a girl like me to fix, and they don't give me a headache. There might be occasions when you find that the position of your feet and legs may stop you from applying your brakes, just push your feet forward and it will be fine. Oh, and from time to time you might need to adjust your brakes and put them back into position, as they loosen and move over time. Luckily for me it is not rocket science, just fiddley and a bit messy, but I can handle that. I should probably also mention in this paragraph that if you happen to change your tyres to something different from what you have on right now, or change the wheel, it may well mean that you will need to adjust the position of your brakes too. Just want you to be aware beforehand.

Can you believe a lot of people (mostly the opposite sex) choose not to have brakes at all !!!!! Geez. Do you think it is the thrill factor or the ego? As for me, I choose brakes, because I like an amount of assurance and simplicity in my life. And, because I have also parked my car in a number of places where my chair would have rolled away had I not had brakes.

At this point I want to warn that having **handles** on the back of our chairs might invite unwanted guests – no, not the creepy crawly sort, but those who would feel free to move us should we be in their way (just as they would a shopping trolley). I would like to point out that moving a trolley with food items in it is nothing like taking control of another human being and relocating them to where someone believes they should be. Whether the person in the chair is a senior member of our community, is awake or asleep, is able to understand the request to move or not – the question needs to be addressed to the human being who uses the wheelchair first! Just as it would be done, if it was someone standing. There is no difference at all, and there is no excuse for it either. Sorry, I know that I am getting on my soap box, however, it just feels like we are treated like half-people.

It is disrespectful when people who are able-bodied park in our 'disabled parking' spaces, it is rude when our wheelchair goes to the carousel in airports instead of coming to us on the plane, it is selfish when able-bodied people exit the disabled bathroom that I have been waiting for, it is excluding us as members of the community when shop owners don't provide wheelchair access, it is rude when shops have six foot tall counter tops and store persons don't stand up to speak to us, and it is disrespectful when people don't communicate with the person who uses the chair. It needs to be addressed every time it happens, or else it will never disappear. And we are the ones who will have to do it.

I have not had anyone grab my chair for a long time now, so I am not telling you that this is going to happen every month. My first chair had removable handles that screwed in and I kept them in the glove box of my car, because I noticed that I didn't need them a lot. I know a number of others who have handles and use them this way, when needed. But even then, it is a pain to return to the car, get them out, and then return to where you wanted to gain access. Chair No.2 and 3 have not had handles on them at all, they do however, have a grab bar that sit about half way down your back rest and Marty and I have found this to be helpful enough. I really do believe that when a person sees handles, they just can't help themselves. Don't get me wrong, I don't mind being man-handled– but I only want Marty to do that! (wink wink)

What would be fabulous is a set of handles that were permanently attached to the chair yet folded down out of the way and were almost non-visible to the unfamiliar eye. A sort of handle that wrapped around the frame of the chair on the back rest, but as I am not going to design them, I'll stop wishing right now.

To be man-handled or not – it's up to you.

When choosing your **cushion** as it is one of the most crucial pieces of equipment you will have, I would refer you to a "seating clinic". Why? Plain and simple – it supports your spine, so it's a tad important! Even as a lay person, I can tell you that a good cushion will have you sitting in an upright position that protects your skin, and has you sitting pretty (Heehee). A bad cushion could have you off balance, increase scoliosis, as well as cause all sorts of problems for your skin. There are a plethora of options and you need to get one that suits your specific needs and body, which are two very good reasons to seek professional guidance. All of the cushions will have pros and cons, some cushions are very temperamental when it comes to air pressure (in planes), some give fantastic pressure relief but weigh a tonne, others are as light as a feather but may have little spinal support. So, make sure you discuss this in detail to ensure you completely understand the options, cost, maintenance requirements, and repair before making your decision.

I don't know what comes to your mind when you think about wheelchairs, but when I think about this subject there are primarily only three countries that spring to mind, and these are Switzerland, the UK and of course, the USA. So, despite the cost and the delay in receiving the goods, more than a decade later I still purchase what was recommended to me by the seating clinic at the spinal unit. That was, until recently anyway. What is not important, is the manufacturer and the model of the cushion, what is important is what I got out of the experience. So, allow me to share this with you.

Up until recently, I had been more than happy with the cushion that I had for my wheelchair – it was lightweight, no fuss and easy to travel with. A big bonus was that I didn't have to fuss with the gauge and air pressure whenever I travelled by air, as a lot of cushions do. It wasn't until this year when my current cushion died that I discovered there were no distributors for my cushion in Australia, and because of this fact, I had to wait for the item to come from the USA. But, that was ok because I really like my cushion. Then the company that takes the orders informed me that when the item arrives in Australia, it would need to go to them first before being forwarded onto me. And I knew what that meant – it would add at least two weeks to the delivery date and until I had it in my hot little hands. Still, I didn't mind because I really like my cushion.

It actually ended up taking close to two months before I was sitting on my new cushion…. And that was only because I informed my local post office that I was waiting for a delivery from America. Unbeknownst to me, my new cushion had been sitting in their depot for almost a month. I was a little ticked-off about that, and I told them so. Yet, that didn't break the camel's back still. What did, was the puncture that I acquired in the cushion (I don't know how) less than four months later.

You see, I knew that regardless of the warranty that I would have to send back my almost-new cushion back to America and wait for its replacement to return back to me. And, I had an idea about how long that whole process might take! Way too long!

Of course Marty tried his damndest to come to my rescue. He attempted to seal it two different ways, first with a mattress repair kit, and secondly with a tyre repair kit – both with no success. Anyway, that is the story… What I gained from this experience was knowledge and the pride of self-reliance.

At first I decided to use just a regular cushion, and it was fine. No, it wasn't perfect, however it did the job – I received no pressure points and it was easy to find. Yet, one aspect that I did notice was that I sat lower in my chair, and that I didn't like.

Then I thought, 'what about adding memory foam to my cushion?' When Marty and I went out looking we couldn't find just a piece of memory foam, but we didn't spend a whole lot of time looking either. What Marty did find though was a memory foam pillow, so we were grateful and we grabbed it. And after we arrived home he used a bread knife (Heehee) to cut it down to the size we needed and inserted it into an old cushion cover of mine. Hmmmm…. When I sat on it, it sank down to almost half its height.

Then I decided to add the cushion I had been using as well.... yet, it was still too low.

But wait, I had still another idea... this time I wanted to cut out the foam (from the non-functioning cushion) and put that with the memory foam together inside the cushion cover.... And to date, there are no pressure points whatsoever. Aaaah.... success! While my current cushion is not recommended by a seating clinic, and there is no warranty to go with it - there are also no valves/gauges to fuss with, and there is nothing that can go mechanically wrong with it either. I have learnt that I can save myself a lot of time, money and worry if I use a tad of resourcefulness, and that not everything that comes with a warranty is worth its weight in gold.

bit five – Buying wheelchairs

Before I finish with this section altogether, I want to give you details to think about when making such huge decisions.

There are so many facets to consider when you are purchasing your very own chair, and especially because, you will be stuck with the same one for at least the next 4 or 5 years, if not longer. I would suggest (if at all possible) speak to another person with a similar injury or circumstance as you, to find out what they would advise. And if they don't want to give you any advice, simply ask them what they do like and don't about their own chair. As you can imagine, anyone that has been in a chair longer than yourself can be a wealth of knowledge.

The Wheelchair Site is a website that I stumbled upon, and I love it, so I thought I would include it for you too. It is an independent website designed to help you choose the right wheelchair to get you going. On each page it explores subjects and offers buying tips on such topics as manual wheelchairs, electric wheelchairs and pediatric wheelchairs, motorized scooters, wheelchair lifts, wheelchair vans, and wheelchair accessories.

www.thewheelchairsite.com

bit six – Schemes available within Australia

The National Continence Helpline (Free call) 1800 33 00 66 or your local continence clinic can provide you with contact details for suppliers of continence products. www.continence.org.au

MASS – Medical Aids Subsidy Scheme

MASS provides access to subsidy funding for the provision of MASS endorsed aids and equipment to Queensland residents (in Australia) with permanent and stabilised conditions or disabilities.

The range of MASS aids and equipment is selected to assist people to live at home and avoid premature or inappropriate residential care or hospitalisation. Aids and equipment will not be provided when the main intent is for use to access the community including school and work. They work on a priority basis, giving first to those in the community with the greatest needs.

Applicants seeking MASS subsidised aids and equipment will need to arrange a clinical assessment by a health care professional (prescriber) approved by MASS. The health care provider authorised to prescribe your equipment can vary depending on the aid required.

Contact your local Community Health Centre or domiciliary agency where health professionals such as physiotherapists, occupational therapists, registered nurses and continence advisors are available to assist you. Together with your health care provider, you can complete an application form and forward it to MASS for consideration for subsidy funding assistance.

On the following page is a list of all the aids and equipment programs, in terms of disability in general, which is provided by the government within each State/ Territory to Australian citizens. www.health.qld.gov.au/mass

Continence Aids Assistance Scheme (CAAS) as of 01 July 2010 was replaced by **the Continence Aids Payment Scheme (CAPS)**. It offers financial assistance to people who suffer from incontinence in Australia. You will need to qualify for eligibility first by submitting an application. If you have any questions about completing your CAPS application form, please contact Medicare Australia on **132 011** and select option 1. www.bladderbowel.gov.au

CRS is not an acronym. CRS Australia is part of the Australian Government Department of Human Services.

The government has provided equipment to people entering the workforce after an extended absence from employment. There is a workplace modifications scheme also, which your employer might find helpful. www.australia.gov.au/people/people-with-disabilities

The Department of Veterans' Affairs (DVA)

DVA provides a range of continence products to eligible members of the veteran community via the Rehabilitation Appliances Program (RAP). A form requesting the continence products needs to be filled out by the assessing doctor or health professional. It is then sent to an authorised product supplier on behalf of the client. www.dva.gov.au/health/rap/rap_index.htm

There is also an **Artificial Limb Scheme** available in all states/ territories for those persons who fit this category. Below is a list of all of the official contacts for each state within Australia.

Australian Artificial Limb Services by State/Territory:

Australian Capital Territory: Contact Mr Bill Stone, The Canberra Hospital, (02) 6244-2475, email Bill.Stone@act.gov.au

New South Wales: Ms Rebecca Kemp, EnableNSW, (02) 8644-2083, email to Rebecca.Kemp@hsupport.health.nsw.gov.au

Northern Territory; Mr Thomas Berhane, Royal Darwin Hospital, (08) 8922-8241, email to thomas.berhane@nt.gov.au

Queensland: Ms Debra Berg, Buranda Shopping Centre, (07) 3896-3770, email to debra_berg@health.qld.gov.au

South Australia: Ms Mellissa Ward, SAALS, (08) 8266-5260, email to mellissa.ward@dfc.sa.gov.au

Tasmania: Ms Kathy O'Dea, Orthotic Prosthetic Services, (03) 6222-7377, email to Kathy.O'Dea@dhhs.tas.gov.au or go to www.dhhs.tas.gov.au and search for prosthetics.

Victoria: This lucky state has more than one contact and so it is best to follow this link www.rehabtech.eng.monash.edu.au/address/Result.idc to find your nearest point of contact.

Western Australia: Mr Ian Burns, Royal Perth Rehab Hospital, (08) 9382-7456, email to robert.burns@health.wa.gov.au
Following are some additional organisations that might be of interest and/or use too.

Amputees United of Australia Inc. gives every amputee in Australia the opportunity to voice their concerns in a more co-ordinated and effective approach at national and state level. Their role is to inform all levels of government, the business sector and the Australian community of the needs of amputees, in relating to their disability and lobby for change as necessary. Website www.monash.edu.au/rehabtech/amputee/AUA.HTM

Limbs4Life aims to empower amputees with information and support. The website provides peer support, provides information on rehabilitation to prosthetics and health; top website. This website is based in Victoria. Phone: 1300 782 231 (free call) Website www.limbs4life.com

Amputees Queensland is a collaboration between a number of amputee focused organisations operating in Queensland; there are 19 businesses listed which is fabulous. The only details given is this website www.aq.org.au/page1.php

Amputee Association of NSW Inc is run by amputees for amputees. It is a not for profit organisation with a number of affiliated branches throughout NSW; run by dedicated volunteers. This web site has been developed to assist all amputees in finding helpful and current information on support and assistance. There is also an online forum which is administered by Limbs 4 Life in Victoria. Website: www. aansw.clientcommunity.com.au   Contact us - Free call 1800 810 969

Central Coast Amputee Association Inc. is a non-profit organisation, which supports, advocates and provides information to people in the Gosford/Wyong area.   Call (02) 4328-1004 or email beryl@ centralcoastamputee.org.au

Amputee Association of South Australia Inc. is located at Level 1 220 Victoria Sq, ADELAIDE SA 5000, call: 08 8410-9255. There is no website for this organization and this is the total of details available. So just give them a call.

Tasmanian Amputee Society provides support and information for all amputees within the community via regular meetings and home visits. Call (03) 6344 6542 or 0438 523 015 or email: phatters@ wiseemployment.com.au

I shared a house with a girl that used a chair as she had lost part of her leg (below the knee) when I relocated to Sydney in 2001. She said that she attempted to use a prosthesis yet found it too painful, and so succumbed to using a chair full-time. I have absolutely no idea what it is like to try to attach an artificial limb to my body and trying to work with it, and I have full respect for those of us who do. What I do know is that professionals will want you to stay out of a chair for as long as possible, and I could not agree more, because muscle wastage increases the less you use your legs and the more you use the chair. Maybe the pain is more psychological than physical, I don't know, but I know that I would love to be able to throw on a leg and stand up again. And if you couldn't tell – that was some tough love for you, because I want the most for you in life.

State	Agency	Contact details
NSW	Department of Health, ENABLE Program of Appliances for Disabled People (PADP)	www.enable.health.nsw.gov.au/padp
QLD	Medical Aids Subsidy Scheme (MASS)	(07) 3136 3636 www.health.qld.gov.au/
WA	Silver Chain WA Health Department – Aged Care	1300 787 055 www.agedcare.health.wa.gov.au
SA	Independent Living Centre	(08) 8266 5260 www.sa.gov.au/subject/ community+support/disability/ adults+with+disability/
NT	NT Department of Health and Community Services	www.health.nt.gov.au
ACT	ACT Equipment Scheme (ACTES)	www.health.act.gov.au/home/ and search for 'ACTES'
VIC	Aids and Equipment Program (A & EP)	www.dhs.vic.gov.au/for-individuals/dis-ability/individual-support-packages
TAS	Community Equipment Scheme (CES)	1300 723 143 www.dhhs.tas.gov.au/services/view.ph

bit seven – Continence Aids

The provision of continence aids through schemes administered by State or Territory governments varies widely. Both the type of product and the amount available may differ depending upon which state the person lives. State/Territory schemes provide a range of equipment to people living in the community who have a permanent or long-term disability.

Buy Wheelchairs – ACT

I could not locate any companies that sell wheelchairs in this state and I asked one of my friends (who knows everything about chair-making) who said that most people go to Mogo in Sydney for chairs.

Buy Wheelchairs – NSW

Mogo Wheelchairs Pty Ltd
Unit 5/42 Canterbury Rd, Bankstown NSW 2200
Ph: (02) 9708 5255
www.mogowheelchairs.com.au

Mogo made my basketball wheelchair and they are great. It was everything I wanted and needed. They know what they are talking about, and build quality products. They make them on-site, so, allow sufficient time for the creation of your chair.

Sunrise Medical Pty Ltd.
Unit 7, 15 Carrington Road
Castle Hill , New South Wales 2154
Australia
Telephone:(+61) 2 9899 3144

Buy Wheelchairs – QLD

Power Mobility
Rod Silvester
Unit 3/ 41 Deakin St, Brendale QLD 4500
Ph: (07) 3889 8921
Rod used to deal with manual chairs & I have bought two through him – he knows his stuff. Now though, Rod is your man for power Chairs.

Dion Reweti
'Wicked Wheelchairs'
P.O. BOX 680, Oxenford QLD 4210

Mobile: 0406 771 265
Dion has helped me on a couple of occasions and I happily recommend his services. Dion is your man for Manual Wheelchairs.

Cerebral Palsy League of Queensland
354 Bilson Road, Geebung QLD 4034
61 7 3637 6360
www.cplqld.org.au/business/ets/wheelchairs
I just thought this might be handy for people with different needs.

Buy Wheelchairs – SA

Wendy Turner Wheelchairs
3 Albert Road, Richmond SA 5033
Ph: 08 8443 8844

Mogo Wheelchairs Pty Ltd
www.mogowheelchairs.com.au

Buy Wheelchairs – TAS

Again, I did some research and came up with a blank, and then asked around and found out that most Tasmanian's get them from Melbourne.

Buy Wheelchairs – VIC

Mobility Plus Wheelchairs
Unit 1/ 23 Bell Street, Preston VIC 3072
Freecall: 1300 011 000
Ph: (03) 9495 1955
www.mobilityplus.com.au

Dynamic Wheelchair Solutions Pty Ltd.
Unit 17/14-26 Audsley Street,
Clayton VIC 3168
Ph: +61 3 9548 8400
www.dynamicwheelchairs.com.au

Buy Wheelchairs – WA

Good Life Medical
25 Stockdale Rd, O'Connor, WA 6163
Ph:(08) 9331 8377
Recommended to me by a friend in the industry.

Buy Wheelchairs – United States of America

Spinlife – Experts in Motion
330 West Spring Street
Suite 303
Columbus, OH 43215
Toll Free:1-800-850-0335 or Phone: 614-564-1402
www.spinlife.com

USA TechGuide is a program of the United Spinal Association.
Here you can submit questions on any aspect of wheelchairs, mobility scooters, equipment, and assistive technology. Their staff will answer your questions and may supply you with additional information and resources that can be of help to you.
www.usatechguide.org

Kuschall
Is a Swiss designer and manufacturer of lightweight wheelchairs, and now it is making their way to America. I personally think they're fabulous and I wanted my first chair to be a Kuschall, maybe I'll get one someday.... (Big grin).
www.kuschallna.com/index.php?option=content&task=view&id=8&Itemid=29

TiLite
TiLite chairs are solely designed with Titanium. Sales representatives claim that titanium chairs are 50% lighter than steel and stronger than Aluminium. Other benefits are that it does not rust, and actually absorbs vibration.

This is the second wheelchair that I have had and it was pretty good, not my favourite though. I do like what this company has to offer though, check them out. This is an American site, so remember to convert the prices.
www.tilite.com

Buy Wheelchairs – United Kingdom

Gerald Simonds Healthcare Ltd.
9 March Place
Gatehouse Way
Aylesbury
Bucks
HP19 8UA
Telephone: 01296 380 200
E-mail: webenquiry@gerald-simonds.co.uk
www.gerald-simonds.co.uk

Nomad
Nomad was inspired by the end goal of giving a wheelchair user, a chair that they could be proud of, and was in fact born from a 'very determined user's own wants and aspirations. This company is based in Wales, United Kingdom.
www.nomadwheelchairs.com

Sunrise Business Park
High Street, Wollaston
Stourbridge , West Midlands DY8 4PS UK
Telephone:(44) 1384 44 66 88
www.sunrisemedical.co.uk/index.jsp

The Sunrise UK facility manufactures and distributes Coopers patient aids, DeVilbiss respiratory products, Oxford patient lifters, PowerTec, and Quickie wheelchairs and Sterling scooters.

RGK
I have one of these and love it for different reasons, being that I can get

clothes guards with it and the back rest folds down in between the two guards; so I'm not wasting time removing and re-inserting them. The framework is much like most chairs – simple and sleek. I chose to have the bare metal look which actually looks pretty good and doesn't clash with anything that I wear, and I don't have to worry about the paintwork coming off meaning that it won't look tired or dated, just scratched. Love it! www.rgklife.com

<u>UK Wheelchairs</u>
This site is mainly an online source of all sorts of chairs, from rigid frame to tilt/recline to electric. While they seem to cater to any need you can imagine, I don't know if I will be buying from them as their chairs tend to the futuristic end-of-the-scale. They do offer a tonne of manufacturers though and seem to offer anything pertaining to mobility.
www.uk-wheelchairs.co.uk

bit eight – Sliding boards/Transfer boards

So let's talk about moving around, from your wheelchair to other places.

Over the course of my life I have seen that I have gained all sorts of skills and tools. Some that I need for my lifetime, like learning how to walk, some that I have used for a period, like in a job, and then there are those tools that are merely a means to an end. These tools provide a stepping stone that help me get to where I want to be, just like training wheels on a bike. Training wheels support us while we learn to balance a bike so that we don't fall off and hurt ourselves, just as a sliding board is there for us until we become proficient at the skill of transferring.

First and foremost, I want to say that we need to give ourselves the time and space to learn without self-abuse and criticism. Treating ourselves like this is not helping us reach our goals. I know that I have said this just a minute ago, but I want to repeat it, because it is important - the sliding board is not the desired outcome, it is purely a means to an end – use it, practice your transfer skills as much as possible, and then take that step to get rid of the sliding board. Yes, there will be moments when you fall, but it is not the end of the world. Get up, dust yourself off and get on with your life. (Yes, this is tough love, I don't mean to offend anyone, but, sometimes it is necessary to aid us in moving forward).

In the beginning, a sliding board will be your new best friend. And regardless of whether we like it or want it, it is a vital part of our life now, because if we can't move around, we won't be able to do anything! But, the only thing that is better than a sliding board is the day you no longer need it!!

The sliding board is usually made out of wood, because it is strong and reasonably priced. The wood has, of course, been sanded and polished so that there is no chance of splintering, and a long rectangular hole has been cut out of one end of the board, so to provide an in-built handle. To use the sliding board you place one end under you (actually your derrière) and the other end onto the bed or bench or spot you want to go to. Then you lift your body as far as you can so that you make your way from one end of the board to the other end. Yes, using the board is a tad daunting at first, and for a while your transfers will be a bit awkward and unsure, but like learning to walk, we stumbled and fell, but eventually found our feet. You will too with doing transfers, and, I guarantee that in time, doing a transfer will be something that you don't even have to think about anymore.

I think for the men it was about who could get rid of the sliding board first. There is no prize for the person who stops using the sliding board first, and nothing for those who take their time either. During my rehabilitation I recall we were loaned a board for the first couple of weeks but were expected to have handed it back to the physiotherapist before too long, and so I practiced lift after lift, on the safety of my bed. Even if you believe you are going to walk again, learning this skill will give you knowledge and help you tick the list, meaning that you will discharge quicker from hospital.

Oh, I have to tell you about my first car transfer, it was a real laugh. Located in the gymnasium was a car, purely for this purpose. Yes, a whole car. It is fantastic that the spinal unit had this available to patients, but when my physiotherapist asked me to complete this transfer from my chair to the driver's seat, I was gob-smacked. I said, 'you've got to be kidding me!' She had a huge grin on her face. I should mention that my physiotherapist wanted me to complete this transfer without the use of a sliding board - I was certain this woman had a sadistic nature. I looked at her and exclaimed, 'But that is like the Grand Canyon to me'. (She stood there, arms crossed, explaining that if I wanted to drive, I'd better get used to it). A few expletives came to mind, but all that I could hear was, 'How on earth am I going to do that?' Not exaggerating, the gap between where my bottom was sitting and the driver's seat looked like it might as well be the Grand Canyon. Yet, I knew that my physiotherapist was absolutely right, if I wanted to drive I would have to conquer it at some point. I didn't transfer into the car that day, but today that transfer is 'a piece of cake'. And in fact, depending on the day, some days I have transferred into and out of my car more than eight times – going here and going there, doing this and doing that.

Oh, and before we finish on this topic, can I just touch on the transfer itself? Thanks. There are a few different ways to get into a car, (a) both legs in first, then transfer (b) transfer first, legs in second (c) one leg in, then transfer, than the other leg in last – these transfers are the same for a bed transfer. Then there are also many different ways to get your chair into the car as well. I used to check out what other people would do when I went to basketball training or games.... How I lift my chair in will be different to how someone diagnosed with T10 paraplegia will do it, and that will be different again to someone with a T4 injury. So, what I am saying is that we have to work out what is best for us and our needs. Remember, focus on what you can do, and not, what you can't!

bit nine - Grates

Where ever we are in the man-made world of concrete and buildings, we will find grates. I am talking about those nasty grates that are found in the ground that can catch our castor wheels if we are not paying attention.

Just like cars don't feel the bump while going over stones, a bicycle will. Depending on the size of your castors, you may or may not have to worry about grates. If your chair has castor wheels (front wheels) that are at least 10 centimetres in diametre, then you don't necessarily need to mind anything. Yet, my castor wheels are similar in size to rollerblade wheels, so I do have to watch-out for grates. Still, it is not as bad as getting the heel of your stilettos caught and ruined – anyone ever seen the movie The *Wedding Planner*, with Jennifer Lopez? (Smiles). That's one thing we don't have to worry about that anymore? Hhmm, maybe there are some pluses. And our shoes will rarely age (unless of course they are white).

There is not really a lot to say about grates. If you are still in the spinal unit now, make sure when the occupational therapist takes you out for a day out into town that you ask them to go over some grates with you. Now, what is next?

During my rehabilitation some of the occupational therapists organised to take a group of us inpatients out with them into the local village so that we could practice all the tools we had learnt and do some things we hadn't, like escalators. We did a lot of different things, had a lot of laughs, and the staff made sure it was a safe and supportive environment for us. What made it really fun was the fact that the physiotherapist's brought their own chairs and we took a big bus taxi. I don't know if they intended it or not, but because almost everyone was in chairs, it made me feel like I didn't stick out like a sore thumb. And that was exactly what I needed at that point in my rehabilitation.

This was one of the fun moments of the whole accident and rehabilitation experience, and I am really grateful to the staff for the opportunity they gave myself and the other patients.

bit ten – the Escalator

We went down curbs and up curbs, over grates, up ramps, down all sorts of ramps, down steps, tried sitting at different sorts of tables, opened all types of doors, and then.... there were the escalators!

I can honestly say that we, the inpatients, were a tad skittish when it came to getting on an escalator – as this was the very first time we had even thought about them. When the physiotherapists asked 'who would like to go up first?' I asked, 'how on earth do I do that in a chair?' So the physios suggested they went up first in their wheelchairs and we could watch them to see how easy it was. After watching them, it didn't look so bad, so we all stepped up to the plate and gave it a go and yes, it was a breeze!

Having gone up the escalator without any hiccups, I was not fearful about coming down at all, however, perhaps I jumped the gun a bit! Let's just say that I reached the bottom before the chair actually did, thank god for the Physio with me on the escalator and the rest of them waiting at the bottom. I have never professed to have balls of steel, which is why I only go down escalators with someone else there now, and being the wuss that I am, I do it backwards.

This is another method I have used for going down an escalator – my friend gets on first and treads water, so to speak on the steps, while I line up backwards to the top of the escalator. My friend grabs the bar on my back rest and guides me to a step, on which I stay until we near the ground again. Then, nearing the ground level, I let go of the rails and allow my friend to pull me off the escalator and away from escalator traffic. If you want to try going down forwards, as it was intended, then you just need to get on your rear wheels and hold onto the rails, and for God's sake, stay still until you reach the end of the ride. If you do use this method, well, you've got more guts than I do! (Big grin).

A lot of shops have signs that don't allow wheelchairs on their escalators, I know it is to protect them in the event of an accident and I agree, when people use them that are not experienced, it is dangerous for both the person and the store. I think the design of the chair might also make a difference to how easy or difficult it is to do this activity, as the typical hospital chair is so cumbersome anyway. I am not certain, but I think, the longer the wheel base of the chair is, the more difficult it would be to use an escalator. But, don't let me tell you what you can and can't do!

I will also mention that I have noticed some shops get a tad uncomfortable when 'we' (people in chairs) use escalators.... I will always argue that it is so much quicker and easier than using a lift, especially when walkers fill up the lifts. I have been told off twice in twelve years for using the escalator (Heehee, I have to giggle). The first time I was told off, was ever so nicely by a store person who informed me where the lifts were located for *people like me*. Now, I could of gone off my head and got my knickers in a knot about the people like me comment and the discrimination, however, I chose not too. I understood that she was probably unsure and fearful, and that she also had to enforce her store policy. However, if the escalator is closer than the lift, I will choose the escalator every time.

Oh, talking about being told off, have you ever seen those mini-trains at the shopping centres that take children on rides around the shopping centre? Well, there is one at a shopping centre on the Gold Coast that I frequent, and occasionally I will have some fun with it. Now, what I am about to tell you is probably frowned upon, but considering the train is moving at less than 1 kilometre per hour and that neither the passengers, the train or the other shoppers are affected, I don't see the harm. So, once in a blue moon (probably once a year) I will grab hold of this mini-train at the very rear and let it pull me along, however, like I said, this is rare because I only do this if the train is going in the same direction that I am heading. The bonus for me is that it saves my arms and I don't have to worry about making my way through crowds, which is a nice change. And, the rare ocasions that I have done this, the people who see what I am doing get a huge grin on their face too. So it would appear that I am actually providing entertainment for the shopping centre. Hhmmm, maybe I should ask for payment for my time and services (Heehee).

<u>My step-by-step process for travelling on an escalator</u> –

- To go up an escalator I just walk onto the steps.

- I pick a plate to stay on.

- Then grab hold of the railing until I reach the top floor.

- I use the rails to help me move from the step I am on, to the actual ground.

- If you have not yet attempted an escalator, I would definitely suggest that you take an experienced person with you for the first few attempts or, at least a friend.

- Be sure to talk about what is going to happen before you even start, so that both are clear about their roles and what you will do, should something go awry. Please try the escalator, and just expect success!

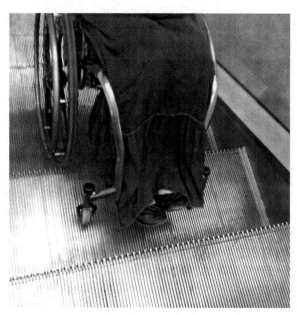

Position on an escalator

bit eleven – the Hair salon

Ok, let me think, what else is at shopping centres that we might like to utilise? Oh yes, hair salons!

Before I get to the nitty gritty about going to a hairdresser, I want to weigh up the pros and cons between visiting an independent hair salon or choosing one within a shopping centre – for me there is only one important point – does it have a bathroom I can access? Again, our lives are ruled by our bladder (big grin). We all know, as women, that when we visit a hairdresser we could be there for one to four or five hours, depending of course on what we are getting done. This is why we will most probably want to visit the 'ladies' during our visit, and most of the independent hair salons that I have been to don't provide a wheelchair accessible bathroom onsite. Your city may differ, but this is what I have discovered. Shopping complexes will surely have a wheelchair-friendly bathroom somewhere inside. And yes, I have had to leave the salon and trek to the nearest bathroom – foils and all.

But back inside the hair salons, as for me, I have never had an instance where I have felt belittled or attacked. In my experience, hairdressers have not freaked out if I preferred not to transfer into their chair, however, if you would like to transfer into their chair, they will probably offer a hand when you are making the transfer. This is what has happened to me every time, anyway. I have to say that in twelve years I have never had any problems at all at a hairdressing salon, and I hope that you have not and will not, either (big smile).

The first few times that I visited a hairdresser, I just stayed in my own chair, and I don't know how it works, because, even with a cape over the entire chair, hair still seems to get into every nook and cranny. It wasn't until one of the hairdressers offered the salon chair that I even considered the possibility of transferring, and now, I never stay in my chair and I am happy because my wheelchair is hair-free!

Let me outline the two choices, we either:

- stay in our chair for the entire process or

- we transfer into one of their chairs and back into our own to make our way to the sink, and again transfer into their chair at the sink, then back into our chair to return to our station, and of course back into their seat for the rest of it.

You might be thinking – 'damn, that is a lot of transfers', but when I do it, it really isn't that much, and let us remember that all the transferring is fabulous pressure relief and exercise! And, transferring out of our chair into their chair clearly shows other people that our wheelchair really is just a means of mobility for us. I really like moments like this, because it helps educate others, which can only be a good thing for the community of wheelchair users. Now that we have touched on the pros for transferring into one of the salon's chairs, let's continue.

TIDBITS

If you do transfer out of our chair and into theirs, I want to point out a couple of things.

- Be sure to ask someone to hold the salon chair completely still (as it will swivel all over the place).

- Know that your shoes will fall off when you are sitting in their chair, like mine do. We can either get frustrated about it or see it as funny!

- Transferring with a cape around you is a bit like wrapping a sheet around you, so when I am moving, I tuck the cape in between my legs so that I can see what is happening with my chair, the floor and my feet.

- The transfer to the sink chair is easy, just a normal transfer. If the chair at the sink does move, maybe you might like to just stay in your chair and reverse into position. Your choice.

Whereas, if you stay in your chair, the pros are that you don't really need to do too much, this will save you time, energy and fuss. I want to point out though, if you do want to stay in your chair, the main concern would be the chair at the sink; as some salons these days have permanent chairs. Best to ask that question before you book an appointment if you prefer not to do any transfers at all. Let me just talk about the sink for a moment - if you stay in your chair at the sink, please note that you will need to lock your chair into position and lift yourself towards the front of your cushion, because you will need to lean back so that your neck and head rests in a comfortable position for you as well as the hairdresser at the basin.

Another option, if you are time limited, or use an electric chair, might be to obtain the services of a mobile hairdresser. They will come to you, and after the initial consultation, they will get more and more comfortable with you and your needs. You will still need to have access to a basin or water from somewhere, however that is something I am sure the two of you can solve. Then, after a little while it will just be like a friend coming to visit, as you both know what needs to be done and how it is going to happen, thereby helping you feel relaxed and at ease.

bit twelve – the Change Room

Alright, because I don't know you, I don't know if you like shopping or not, I still love it even though buying is more of a challenge. I probably do more window-shopping than actual shopping, but let's talk about change rooms because when you are out shopping, there is a good chance you might need to use one.

Since my injury, I have checked-out change rooms in Australia, England, Paris, South Africa and the USA, all of which are pretty much the same – small and squishy. Yes, sometimes there will be a wheelchair accessible change room, however, that is usually in the bigger department stores, and might only be on one floor. Or, as I have also discovered, the wheelchair friendly room is used as a storage room. So, I am sorry to say that the dilemmas are the same the world over gals!

It just crossed my mind, what do mothers with prams do? If us women in chairs can't squeeze into change cubicles, how can mothers with prams? Hhmmm. Momentarily, I thought we should do something about those of us who are size discriminated but, just like parents have to pick their battles with children, maybe we need to also. There are surely more pressing issues that would get postponed if we had a go at everything that was awkward for us. Not good, ho hum.

As it is difficult for me to get into change rooms in the first place, it is actually quite good for my bank balance, just not that good for my wardrobe or appearance (Hhmmm). But seriously, it does narrow things down very easily, which is good and bad. I don't know about you, but if I can actually find a change room, I only try on items that fit the top half of my body, because trying on trousers or skirts in a change room is just too much effort, hassle and time. It is way too much effort to take off my shoes and everything else I am wearing on the lower half, put on the new item, take off the new item, and put my own things back on again – all the while, in my chair. So, my personal preference is to take skirts/trousers home so that I am able to try them on whilst on my bed. But please don't let me influence you, maybe I'm just being lazy (Heehee). You need to try it and make that decision for yourself. It is definitely do-able.

Of course, when I am travelling I can't return anything, so it is a different story. If the garment was extraordinary I would probably take the time and make the effort to see if I want to buy it. I guess it will depend on time and energy. When at home, in Australia, I only buy at stores I know will take returns if the item does not fit. Before purchasing, I would recommend that you explain that it is difficult to try items on in the store change room and see what the store person says. Usually, I find that they really do understand. It is a good idea to get a name on the receipt, in case a refund is needed.

Talking about fashion, I want to mention a spirited blonde who happens to be making a name for herself in the USA, and happens to use a power chair herself - Tiffiny Carlson. To Ms Carlson's credit, if there is anything in the world to do with chairs and women – she is all over it in terms of communication. This woman is the voice for many an article on the big disability websites in the USA, and years ago when I first stumbled across her website, I discovered that she wrote an e-book titled, *Wheelchair Fashion 101*. To date, I have not read this book, but I have checked out her website over the years, and from her posts, it seems that she knows what she's talking about. So, I have no doubt you will be able to grab some great tips from her website and book. You can find her at www.beautyability.com

I recall when my mother first sat me at one of those ancient Singer sewing machines, she was showing me how to sew clothes for my Barbie-doll-lookalikes long before I was old enough to even reach the pedal. And, because I loved the creativity of sewing, I naturally followed that passion into high school and beyond, all of which has given me knowledge in garment construction, design and fit.

It is not too difficult for me to tell if an item is going to sit right in a chair or not. For each of you, I would suggest trying on a lot of different styles and really look at why the design of the garment makes it look like this or that, think about if it complements your face shape, and consider how it might look better for you. Yes, looking good in a wheelchair is more of a challenge, however it is definitely not impossible! While we don't have to worry about whether our ass looks big in this or that, there are a lot of other things to consider when we are making a purchase.

TIDBITS

- Do the sleeves make my shoulders/arms look bigger.

- Does the design of the sleeve allow for a comfortable pushing movement.

- Is the item easy to put on and get off.

- Does the fabric allow for ease of movement.

- Where are the zippers? Zippers at the back make it more time consuming to undo and redo, in the bathroom.

- Where are the pockets? Pockets in the front will add bulk.

- Does the design of the front of the garment add bulk or weight.

- I steer clear of fabrics like Taffetas, as they are stiff and just don't sit nicely.

- Super soft fabrics, like chiffon, will probably tear with any sort of pull.

- Watch the length of sleeves, the longer they are the more they tend to rub on the wheels when pushing.

- I have found the best fabrics to be jersey, cotton and polyester, as they allow movement, fit the body well, thereby, don't exaggerate our size.

- Skirts with layers give the appearance of movement (from their design), and I have found them to be a lot more flattering to our legs, than simple straight skirts.

- Those elastic belts that are popular will pull us in and give us much needed shape, but not if we have any cuddly bits. They will do the reverse and highlight what we want to disguise.

- Watch the length of your skirts, as some of mine get caught in my castors and that is no fun either.

bit thirteen – Shoes!

Shopping for shoes is a whole other ball game and rightly deserves its own sub-section. If you live in a warmer climate like Australia, you will probably notice that your ankles, feet and legs will swell in the summer months of the calendar. Fish oil capsules will help with circulation, however, I still notice swelling albeit not as much. So, because we will share this wonderful feature, allow me to give you a tip: I generally do not buy shoes with straps around the ankle as it makes me look like Miss Piggy (Do you remember the Muppets?) Oh, unless of course I am wearing them before Noon, or mainly in the winter months. It might be different for you, however, I have found that in the morning my feet are at their best, yet as the day goes on, they tend to get bigger and bigger. So don't be surprised if you buy your shoes in the afternoon and in the morning they fall off your feet – insoles are handy.

Now, due to the swelling I have found that I now need shoes that are about 1.5 or two sizes bigger than what I wore in my previous life. The style of the shoe may influence the size you choose too. Shoes with pointed-toes need larger sizes and I tend to buy more round-toe shoes nowadays, mainly because my toes do not get as marked. You might be different, just be mindful and look at your feet regularly.

When I am trying on shoes I put my fingers inside the shoe and move it around the entire foot so that I can ensure the shoes are not too tight against my skin, and if I can do this, it shows me that there is sufficient space around my foot too.

I want to stress here, that you need to be very aware that shoes will rub on your toes and heels, and that this rubbing may cause pressure sores, or at least marks that could turn into pressure sores. You don't want that, it is not fun being without shoes for weeks and weeks while you're waiting for your feet to heal. Trust me, I have experienced this too. I saw these gorgeous white and pink sneakers and fell in love with them instantly. So I took them home, wore them for only three or four days and bang – pressure sore on the heals (both heals of course!)

So guess who had to go without shoes for the next 3-4 weeks? Yes, not happy Jan! Not happy at all. The only thing worse than being in a wheelchair is looking stupid in a wheelchair, and if you can't wear any shoes..... Well, I am sure I don't need to tell you what you will look like, especially if you still have to go to work.

Reluctantly, I forced myself to give away a pair of my most favourite and gorgeous cherry red pointed flats to a friend. Why? Well, I had noticed that each time after I wore the shoes (even for just an hour) my toes would always have red marks on the top of the knuckle. I figured that the shoes must be rubbing against my toes and that is not good full stop! If it happens for prolonged periods of time it can lead to pressure sores and we do not need that either. Our heels and toes will be the main points to watch with feet, basically watch any area where bone can rub on something. Be certain to dry in between toes completely after a bath/shower, as moisture can also cause problems.

My cherry red flats were one of my most favourite pairs of shoes and of course, it was a struggle to make that decision. My friend was very happy to take them off my hands though. As she received them she said to me that most of her wardrobe now comprises of a lot of memories of me. I chuckled and smiled because I knew that it was true. After training as an image consultant in the USA and Australia, I discovered that I had a lot of colours in my wardrobe that did not compliment my skin, hair and eyes, so all of my friends graciously accepted items I no longer wanted in my wardrobe.

I don't know what you used to wear pre-accident, but I just loved high heels, the height of the heel never scared me, however they had to be sexy and feminine. Doing character dancing and tap dancing as a young girl, heels never scared me, and like most little girls, clip-clopping around in my mum's shoes was one of my favourite past times.

Nowadays, I mostly stick to flats, courts or wedges, as I have noticed my feet are prone to roll with the really thin high heels. I love wedges particularly, as I don't have to give up the height and my feet usually don't roll because they have more of a foundation. But that is just me, you might be different. On occasion I will put on some high heels, but only when I know it is not going to be more than an hour or so, as I also get a sore back. I don't understand how that works because I definitely can't feel my toes, yet I can still get a back ache – unfair God! Being in a chair doesn't have to limit you with shoes, it just depends on what you are willing to endure.

Another thing to consider when buying shoes is how they will sit on your foot plate. Let's take my first chair for example: the foot plate consisted of two bars that sat parallel and joined at the sides. It did not have any covering on it and it was quite tricky to work with, in terms of shoes. A lot of the time the heel of my shoes would fall down behind the back bar, which made it look like my ankle was being choked. I believed that when this happened, circulation was affected so I made the decision not to wear heels in that chair.

The chair I have now has a plastic platform covering the framework of the foot rest that my feet and shoes can sit on top of. I find this a better design because my feet can sit flat and there is something for my shoes to sit on. Personally, I have discovered that if the shoes I am trying on in the store don't stay on, they won't stay on at when I am out and about either. I know (from lots of trials and errors) when I'm moving and going over various types of surfaces (cobblestone, timber decking, bricks, tiles and grass) that I will be forever putting my feet back on to my wheelchair footrest. This is fine once or twice, but it gets a bit tiring when it is every couple of minutes for an entire day! But, again, this is what I have decided.... you need to decide for yourself.

One day, I thought I had come up with the best idea when it came to wearing heels in a chair.... this great idea lasted for about a day, until I tested the theory – epic failure!

Now, you know that I am not the kind of person that gives up without a fight, right? So, it was only natural for me to come up with a tonne of different ideas about how to wear the shoes I want without them falling off balance or off my foot plate. I pondered and thought, thought and pondered about this dilemma and came up with – Velcro! I purchased some Velcro from a fabric store, stuck one side of the tape to my footplate (after trying a lot of different shoes on the foot plate and coming up with the best position) and the other side of the Velcro to one pair of heeled shoes I adored. The concept turned out to be far more practical and effective in my head than it was in reality. Much to my shock, the shoes did not stick to the Velcro like I was convinced it would, and my feet fell sideways and also off the plate just as they had, thousands of times before! Ho hum. The Velcro had zero effect. Dismayed and dumb-founded, I gave up skinny-high heeled shoes.

And, to this day I am sorry ladies, to say that I have still not come up with any more ideas to solve our high heel quandary.

bit fourteen – Shopping for Groceries

Another type of shopping that we have to do is grocery shopping, so let us consider that. I don't know if you are like me and just like to get it done and get out of there. And no doubt you would have worked out your shopping options by now, but let's just go over them together just for fun -

- I used to order my household items, like detergent and cleaning liquids, via the internet and have them delivered, but then I moved to an area where they don't provide that service – rural areas are always hard done by (heehee).

- I could do the shopping myself in store and then organise to 'pick-up' the goods after I finish shopping. In my experience, I have found it useful to ask for a number to call so that I don't have to get out of the car to ring the button at the parcel pick-up section. At the parcel pick-up area, I have my docket ready and as they are packing my boot, I ask them to place the groceries near the door of the boot, to make it easy for me to reach them from outside the car.

- Another option is *home delivery.* After I go to the grocery store and do the shopping myself, I then ask them to deliver it to my home. It saves me all of the hassle of getting the groceries from my car into the house. A great option if I don't need anything straight away, as it might take hours.

- In the past I was informed that a staff member could accompany me around the shop with a trolley to assist me and help me to the car as well. I tried it once, but I think the staff member must of thought that I didn't have anything else to do with my time, so it took much longer than had I done it myself. Needless to say, that was the last time. Oh, the staff mentioned that this service is only available outside of rush hours. Every store is different, so I would suggest you go and clarify when their rush hours are.

- I usually do the shopping myself in store, then ask the staff member if someone could kindly help me get the trolley to my car. This takes time for the staff to organise, so make sure you ask as soon as you get to the check-out, that way you won't be hanging around waiting for someone to come.

- Sometimes I just do small shops more often, depending on how much I need. I just sit a basket on my lap and run through the shop.

- Finally, there are times when I do it this way too. I organise a trolley in the middle of the store first, usually at the front near the check-out counters. Then I carry a basket around on my lap, fill it and run it back to the trolley. Then when I have everything I need, I move the trolley to the nearest counter and get the goodies onto the bench. This can be time consuming, however, compared to option 5, I think it is quicker.

I have to add that those grocery baskets can get very dirty with everything that gets thrown into them, which is why I use one of the many recycled grocery bags to keep my clothing stain-free. I simply sit one of those bags on my lap under the basket. After all, I know that I don't want a bottle of bleach leaking onto my lovely skirt, and maybe you don't either.

Oh, passer-bys are very kind and only too willing to assist obtaining items that are outside of my reach; helping someone makes people feel good. On more than one occasion, I have asked someone to reach something for me and they see it as a compliment as they are usually asking people taller than them. So, I have put a smile on their face at least. I am sure you can recall a time when you were able to do something for someone else that helped them, and you might remember how it made you feel to give for no reason other than just 'giving'.

I am going to ask you a favour right now.... every person in the world needs assistance from time to time, whatever that may be. People in wheelchairs are no different, as much as we won't want to ask for it. To the majority of the community we are all the same, us people in wheelchairs, so when we decline another's help, depending on how we do it, they may or may not decide to offer help again to another person in a chair. So the favour I am asking you, is that when you refuse assistance, please be gracious about it.

I'll show you what I mean by telling you about something that happened to me when I was out one day. I was out and about running here and there, getting things done when I noticed that my fuel gauge was low. So I pulled into a service station that I use a lot, as I was on my way home anyway. By this time, I had not taken time for lunch and I was feeling tired... I would have welcomed assistance from anyone, and as I looked around I noticed two service attendants out near the fuel pumps. I thought to myself, 'gees, it might have been nice if one of them had offered to help me'. Then, as it happened one of them did come over to me, almost as if she had somehow heard my thoughts – it's spooky when that happens! Anyway, the attendant did offer her help but I had put my chair together by this time, so I thanked her for offering but said something about it being a little too late. Nothing spiteful or rude, but I wanted her to know that her help would have been welcomed before, yet not now. She seemed to take my hint okay and we chatted some more, then she left. Now, I was pumping petrol into my car when she came around the pumps a second time, stopping at mine again. This time, the attendant told me about how she had offered her help before to another person in a chair and had been bluntly told off.... now I can understand both sides here. The person in the chair feels defensive about being in the chair, however, I can also see why the attendant was less inclined to offer her help again. Yet, this is precisely why I request that you and I decline nicely, because who knows when we might need a little bit of help in the future...

The way I look at the person asking if I want help, is that they are offering to serve, and that is very kind. So, I thank them for their kindness and say, 'no thank you this time'.

bit fifteen - Cinemas

One of my favourite things to do is go to the cinema!

Now, let me tell you right from the get-go that each cinema is going to be different, and even each theatre within the same cinema complex might vary in design and facilities. So please don't go in with certain expectations in mind, because if you do, you might well be disappointed, like I have been more than once.

We probably need to talk about just getting into the cinema first. Most cities around Australia provide access to people who use wheelchairs, even in the smaller towns like Lismore (in the

Northern Rivers area). Yet, I will say that I have noticed that when the population drops below 20,000, access does seem to diminish. I have not travelled Australia-wide to find out if this is the case for each state, but, it just makes sense that the smaller the town - the less government resources are available.

I need to warn you that just because the front of the cinema offers wheelchair access, does not mean that everything else will be fine and dandy inside. That was my mistake when Marty and I went to a local cinema that we hadn't been to before, in a gorgeous little town near the beach. I guess because the cinema was built inside a 3 story shopping centre that was very wheelchair friendly I assumed the cinema would be too. My bad. But, can you believe it, it wasn't until after we bought the tickets, ice cream and Malteses and made our way to our screen that we noticed the eight steps leading inside. We are not the kind of people that are going to let that ruin our night though, and it was a lovely night indeed. Yes, Marty had to go in and find two chairs, then come back and sweep me up into his arms and carry me inside, but I just felt like Cinderella, instead of disabled and discriminated. Be sure though, that after we enjoyed the movie I suggested to the staff that it might have been best if the they had informed us of the lack of access before we purchased the tickets and everything else. Apparently only two of the six theatres, in this cinema, have ramps leading inside – and this was in 2010! I am astounded.

I miss the freedom that goes hand in hand with spontaneity, and no, we would not have been taken by surprise if we had called the cinema ahead. Marty and I wanted to be spontaneous, and when you want that, you have to be open and flexible to anything that can happen. So, we were open and we had fun!!

Okay, now that I cleared that up, let's talk about the inside of the theatre shall we? After the ramp into each theatre, you will arrive at a mezzanine level and this is the only location for people who use chairs to sit, unless you can walk a little.... Grrrrr – utter jealousy (Heehee). Of course there are some of us who will sit in our own chair for the movie, and there are those who will transfer out of our chairs and into the theatre's. So, the designers of the cinemas have taken away a few chairs for us so that we can just wheel into position and sit next to our friends, if that is our choice. The people who design these places must not assume we have a lot of friends as there are usually only two or three chairs together. God forbid I have more than three girlfriends (Heehee). Proving yet again, that the world we live in is not entirely perfect yet, and we need people in chairs who are engineers! (Heehee).

When I go to a cinema with my friends or family, I will always get out of my chair and into one of the seats for two reasons, (1) because I payed for a chair, and possibly the more critical reason, (2) their chairs are more comfortable than mine. As you know sitting in our chairs is painful and uncomfortable for long periods of time, and if I sit in the cinema chairs I can slide down the seat, relax and really enjoy the experience. I realise not everyone who uses a chair is able to transfer by themselves, but that means you will be able to invite one more friend! (Winks).

Be sure to check the arm rests on the chairs (the ones with the spaces next to them), as the arm rests may actually lift up. Otherwise, should the arm rests be bolted down it is still possible to transfer, just position your chair as close as possible. It's only a 90 degree transfer and very do-able (Heehee).

Oh by-the-by, in England, if you ever find yourself at the cinemas, your companion may be able to get in for free as the cinemas do not charge the carer of a person in a wheelchair. This rule is wonderful, kudos for England! Unfortunately, I know that Australia does not have the same principle towards their residents who use chairs – shame, shame, shame. As for the USA or Canada, I have no idea – sorry women. Next time I go overseas, I have to remind myself to make time to check out the cinemas so that I can give you the low-down.

I just recalled something that just blew me away when I found this out, so I will share it with you because I know it will give you a giggle.

I just remembered that I have been to the cinemas at one more place overseas. Back in 1994 I was in Japan for a couple of years on a working-holiday visa, I have to tell you this story – it is hilarious.

I was teaching English at the time, and in hindsight I realised that I enjoyed helping people to learn and grow. But that is not the point here. My boyfriend at the time and I had decided to try something different and go to the movies. We knew it would be in Japanese, but found out that they had English subtitles at this cinema in the city, so we made the trek and were very excited about it. Right now, I can't recall the suburb it was in, but I do remember that it wasn't too difficult to find even though there was not a lot of signs and didn't look at all like the cinemas in Australia. Yet we found the cinema and looked around for the booth to buy tickets but couldn't see one. So we went back downstairs to the entrance and discovered that the tickets were sold from an automated ticket machine. Self-serve I guess. We waited a while before the doors opened and then people just came flooding out of the cinema, like they do at a concert or football game. It was then that we realised there was something missing. Then it dawned on us. Where was the person that stands at the door to collect the stubs and permits entry into the theatre? As the people were racing towards the doors, dodging those who were trying to exit, the penny dropped and we started scrambling forward too. Inside we saw the seats filling as quickly as they were emptying, so we grabbed the first two we saw. When we located a seat and saw the advertorials reeling, we looked at each other and laughed our heads off (It was absolutely hilarious!). As we talked about it, we realised that the ticket machines just keep selling tickets, there was no limit. It kept selling tickets regardless of whether you get a seat or not. Actually acquiring a seat depended on how quickly you made your way inside the theatre, and of course your level of determination. I still get a giggle now, as I sit here writing about it.

So, the moral to the story - Expect the unexpected! Heraclitus, (c.535 BC).

bit sixteen - Restaurants

Now, I hope you won't let a silly thing like a wheelchair stop you from going out to places like restaurants with your family or friends! It shouldn't.

We all know that a lot of our life revolves around gatherings with food at the centre of them, such as weddings, birthdays, christenings, funerals, Christmas, New Years, Easter, and well, almost all aspects of our life. This means, that if we stop ourselves from attending these functions, we are missing out on a lot more than just food, aren't we? (Big grin).

And just because we use a chair now doesn't mean that we can't be a part of these celebrations! In fact, I would argue that it is more crucial now that we put in the effort to go, because not only does it benefit us and the people who we mingle with, can I be so bold to claim that it also benefits society in general. Each time we go out and talk to someone, we change the world. One person at a time!

'What can we change by going out?' I hear you ask. Ok, let's consider it. When we go out, we are interacting with people who have probably never had anything to do with someone in a wheelchair who isn't 70 years old. Just by getting out of the house, we are showing members of the community that we don't just sit around home twiddling our thumbs. We are showing them that we are independent, can contribute to our families, our friends, heck, our society in general, and wait for it that we are just as interesting and fun as people who don't use chairs!!! And, so going out is vital for us, our friends and for the community at large, because it shows the world why we need access, inclusion and equality.

With that cleared up, now we can chat about restaurants.

Like most things we want to do, there are two main considerations – (1) access and (2) bathroom accessibility!

In a perfect world every single business would accommodate all human beings regardless of age, ability, disability, ethnicity, gender, stature, or socio-economic status. But, we all know it is not a perfect world yet, so we need to work with what we have right now (and try to improve it every day).

I think the first question we need to ask ourselves is this –

Q. Do steps make a difference to us or not?

Permit me to explain what I am trying to ask. When I was new to the whole paraplegia thing, I made the decision that only businesses that provided for me and my needs deserved my custom (and dosh). I think it is only fair, because these shops have made me feel welcomed and included. And I don't believe that it is impossible for any place to design access for prams or people in chairs. That is why personally, I will still stick to this principle. However, each of us will have a different opinion to the next person, and that is our right, so please understand that you can choose one or the other or both – neither is right nor wrong. So my question to you is, 'what decision will you make about shops/restaurants that have steps?' Will you avoid these stores/restaurants, or will you simply ask for assistance to get inside and back out again?

I can see how some people in chairs would see steps at the front of a shop/restaurant and just say, 'well, I'm not going to let a few measly steps stop me', and ask for assistance to get inside. Every now and then I think, 'I'm not going to let them tell me where I can and can't go' and get the help I need to get inside too. If we made a purchase it might be a good time point out that people in chairs, moms with prams, and the elderly could bring them more business. Who knows? It might make them re-think accessibility to their business.

In the beginning (of my new life) I used to be self-conscious, irritated and almost angry about being lifted up stairs in order to get into restaurants or such. It used to be about everyone watching me, feeling embarrassed, losing my independence, and the fact that society doesn't include us people in chairs. I guess other minorities would understand what I'm saying here, it's just that I've just never been a part of a minority before. I would wonder why it seemed so incredibly difficult to provide a ramp instead of steps. It still tickles a nerve, but over the years, I have realised that change takes time and perseverance; nothing can be done to alter the steps or the venue at that precise moment and getting angry at the staff in front of me, does not change anything, because they don't own the business. Yes, we need to stand up (heehee) for our independence, our rights and our feelings and demand physical inclusion into this world, however, I don't feel that getting bitter, sour and angry about it helps the dilemma or our cause!

You will not go through life without experiencing one moment when you will need a helping lift.... like when Marty and I went to the cinema and there were a tonne of steps in front of us. He had to just pick me up and carry me inside because when we were purchasing our tickets, the staff member omitted to tell us that there were steps into that specific theatre. The movie previews had already started and we were standing outside thinking about what to do, and then, I just asked Marty to scoop me up and said, 'let's just do it'. He told me later, he loves it when he gets to pick me up because he feels like my knight in shining armour! And, as for me, I get to feel like Cinderella, so, being picked up in order to get somewhere doesn't have to be a horrible experience. I imagine for men it might be a different kettle of fish, yet sometimes you just have to do, what you have to do! I have also come to realise that attitude matters. Let me clarify this.

TOOL – CHANGE YOUR GLASSES

I don't know if you wear glasses, but at some point in our life we will all put on a pair of sunglasses, which is why I am going to use this analogy to translate what I mean.

Some people wear glasses for fashion and others for function. We all know that it is the lens that is the most vital aspect of the glasses because they are the instrument which makes it

---

possible for us to see the world. And, I am sure that you realise that the lens can colour our world too. Have you ever heard that French song that is about seeing the world through rose-coloured glasses when you're in love? Well, most of us, I am certain, have experienced something like this – when we cannot see reality for the love-coloured lenses through which we are looking. In fact, I would also claim that we wear a multitude of lenses to look at the world, not just when we are in love.

Have you ever had an argument with someone and continued on with your day doing whatever you had planned and discovered that other things, throughout the day, would come up that would annoy and upset you too? So the whole day would turn out just yuck? May I suggest that these days we are wearing grey-coloured glasses, coloured by frustration or anger. Would this not make sense too?

If we see the world through lenses, and these lenses can and do change their colour, it makes sense then, that it is possible we can proactively change them ourselves at our will. And that is great news, because no longer are we a victim, but in fact, a captain instead.

What if, while we were being lifted up the steps into the cinema, rather than focusing on all the negative aspects that we can find – preferably, we concentrated on the kindness of the person helping us? I think it is necessary to remind ourselves that this person does not need to perform this service for us, we are not paying them, and they are not our employee. Rather, it is only out of the kindness of their heart that they are offering to serve us in this way. No, don't worry, I am not telling you to just let everything go, I am not telling you that our rights are not significant and we need to be a doormat.

We can still be frustrated with society and the world in general. But, I am encouraging you to value the kindness and genuine care you are experiencing from one human being to another. And that is a wonderful thing.

In the beginning of my new life, I continuously worked on my thoughts, beliefs and self-esteem, almost daily; changing negative to positive or just less negative, bit by bit, day by day. And what you find works might be different to what I did – the same method/tool is not going to work for the entire population, that just isn't feasible. We are all so entirely unique.

For me, it was self-talk mixed with lots of visual work I did in my room, so that I could see it every day. For you, it might be writing, or it could be physical exercise – who knows? I don't. But, what I do know is that you have to keep trying until you do find something that does work for you. The first technique you try might not work, nor the second, nor the third, nevertheless, you have to be committed to yourself! That is what I know.

The bottom-line simply is – making a decision and sticking to it. And if you lose focus, reminding yourself and starting all over again and again and again. You only fail, when you actually stop trying....

'A failure is not always a mistake; it may simply be the best one can do under the circumstances. The real mistake is to stop trying' by BF Skinner, US Psychologist.

Now, let us get on with the second consideration – accessible bathrooms.

An accessible bathroom is another necessary aspect of going out because it is basic science - if we want to drink = we need to pee. No insult intended. Now, let me state what I have found in the real world.

There are three main strains of restaurants out there, (1) those that provide wheelchair accessible bathrooms, (2) those that think they provide wheelchair accessible bathrooms, and finally, (3) those restaurants that don't even care. If this last one sounds a bit harsh – it is meant! If these restaurant owners suddenly needed a wheelchair, they would be the ones kicking up a stink, but I'll get off the soap box now.

It seems that I have started with number three (3) already so why not just continue with it. We will recognise these restaurants by their lack of ramps, their lack of warm invitation to us as we enter their establishment, and their apparent lack of care or concern for our needs. These types of eateries will offer you a seat at the table nearest the front doors so that their other tables aren't bothered, they won't consider your preferences. I have been in my fair share of plush and sublime restaurants all over the world that look pretentious, but bend over backwards to make me feel welcomed and at home. I am not talking about these restaurants, I am talking about the ones who think they are too good for everyone except the beautiful crowd, I am talking about the restaurants that don't seem to genuinely care for our needs. Heck, if any restaurant doesn't make us feel welcome and provided for, I don't think that they deserve our money!

Next we have type two (2) restaurants who pretend to provide wheelchair friendly lavatories or who think they do. When we ring these places and enquire about bathrooms, the staff will proudly claim to cater for us, but usually on arrival I find that their wheelchair accessible bathroom is up two steps or down three steps, or is jam-packed with all of the cleaning products known to man. Because I investigate these facilities first thing when I arrive, I am not caught out, and can monitor my beverages or make alternative plans. If we stick to the newer places, we are almost guaranteed the basic facilities. And well, there is not much to say about the restaurants that do include us in their design other than, well done and thank you! We will most certainly be coming back.

When I venture to somewhere new I will usually locate a number and enquire about their facilities for persons using chairs beforehand with a phone call. And, when I call, if I am told that there are no accessible bathrooms I ask about the businesses surrounding their establishment. If I am informed that they do have a bathroom for people in chairs, then I usually ask a few questions in order to get a concrete picture if they are actually accessible. You have to laugh sometimes, because there has been more than one occasion when the bathrooms were supposed to be accessible but actually weren't.

The sort of questions I might ask are –

Q. Are there any steps getting to the bathroom?
Q. How many steps are there going into the bathroom?
Q. Do mothers with prams use this bathroom? (If they can, so can I).

I ask these types of questions because most people who walk do not even notice steps at all because they are so inconsequential to them. God, how I miss that – not worrying about little things like steps and such (Smiles).

Oh, by-the-by, most hotels offer wheelchair friendly bathrooms, as do petrol stations and shopping centres should there be any near the restaurant you are enjoying.

In Australia we can also use this website www.toiletmap.gov.au to locate bathrooms around the country.

For those visiting the United Kingdom, visit this website www. visitbritain.com/things-to-see-and-do/things-to-do-for-people-like-me/ physical-sensory-needs/practical-information/accessible-toilets.aspx

For those of us visiting the USA or anywhere really, I stumbled across this website www.thebathroomdiaries.com that claims to list toilets around the world! Yes, I said around the WORLD. I was somewhat dubious about its claim, so I checked out how true it is for Australia (specifically the cities that I am familiar with), and even though it lacks a truck load of towns and toilets, the information that they do make available seems to be accurate. Wahoo!

Then I checked out how much information it supplies for the USA and it had so much more, which is great for travellers. There is also information provided that indicates if it is accessible for people with disabilities, just keep in mind that America uses the term 'handicap', instead of 'disabled'.

When you are dining out, do you transfer into their chairs or not? Well, sometimes I do and sometimes I don't. It will depend on if it is just a quick meal, or if there are no time restraints. Also, I will consider how comfortable the establishment's chairs look and compare them to mine. One last aspect I ponder, is how much drinking I am intend on doing, because there will be a few transfers between my chair, the restaurant chair and the bathroom seat. I adore booths so I will always transfer into them, and they never feel too uncomfortable. For me it just depends on how I am feeling basically. So see how you are feeling, give it a try, and see how good it feels to sit in something else when you're having dinner, kind of like taking off your shoes when you are having dinner. And, it may be psychologically positive as well, because you might feel more like everybody else, as you are doing the same thing as they are.

Something that can only be beneficial is letting your friends/family members know about access and bathrooms. They don't need to know the gory details, just an overview really, so that they can choose restaurants that let us get inside and have a drink with our friends. Just like my friend, Miss Earl Grey, who used to be a vegetarian for years, I wouldn't go booking a reservation at a Steak House restaurant if I want her to join in would I? Course not. Everybody has rights and everybody's rights deserve respect. Now, our friends need to consider our needs too. And don't be embarrassed when you inform them of what you need, just remember the vegetarian story, ok.

Other than that, I just want to say 'get out there and cause havoc ok!' – You're still alive.

bit seventeen – let's talk Sleep!

As you will know, in hospital/rehabilitation, the staff will give you advice about every single topic – including how to sleep!

What I want to tell you here is that after you are discharged, you will have the freedom to do what you want, but you will also have the sole responsibility of caring for and protecting your body from harm. I want to stress that you will need to pay very close attention to your body – look, listen, feel, check, and think about everything you are doing. Your body is not the same as it was before, in any way. You need to become familiar with your body as it is right now. I would rather you check more often than not, so as to safe guard your health and body.

As for me, I have worked out that I can sleep on my side, my stomach, or on my back, and I do not need a dozen pillows stuffed between my legs, under my ankles, or even at my back. However, that doesn't mean that you won't need them.

I also worked out that I did not require those egg-shell overlays for the mattress either, but I do have a very cushy latex bed that I miss when I stay in hotels. What I do strongly suggest is a waterproof mattress protector, no make it two. I say two, because while you are cleaning and drying one, you can use the second protector to avoid any in-between mishaps. Oh, but let me share a lovely little thing that makes a great extra for your mattress. It is called 'memory foam' and it is lovely-jubbeley – it will minimise the risk of getting pressure sores on any part of your body and make your mattress feel like utter heaven. In Australia it is available from Harvey Norman for around $300, but it should be available from department stores like Big-W or Target. If it isn't, then just make your way to a bedding store. I was advised to put the 'memory foam' inside an old doona cover to make it easy to keep it clean and I have to agree with this idea and have found it very useful. And yes, I have taken off the doona cover and put it back onto the memory foam myself – so, it is do-able.

Now, there will be times when, like everybody else on the planet, we will fall sick. Now as much as I personally feel we deserve a 'get out of gaol free card' against all forms of illness and general horrible moments – the reality is that we have to put up with life, the same as everybody else on the planet. Unfortunately, we are not protected from food poisoning, stomach bugs, diarrhoea, or anything else that can and will happen. So, for moments such as these.... I hang up my self-pride and take care of business! And if that means putting something on that keeps me clean when my body is weak and poorly, then so be it. As much as I cringe at the thought of wearing those incontinence panties, it is less painful than spending an hour cleaning up everything I come into contact with (if you know what I mean) when I am not at full-strength.

bit eighteen – Picking a Car!

For me an enormous part of re-claiming my independence was getting a car.

Upfront I want to let you know that in no way am I promoting the Mini Cooper at all. They have not sponsored this section, this book, or me at all in any way. What I am doing is simply giving you the information that I have gathered from personal experience.

I have just found that the Mini happens to have a lot of the features that I look for in a motor vehicle. That said, I will also say that when I purchased my 'off-the-showroom-floor' Mini, I had hoped that it would be better than any car I had ever had in my life – mainly because it was a completely brand new car. Yet, to my disappointment, I must inform you that my Mini has had to be garaged a total of eight times within a two year period. This is more than any other car that I have previously owned at all. And all of my prior cars have all been used ones, at least four years old when I bought them.

But, let's just get into it then.

Because I want my life to be as easy as possible, there are four points that I always check in order to ensure that I am getting a car that will be practical and me-friendly.

The four aspects include –

- The height of the seat,
- The degree that the driver's door opens,
- The size of the boot and
- How far the driver's seat reclines.

If you allow me a few minutes, I will go through these points with you and explain why these specific aspects are important to me.

If the height of the driver's seat is equal or similar to that of our chair, it will mean that lifting the chair in and out of the car will be far easier than if the seat of the car is higher than our chair. I will mention that when I am lifting my wheelchair into and out of the car, to a certain degree I am leaning out of the car, which means that a higher seat will only increase my lack of balance and effort. I have found that the higher the seat, the more I have to hold onto something to stop me from falling out of the car and the trickier the transfer. Of course, when we are fit and healthy, the height of the seat won't matter, but we all have had days when our neck, hands or shoulders are not 100 per cent.

Also, when we are lifting our chair into the car more than once a day, it is going to make a big difference. Just to go to one location, we need to lift our chair in and out of the car four times – into the car, out at the location, back into the car, and out again at home.

With two door cars I have found that the doors open much wider, meaning that we can get the chair closer to the driver's seat and we will have more space in which to break down the chair. I have attempted to break down my chair when the door space has been ridiculously small and I can tell you right now, it is no fun at all. And let me tell you that when we transfer into a back seat (of a sedan) it is even worse, do-able, but no fun. While I was doing some research, I found out that it is possible to increase how much a car door opens, but I would check that with your mechanic – I thought this was pretty exciting news, so I wanted to pass this onto you.

Next, I will tell you why the boot of the car is worth taking a real good look at. I liken having a wheelchair to having a pram – they are both annoying, cumbersome and time-wasting, however the only difference is that you will not have a pram for the rest of your life. I have tried car, after car, after car, and very, very few have the amount of space in their boot that can take my chair all set-up. However, with the back seats folded down, the boot of the Mini provides sufficient space for my chair to go in whole, and i love that because that means that my passengers only have to lift the chair into the boot – that's it! And, I don't want my family or friends to have to fuss with my chair every time I get into or out of my car when we go out together, so that is why the boot is so important for me when I consider a car.

The Mini Cooper is also a very easy car to park, and if forced to, I can even get my chair out of my car in a 'normal' parking space. In this instance, I would park all the way over to one side of the space. I don't like to do that though, it doesn't leave much room for the next car owner, and there is no guarantee that the next car to park next to me will leave the same space.

Another important feature to look at in a car is the amount of recline of the driver's seat. The more the driver's seat reclines, the easier it will be for you to lift your chair inside the car by yourself. I am a huge fan of old cars, so once I bought a 1990 Mercedes sedan, and loved it to pieces.... except for one very crucial aspect. The handle that helps the chair recline had to be twisted around and around and around and around, approximately four or five times every single time I wanted to get into or out of the car. I have to say, it took a toll on my wrist. Now unlike the Mercedes, the Mini Cooper has a simple flick mechanism, so to decline the seat is only a mere flick of the wrist - pure bliss to someone who uses their wrists in every action.

One more factor that might make putting your chair into a car more of a challenge is the distance between the steering wheel and the door frame. In a two-door car, the door frame is so much larger, however, in a sedan you will find the door frames slightly smaller. I recently attempted to get my chair into the driver's side of a BMW 320i four door car, and while it was possible it was a tight squeeze. And on a day-to-day basis, I would have to be really careful about how I would lift the chair inside. Yet, if you prefer the space a sedan provides, I guess you have to compromise in other areas and vice versa. In the end, it comes down to what's more important for you!

I should also mention that the modern Minis have some sort of fancy technology that makes it fabulously easy to manoeuvre the driver's seat forward and backward without too much effort. Gotta love that!

I want to talk here about some of the other cars that I have had or wanted to own.

I don't know about you, but I am an 'old school' girl from way back with a love of everything old, be that fashion, jewellery, hairstyles, houses, furniture or cars. So before I reluctantly purchased the Mini, I was day-dreaming of having my own FJ Holden to cruise around in. Every time I saw one parked somewhere or driving around past me, I would 'ooh' and 'aah' over them and then picture myself enjoying the whole experience. Then I wondered what was stopping me from having my own. So I went to look at a couple of them to find out more about the practicality of having and using an FJ.

Alas, it didn't take long for me to decide that it was a bit of an ask – even for someone as positive as me. I would need to add equipment to help the front seat move forward and backward without too much effort on my part. I would need to alter the front seat so that it can recline with a flick switch. It would need to have an automatic transmission, and ideally, I would like to add cruise control and power steering. A big reason why I chose a Mini is because it gives me a car with a retro feel but with all the conveniences, practicality and features of a modern car.

Now, at one stage of my life (post-injury) I gave into a weakness that I had instead of being practical and ended up being a regretful owner of a red SLK230. This was a used car, and one I had later discovered had been in an accident that the previous owner omitted to tell me. Regardless of how much I loved driving around in this car with the roof off, no matter how much I enjoyed this car and wanted to keep it - it was a completely un-realistic, un-practical, and plain stupid choice.

Why? Well, the main way that we (people with limited mobility) can get our chair into the car is by lifting and swinging the chair across our body and sitting it into the passenger seat next to us. I have worked out that by reclining the driver's seat enough we can fit the chair between us and the steering wheel. In the SLK230, the driver's seat does not recline at all - thereby making it very tricky to move the chair across our body. This might not be something that is enough for you to consider this car impractical, but I did — especially considering that I get in and out of my car umpteen number of times each day. Ultimately, it is your life and your choice.

I have decided that it is important to add up all the things that are going to take a toll on our body (on a day-to-day basis) and weigh up the choices that way.

TIDBITS

- Cruise control is a huge help on highways and it means that I won't be tempted to exceed the speed limit. It is another pain-saving device for my wrist.

- Seat covers in the car will mean that 'accidents' won't stain the vinyl or leather, and I also put a 'bluey' between the seat cover and seat.

- When it is raining, a face cloth in the glove-box will mean you can dry your tyres as you put them inside.

- Watch out for leg spasms when you are driving. I have had one when driving and it was a scary, because at first I didn't put two and two together and had to pull over. It has only happened to me once, however I just want you to be beware that it can happen.

Now that you have a car, let's consider how you are going to **get into your vehicle.**

You may still be using that that piece of wood that helps you get from A to B, yet at some point you will need to start doing proper 'transfers' that the physiotherapists have taught you. Hopefully it will not be too long before you lose that sorry excuse for a security blanket so that you can start to have a life filled with so much more.

I have concluded that there are three ways to get from your chair into your car - see what you think. (I use a right-hand drive car in Australia and these examples are of me getting into the driver's side of the car).

A. Put your chair as close as possible to the car. Secure brakes. Move your bottom towards the front of your cushion. Place both your feet on the ground toward the car. Place one fist (left) onto the driver's seat and one fist under your bottom cheek (right). And when you feel safe and comfortable, make the transfer.

B. Put your chair as close as possible to the car. Secure the brakes. Move your bottom toward the front of your cushion. Place both your feet inside the car, onto the floor of the driver's side. Place one fist (left) onto the driver's seat and one fist (right) under your right bottom cheek. Make the transfer.

C. Put your chair as close as possible to the car. Secure the brakes. Move your bottom toward the front of your cushion. Place both your feet inside the car, onto the floor of the driver's side. Place one fist (left) onto the driver's seat and your right hand will grab onto the roof of the car. Make the transfer.

I want to reinforce what your physiotherapist taught you, that is – be conscious of where your head is and where your feet are, because both play a part in the success of any transfer.

bit nineteen – Service Station.

Now that you have a car and you can get into it, you will need petrol in order to get where you need to go.

There are times when I pull into a service station and pray that I lived in the 70s when service stations were serviced, rather than self-served, like they are today. Yet, in some rural parts of our blessed country (Australia), I have actually stumbled across the *serviced station* – what an experience to behold. It was just the other day my girlfriend and I went for a drive to a gorgeous little town just north of Byron Bay, called Mullumbimby, when we had the opportunity to experience the mythical creature known as a service station attendant. And to our pleasant surprise, we sat in our cars while the service person filled our tank. Funny isn't it, that in 2010 we pay more for petrol, yet we get less service now than our grandparents did! A lot of jobs were lost with this progress. Makes you stop and think about if we have progressed or not....? Well, anyway, my girlfriend and I felt like royalty for about five minutes, which was utterly wonderful.

Back in the real world though, you and I will need to get out of our car and fill our own tanks when petrol is running low. Some would look at it as a right pain in the neck, and sometimes it is, and then I remind myself of the people (who are physically less capable than us) who are not able to fill their own tanks, and that puts things back into perspective for me again. I say, be grateful. You have the freedom to do it, so be thankful that you can!

- As you pull in, remember to leave sufficient space between the car and the bowser. Park too close and you will need to ask someone to fill it up for you, or get back in the car and move it into a better position, and that can be a pain in the neck!

- In my experience, even if you pull up to a service station that has signs offering assistance for people with a disability, they won't put two and two together and may not come out to assist, especially if you are a young person. A lot of people only associate disability with the senior members of our community. However, if you were to stick to the same service station they might remember you and come out to help, but this will depend on whether or not you arrive during a busy time of the day.

- I bought an air-compressor at K-mart, just in the motor vehicle section. I have found the car is the best place to store this piece of equipment as I can fill my wheelchair tyres before or after I go out. It was pretty cheap and it saved a lot of time and energy running around service stations trying to fill my tyres. So, now I no longer have to wait in line at the service station, or worry about the hose nozzle not fitting my tyres. Well worth the dollars, I say.

- Over the years I have noticed that with all of the lifting my chair in and out of the car, some damage has occurred to the car. There is the odd scratch and bump inside the car in front of where my wheelchair sits, yet mostly, it is to that part of the car that we would usually step over to climb inside. I have thought about what I could do to avoid this damage, and I would either get some soft leather or vinyl (maybe from a fabric shop) that I could drape over the side of the car prior to lifting my chair out or in. Definitely something like this is far cheaper than getting some paint work done! (Winks).

We worked out that when we use Marty's car, BMW 320i, it is possible to slot my wheelchair, intact, inside the rear door to sit directly behind him in the back seat. This means that he doesn't have to fuss with my chair at all – quick and pain-free. We put a blanket over the back seats so to protect the upholstery. It is a lot quicker than dismantling it and re-constructing it each time I want to get out of the car, and when it is raining, that's important.

bit twenty - day-to-day basics.

Folding bed sheets

Some people in chairs might think they can now get out of doing a lot of the housework because they are sitting down, but I'm here to say - you are more than capable. And that is a great thing, believe me!

When I was lying in the hospital bed post accident, contemplating my future, this was one of the questions that were circling around and around. I was oblivious about people in chairs... I had not seen any young and healthy people in chairs, not seen anyone like me and the other girls. Of course, it was only natural that I was anxious about what I could and could not do.

However, it did not take me long to see that I could still be independent, some things might take a bit longer, and yes, other things will be frustrating and take more patience, but I was and am still capable! And so are you!!

Being in a wheelchair did not give me a 'get out of gaol free' card and that is a good thing. Why? Well, because I can still feel of value. In my experience, I have come to believe that humans need to feel wanted, useful or that they contribute in some form – in the home, at work, or within a relationship. If we are not able to satisfy these feelings, I fear it would not take long for our self-worth or esteem to deteriorate. If you have not lost an arm or a hand, then I am happy to tell you that you can still make your bed, vacuum the house, do the washing, fold big items like sheets, duvets and blankets, and anything else that might take your fancy – and I know this, because I do these every week.

TIDBITS

- I definitely shake out the sheets as I make each fold, this ensures the sheets are hanging straight and not crumpled somewhere in the middle.

- I usually fold them to my side because I don't want them to touch my tyres – yuck. I don't like marks on my clean sheets. Like riding a bike, the more times I did it, the more I felt comfortable and confident doing it.

Making the bed

Ok, there are no secrets here either. Just a few things I want to mention.

Put all of the bed items (duvet, pillows etc.) clear of the track around the bed to make it easy on yourself. Ensure that your bed side table is positioned so that you can get close enough to the mattress corner. The last corner is always the tightest to put on, I find it less of a pain in the neck if I leave one of the outside corners till last. I think it is because I can get physically closer to these corners and thereby, apply more strength. Who knows? That's my take on the bed, but you work it out for you.

I have found that having a mattress protector on my bed saves me a lot of time and money – I don't have to get a dry-cleaner in to clean the mattress, I don't have to wait all day for them to show up, and I don't have to wait all day for the mattress to dry either. You will find that there are two types of mattress protectors, one is fabric with a waterproof backing and the other is all plastic like an oversized garbage bag. Not difficult to know which one I choose, right. I choose the fabric mattress protector as I don't want to hear that plastic sound every time I move, and I don't doubt that it is the more comfortable of the two anyway. They should cost less than $100 each, however it will save you in the end.

It is always a good idea for your bed to be a similar height to your chair, because if the bed is too high or too low, it will make a difference when you transfer on and off, especially when you get up in the middle of the night and you're not fully awake. Also, we will not always be at optimum health, are recovering from surgery, sore from exercise or just exhausted, and this is when the height of the bed will be very obvious, making a simple transfer more of an effort than it needs to be.

I like to have a lamp next to my bed or make sure I can reach the light switch from the bed. As I like to see what I am doing when I am getting into and out of my bed. Anyway, it's something to think about.

I always keep some essentials near my bed eg: a small towel, hand wipes, gloves, garbage bag, and of course, hand cream.

Some people in chairs have seen the need for an intercom and door release system, installed at the front door. I can see how it might make anyone feel safer, and make life a bit simpler. Ideally, you want the internal unit to be installed within the area you spend the most amount of time, like near your bed or in the kitchen. At one place that I rented, it had an intercom unit and the main point that I noticed was that some people don't wait very long. God forbid I was ever on the lounge or on my bed....

Carrying a drink

Ok. Again, like most topics we chat about, there is more than one way to skin this cat (oh my gosh, who in the world would skin a cat! How utterly horrible). Anyway, (a) one way to carry a drink while in a wheelchair is to sit it on a tray that sits flat on your lap. Another way, (b) is to hold the drink in a hand, use the other hand to push the respective wheel, and then swap the holding and the pushing motions between the two hands.

With suggestion (a), if my drink is sitting on a tray and I need to change rooms, chances are it might spill on the try and perhaps on me, while the second method (b) is considerably slower, however, if the drink does spill – it won't be over me! I also want to mention that when I have been out shopping and want to walk around with a drink, I would have no idea where to get a tray from that I can keep with me, so the idea of (b) sprung from necessity and I have found it to be effective so far.

When I am holding a drink, I don't move at a hundred miles per hour and therefore, people can see that I am carrying a drink, but I would suggest that you keep your head up, hold your drink out to the side of the chair and watch out for everybody.

Sweeping

A chore we will all miss is this one – not!!

I don't know about you, but I was not thoroughly dismayed when I realised that I might not be able to do as much of the housework as I used to. When I first returned to Australia, I was living in a hostel and so didn't really need to do anything really. Then I moved into share accommodation with other people with disabilities, we had homecare staff that did general sort of cleaning duties. One year later I was out on my own, and again, I received domestic assistance from the government with the big stuff like vacuuming, moping, cleaning mirrors and such. It wasn't until I got my own home that I said, 'sod this' and just did the house cleaning myself, as best I could.

Regardless whether you choose to do it yourself or pay someone to do it for you, I want you to know that it is possible when you are sitting down to do, not all, but most of the things we used to have the freedom to do – like vacuum and sweep.... it just takes patience and a bit more time.

Now, I will tell you that sweeping from our position will feel a little awkward at first, however if you pursue it, it will get easier. There are a few different ways to do this chore, below are some tips from me, but you will probably work out your own way of doing it when you give it a whirl.

TIDBITS

- I position my chair as I would have, my body – facing the direction I am heading, but at an angle. If the dirt area was at 3 o'clock, then my chair would be at 7 o'clock.

- I lock the chair into position, to ensure I don't move as I make the sweeping action.

- Use both hands to hold the broom, as this will make for a stronger movement.

- Place the broom in front of you, on the ground, and sweep towards your direction. Yes, it is a slow process, but give it a go and decide for yourself what is a priority.

Hand-held vacuum

Like any partnership, you can work out with your flatmate or partner what you can do and what they can do, in terms of housework. As independent as I am, I have decided to leave the vacuuming to my partner, while I clean the toilets and bathrooms. But, being a woman I can't help myself and always want to tidy up a little between cleans. This is why, over the years, I have purchased a couple of those hand-held vacuums. They are small enough for me to carry around and generally have enough power to actually be useful. I will warn you that they don't last that long off the charging unit, and anything less than 18 watt vacuums won't have enough oomph.

Your Wedding ceremony

It does not matter if you have 'saved yourself', it does not matter how young or how old you are, it does not matter if you use a wheelchair, and it does not matter if you have been married seven times before – this one particular moment between you and your partner will never happen again, thereby making it special! Which is why, when you are considering such a momentous moment, it ought to be (and deserves to be) everything that you both want it to be!

To me, weddings are much like birthdays – no-one else has any right to tell you what to do on your big day! (I guess if they are paying for it though, that might be a different story). It doesn't matter if the bride wants her bridesmaids to wear cowboy hats and boots, or if the groom wants to get married in the middle of a football field, it is completely and utterly their one day to have it any which way tickles their fancy. Some people have a ceremony on a beach, others have an enormous gala event with hundreds of guests, and for us ladies who use wheelchairs, it is no different – our wedding day is the one day where all of our dreams can, and ought to come true!

When I am planning my big day with my Mr Right – you know I am not going to let anything come between me and a wonderful day. And I don't want you to either!!

Now, just because us ladies use chairs, it does not mean that we can't look super glamorous and feel like a princess on our wedding day. And if you think any different to this – stop it right now! Or else I'll come over to your house with a fire-engine hose to blast it out. I know it is possible to look absolutely gob-smacking, because I've seen it and I want to say that it is necessary! It is necessary for you, it is also necessary for your husband-to-be, and necessary for everyone else who sees you on this day.

Why do I say necessary? I say it because we are still women (despite what we have or don't have), because the media bombard us with ideas of how a bride should look, because how we look affects how we feel about ourselves, because our husband-to-be deserves a princess, and because everyone else needs to see that we are not defined by the chair – we are women, first and foremost! We need to do this for our self-esteem and self-worth, so that our husbands can glow with pride and for those around us to really get that we are more than the piece of equipment we sit in.

You might want to dress up your chair for the day and get a white satin back rest and cushion cover, like I have seen some people do. You might twist flowers around your chair's spokes, another idea I have seen - do it! You might want one of those big foo-foo dresses that are two meters in diameter, or you might prefer an elegant satin sexy little number instead – go on, do it! Or maybe on this day, you might want to keep your wheelchair out of the picture all together? Do it. I say we are only limited by our guts and our imagination really, so do whatever makes you feel good and you won't have regrets in years to come.

When you are shopping for a special dress for this wonderful day, I would advise you not to let anyone make you feel silly, and if they do, they don't deserve your custom. It might be a bit of a challenge to find a dress off the rack that fits you down to a tee, but don't give up if that is the case ok. Another option is to get one made, and depending on who makes it, it doesn't have to cost an arm and a leg (Heehee). I really want you to understand that you are the only person that can stop you from having a spectacular day! So don't!!

TIDBITS

- You will still need to use the bathroom on your wedding day, so, when considering a dress design, keep this in mind. If you designed the dress as separates, it might make this function somewhat less stressful. But, that's your choice.

- Mind the dress length, as you don't want it to get caught in your castor wheels all day and night long.

- Strapless dresses still fall down on us, just like they do on every other woman, but there is always a way around it if that is your preferred style.

- Be mindful of the length of sleeves, they could annoy you all night long if they are too tight, long, or fall down all the time.

- If you choose a satin or silk fabric, be aware that you will slip n slide on the cushion.

- A corset built into the dress will help hold in your stomach.

- Have a side zip on your skirt, if possible, to ease dressing and undressing.

- Wear 'stay-up' stockings, to ease re-dressing after bathroom visits.

- On this one day you might need some assistance when going to the ladies, just like every other bride does – so we are no different!

- Create a specially made cushion cover out of lovely fabric to compliment your dress. Remember, if it is made out of satin or silk, you will slip 'n' slide.

- On this day, consider letting someone (like your father) push you down the aisle so that you can just sit there and look stunning for your groom!

One way of keeping your chair out of the picture is for you and your partner to both sit on chairs in front of the celebrant to make your vows. If you are using a resort, they may well have two high back velvet chairs, or perhaps these could be hired and delivered on the day. I am sure someone in the party, like a groomsman or family member could oversee the arrangements. I saw two red velvet French Louis chairs used once, they were positioned at the end of a red carpet and the signing table was located behind the chairs. So it was a simple turn in the chair for the bride to sign the documents; meaning that the bride can stay put and won't need to get back into her chair until leaving. In a church, it might be a bit of a different set up, and you might very well need to get back into your chair to access the signing table. Transferring won't be one of the things you will want to do ten times on this day, considering the dress and all.

On this one day, I would encourage you to ask someone you love to not only escort you down the aisle, but also help you down the aisle (yes, push you). Give them the honour of doing this for you, it will make them feel special (and useful), and you know that they would love to do this for you. As for you, the only thing you need to be concerned about is looking as pretty as a picture. Right? And if you normally use an electric chair, perhaps on this day you might consider using a manual chair so that there is more you and less chair... I am sure your bridesmaids, father or husband would love to be there for you, eg: help you move around.

You might want to hold a bouquet of flowers like a lot of brides do, or you might like to do things a little different, like wear a corsage around your wrist. The corsage could be something you have organised, or it could be a gift from your mother or father, but it is a sweet idea that I saw once. You can still wear a garter, and it is nice to keep traditional aspects to your wedding day – it is all just a bit of fun anyway, isn't it? And I know you don't need me to tell you to wear anything you like when it comes to undergarments, but just remember, it may be a tad constricting, uncomfortable and bulky. Maybe you might want to keep it simple under your dress and then change into something special for the night? Just have fun with it.

Think about if you want the chair in the photographs or not, and talk to your photographer about this beforehand and make certain he or she understands your likes and dislikes. Remember, there are some people out there who have no experience with gorgeous young things in chairs like us, and we might need to spell out that we don't want photos of us transferring and such. It is your day and this is when your dreams come true!

So, with that said, I think we have covered just about all of the issues we might face in the outside world. And if I have missed something, it is only because it hasn't happened to me yet (Cheesy smile).

Make this life everything You want!

Violet

Chapter seven

Your life is Your choice!

bit one -You and only You!

When a girl is brought up without the tenderness and gentleness of a mother figure, it is no surprise that she will assume a lot of the masculine traits, habits and beliefs of her father. This is what has happened to me, and I have found this to be neither good, nor bad, it's just different. What I can see though, from hindsight, is that if it were not for losing my mother and growing up on my own – perhaps I would not have turned into the person that I needed to be today. I shared this information with you for a point, and that is, that I want to apologise (in advance) if I am too direct, too blunt, or hard-nosed in my approach.

In no way do I intentionally want to cause pain or hurt anyone's feelings. Trust me when I say that I am not giving you anything that I have not already given myself x 10.

Research indicates that every single year, 40 million people around the world (almost 400 hundred Australians per year) who lead fun, interesting and full lives, find themselves injuring their spinal cord and using a wheelchair – and it is never a deliberate or intentional outcome. I have heard dozens upon dozens of stories from people just like me, the world over. Some people have ended up in chairs because they have fallen down stairs, others have fallen off stools, some were pushed off fences, some have had things fall on them, some of us are sports people who were just unlucky, but, no matter how it happens, I have never heard of it being a desired outcome. None of us want to be in a wheelchair, and would surely give up something, anything, just to be able to walk again or walk for the first time.

What I am going to say to you might hurt, "what has happened has happened!"

Let me say that again, "what has happened has happened!"

And one more time for good luck, "what has happened has happened!"

No, I don't have Alzheimer's or some disability that causes me to repeat everything three times – gees, the book would never get finished and you would probably throw it in the bin very quickly. But, I said that statement three times, because sometimes, I have to go over things a lot before I really get the meaning and for it to sink in. The above-mentioned statement was something that I actually had to repeat and repeat and repeat to myself on a daily basis in the beginning, until I noticed a change in the way I felt about my new predicament, and how I perceived my new way of life. What I soon realised though, was that no matter how long I ignored and denied the events and subsequent outcomes, it did not alter what is now my new reality. Sure, getting to a space where I accepted my new circumstances 'did not happen overnight..... but, it did happen'. (Heehee) Please allow yourself to feel, but also, allow yourself to heal too.

I think my friends would agree with me when I say that I am a pretty resilient sort of person, but, when this (the spinal injury) hit me, I will be honest and say that I was 'out for the count'. For some time, I was very unsure about what my life would be like, about my future, and in fact, if I even wanted to live like this. But, in the beginning there are so many emotions going on inside of us that I think, even with positive stories and examples, it takes some time before we are ready to really hear them. Have you ever heard someone say something like, 'it's just not the right time'. Well, one day I actually grasped what that meant and understood that I could not force everything to happen when I wanted it to. Up until that time, I just thought that it was necessary to plough through with fierce determination. Then I had the 'ah-ha moment'. It came when I was mentoring a woman in a spinal unit and for the life of me could not understand why she could not see that she could still have a great life, as I was living and breathing proof sitting there right in front of her. And still, she just couldn't get it. I had told her everything that I had done in a chair, all the countries that I had travelled to in my chair, and all the fun things that I had done in my life, in a chair – still nothing. And finally one day I got it - I realised that she was just not ready to hear it. This woman, as all of us, needed time to be sad, mad and everything in between, before she could move forward.

The lesson for me was that – I have to allow people to feel and only when they are ready, they will heal.

I believe, in order to heal, we first need to get a grasp of what has happened and the consequences of the event.

No matter what we lose, whether it is our keys, a job or parts of ourselves, because we are humans and not robots, we can't help but feel. I remember being in the physiotherapy unit one day and looking around the room at all the other patients and thinking, 'everyone is so different'. But, I wasn't talking about the individuals themselves, I was thinking about what they were going through and where they were emotionally. As I looked around, I saw pain, humiliation, anger, despair, sorrow, and acceptance – with each of us on our own path. And as much as there are similarities between all humans, I feel that we have to remember to allow differences too.

> *When I consulted the Macmillan dictionary, it defines 'dead' as – no longer alive, not working, tired/weak/ill, having no feeling, showing little emotion, when place has no life, no longer being used .....*

In movies we have heard characters claim that family members who have crossed them 'are now dead to them'. When we are cleaning out the fridge, we often say that the broccoli is 'dead' because it looks like it has lost its life and goodness. And when the car won't start, we always hear the words, 'oh, the battery must be dead'. So, it makes sense that when we can no longer feel or communicate with parts of our own body and we seem disconnected from them that it feels as though those parts of us are 'dead'. Which is why I liken paraplegia or quadriplegia to a death – our limbs are visible but they are lifeless to us now.

Professionals have identified that despite individuality, people who experience a significant loss (i.e.: a husband, a marriage, or a body part) will move through a distinct set of emotions, starting with feelings of shock, denial and disbelief, followed by feelings of suffering, anger, resentment, isolation, then will move to a bargaining-like state, that is followed by a period of despair and sadness, even depression, and finally arriving at the healing place of acceptance.

Some professionals state there are five stages while others claim there are seven, I think it is ridiculous to say that everyone in the world will experience a definite 5 emotions. Then professionals continue to outline the type of emotion and the stage we will experience each emotion. Again, how impossible is it to make such a generalisation about every human being on the planet, regardless of their culture, age, gender and nationality.

Have you heard that song....? 'You say pot-ay-to and I say pot-ar-to'? Hmm... showing my age here. Anyway, I don't know if I experienced each emotion at the according stage, however, I do know that I did go one-on-one with some of these feelings, but in a less succinct and constructed manner.

Because everyone is different, they are going to experience their feelings individually. Some people like to talk things out, and some people like writing about their feelings, some like to go for 5 kilometre jogs, and some like to cook.... pain kept inside is not healthy for the mind, or the body, so I urge you to find something that lets you release. I like swimming – when I am in the pool, it is just me and the water, still and peaceful.

I would encourage you to find something that allows you the opportunity to express and release how you feel, such as –

- Consulting a professional eg; social worker, psychologist, counsellor or join a support group.
- Drawing or painting – it doesn't have to be perfect, it is only for you.
- Write without editing or thinking – just put pen to paper.
- Hold a pillow and scream into it, scream in the shower or inside your car.
- Meditate or pray,
- Do something physical....... but, just do something.

Let me round off and say, that when someone ends up in a wheelchair it doesn't have to be a passive life in which we sit around watching everyone else do the things that we want to do. I know this could be one of the thoughts going through your head, because initially, I imagined this too. And of course, it is only natural when we are stuck in a hospital with no resources to offer any positives about our new life.

Living successfully without the ability to feel the grass beneath your feet or the sand between your toes is not done with ease – it will require you to love yourself utterly and disregard the media and all its hocus-pocus about beauty, it will require you to have a 'this will not beat me' attitude and you will need a 'motive' to pick yourself up when days go haywire. *(I chose the adjective 'successfully' to depict the chasm between merely existing and really being a part of life).*

We are only as 'disabled' as we let ourselves be! Personally, I have seen a lot of people in the world with perfectly functioning spinal cords that are actually more disabled than I am, because they disable themselves!

Now let me tell you what is very exciting!

We have the power to create it - our future, the way that we want it whenever we want to. In fact, each time the sun dawns is a fresh, brand new, untouched day where nothing has happened yet and everything awaits us. But, and this is where it gets even more exciting - we don't have to wait till the next sunrise to make a fresh start.

Every tick of the clock is a new opportunity for us, because if we do not like what is happening, every second that ticks by is a brand new possibility, opportunity or chance to change things to how we prefer it to be.

'You become what you think about' – **Buddha.**

bit two - The Past.

The past is exactly that, a moment in our lives that is now behind us, just like when you are driving.

Let's say we get in our car and drive to Brisbane. On the way we pass lots of smaller suburbs, yet when we finally arrive at our destination it is physically impossible to turn our head and be on the Gold Coast, because we are physically in Brisbane. I do not believe that we can live on more than one plane at a time. I do not believe that we can successfully live in the present and the past at the same time. I would like to emphasise the word 'successfully', because obviously we can live in the present and the future or the present and the past, if we choose to, but it won't get us anywhere other than 'stuck'. I have a theory that living in more than one dimension at a time is what leads us to procrastination and or depression. But that is all I want to say about that, right now.

You have to choose - you have to choose to live in one dimension only. Remember that famous phrase – "You can't have your cake and eat it too" (John Heywood, 1546). I'm going to suggest that this phrase exists because it has been proven to be true and that is why this phrase is still in use today! It has stood the test of time. I want to propose that we cannot live in the present while all of our thoughts are of the past or the future – that is having your cake and eating it too.

The dictionary defines the past as...... *a time that has elapsed.*

The past is not the present, nor is it the future. The present is not in the past or in the future, and the future is not in the past or in the present. They are all separate and distinct planes. The past is the past and that is where it is meant to be.

I love yoghurt, especially the ones from organic stores, they're so rich and creamy. As much as I love yoghurt, when it passes its expiration date I am not going to think twice about eating it. Sure it might still look good, yet you don't know what has started changing inside its molecular structure. Once the yoghurt passes its life span it is not going to do our body any good at all. It is losing all of its goodness and vitality. Of course I might want to indulge, but I will probably pay dearly for my stupidity a few hours later.

If you aren't a yoghurt-lover, let me try something else. When you look at the design of a car you can't help but notice that the windscreen in the front of the car is the largest window in the entire car. We cannot drive a car forward when we are solely looking in the rear vision mirror or even the small side mirrors, can we? Sure, we do need to look back at times to see where we came from, learn from what has happened and see what is behind us, however, if we are wanting to move in a forward direction, we must look out through the windscreen that is directly in front of us.

When we are living in the present but holding onto past memories and events, this is when we are most likely to run our car off the road into a ditch, metaphorically speaking of course. It is only natural to go over past events in our head, we have all done it. That is not what I am talking about here, it is when we can't think of anything else but those past events and find it difficult to step out of those thoughts, that it might become a concern. Let me give you an example of what I am talking about.

Side track:

A neighbour that became a friend, Miss Double Shot, and I were sitting down to lunch one day and I think we were talking about seminars for some reasons and then she started telling me about one of her friends that did an Anthony Robins 'Date with Destiny' week-long, change of life seminar. I'm sure you know the type. I don't know if the point was the seminar or the friend, yet she went on to tell me about this friend of hers that up until that point had been really struggling with stepping out of her past and what was her past life. Miss Double Shot relayed how each time she met up with her friend, the friend just seemed more and more miserable because the friend could not come to terms with her divorce. The entire conversation with this friend was around the divorce and her past. The friend could not step out of her thoughts of her past, they literally consumed her, meaning that Miss Double Shot felt less and less inclined to spend time with her. This is what I am referring to when I say 'running our car off the road and into a ditch'; this friend was pushing her friends away because she was living in the past.

When we love someone, whether it is a friend or sibling, we allow them more than we would anyone else, right? We give them more patience, more understanding, more money, more time etc. You get my drift, right?

I want to warn you that should you continue your determination to be depressed, be sure that your friends will call you less, spend less time with you, and as a result, sooner or later, you will end up alone. And I am here to grab you by the shoulders and shake you ferociously and tell you that 'only You can change this situation'. You can take the first step by seeking help, seeking advice, seeking knowledge - just do something!

I apologise for being in your face, I don't like or enjoy doing this, but I don't want you to end up alone, wasting your life and basically giving up before you even start (so you need to know that this comes from a place of care and love).

Now, I am not saying that when something horrible happens, we need to just put on a mask and act all happy - not at all, that doesn't help anyone. What I am saying is that you need to feel your suffering, your pain, your heartache. I just ask you to remain present, see where you are, look around you and know that you are still here, you are still breathing, and because you are here, there is only one direction - forward! Life does and can go on.

If you have read any of the books by Eckhart Tolle, you are aware that he describes our mind as simply another muscle, like in our arms or in our legs that need to be exercised, strengthened and given instructions. If we did not have some form of control over the muscles in our body, then we would be like jelly; our arms and legs going all over the place, doing whatever they wanted to do. So too, our mind needs discipline. It is up to us to take control of it, instead of it controlling and directing us.

Check out *The New Earth* by Eckhart Tolle, I got a lot out of it and you might too. (You might also like his other book, *The Power of Now*).

<u>TIDBITS</u>

- Only we have the power to be the guardian of our mind.

- Only we have the power to break old beliefs and thinking patterns that do not serve us.

bit three - Value the gift of Life!

For all the things that we learn about in school, I don't recall learning how to value our authentic selves, those parts of us that cannot be bought or priced with a dollar figure. Yet aren't these the aspects of us that will get us through some or all of life's challenges that will take us to the brink and back, stretch us, test us and truly define who 'we' are as humans?

Knowing who we truly are, what we stand for and believe in, what makes us different to the next person, what we care about and don't, acknowledging and embracing all the parts (strengths and weaknesses) that create who 'we' are – all of these bits 'n' pieces of our core are the greatest asset any one of us can fully realise. Builders lay a concrete foundation when building a house, shed or office, because it is durable, can withstand great pressures and will not thin out over time – knowing 'who we truly are' gives us that same solid foundation to start from and build onto, it can reassure us when people make accusations, we can fall back onto it when we are tested, and it will withstand any storm that life throws at us. And there will always be storms.

So, now I want you to go out and celebrate the fact that you are actually still here. And I don't mean by going out to the movies or a restaurant. I really mean make a party of it - invite everyone you know, get sloshed, have a "I'm alive" cake and get some champagne too! This is something worth making a big deal about!

Ok, I know some of you may be asking, 'Why do I need to celebrate having a life like this??'

Well, let me say it very plainly – you almost lost the opportunity to be here and the chance to experience all that is part of this thing called 'Life' – like the chance to be near the ones you love, the chance to feel their embrace, share their smiles and the future moments with them. You almost lost the chance to experience emotions like passion, pride, joy, jealousy, love and lust. No, life is not perfect, yet there are so many wonderful opportunities, aspects, people and experiences in it, why would you give that up?

But, regardless of how you may feel right now, I think you are a survivor! Whether you were born with the disability, gained one from surgery, ended up in a wheelchair because of an accident or a disease – you and I are still here, so why not make it worth your while!

Being here means that we can still enjoy the people we love, watch the sunrise, enjoy a hot chocolate, go snorkelling, go horse riding, ski, eat a hot cookie right out of the oven, cuddle up with someone on a cold winter morning, enjoy the smell of fresh cut grass, go to the movies with a loved one (girlfriend, boyfriend, mother, father)...... need I go on?

So, because you have been re-born so-to-speak, you have the very exciting opportunity of re-creating your life. Have you seen that movie called 50 First Dates with Drew Barrymore and Adam Sandler? It is sort of like that, your slate has been wiped clean and you have a fresh start. Perhaps you didn't want a fresh start. Perhaps you liked your life just the way that it was. Well, me too. But we are simply dealing with the facts that are in front of us right now.

Of course it is pretty obvious that this new life will not be the same as your last life, to me it is just different, nothing more and nothing less.

bit four - Positive Thinking doesn't cut it.

One day I was speaking to a girlfriend as she was challenged with being pregnant for the first time. She found the immense changes to a woman's diet, body and life in general, very trying. She shared her frustration and fears with me, after which, I reminded her that this moment will pass in a very short period of time. So, I asked her to put up a reminder somewhere in the house of the light at the end of the tunnel – the D-Day as it were. D – as in delivery (Heehee). She sighed and replied, 'I know, I know. I've got to be more positive'.

It was in that exact moment that I had a light bulb moment.

At that point I realised that being positive is like using an exfoliate – sure it will scrape off all the dead cells on the surface of your face, but if you really want to make a difference to your skin's appearance, you have to attack it on every single level and in every way possible. Meaning, you really do need to drink 2 litres of water a day, eat foods that give you nutrients, cleanse, tone, moisturise, exercise, bla bla bla.

Then I realised that positive thinking will only get you so far, but really changing the way you think, speak and perceive, to a more responsible, resourceful and powerful mindset is a far more effective and sustainable tool that will truly result in life-changing outcomes.

To me the whole 'being positive' thing is like when I was first in a chair. In order for me to leave the house, I had to psyche myself up and almost chant to myself 'I can do this, I can do this, I can do this'. And sure it worked, it got me out of the house and I was able to do what I needed to do for that moment, but if I wanted to actually feel better about myself and have a deeper impact on my self-worth and esteem, I would need to do a lot more work. I needed to attack it on a variety of levels, like do visualisations, create pictures and phrases around my house, use affirmations all day long, and do it enough so that it all sinks into the essence of my being.

No, it is not easy – which is why a lot of people might start it but slowly it fades away. Yes, it will require persistence, repetition and constantly being conscious of everything you say, feel and think – which can be exhausting – which is another reason why people don't keep it up. However, just like the campaign advertisement for Pantene, 'it may not happen overnight, but it will happen!'

There are so many great books and seminars that can help when it comes to changing old thought patterns, hmmmm, where do I start? Let me tell you this though, there is no one magic book or magic wand that will do it for you. You can buy all the books you like, yet at some stage, the only way things will change, is if you actually put into practice what you are learning on a day-to-day basis. You must put in the effort in order to get something out of it!

bit five – Choose your thoughts wisely!

There are no good or bad events in life – there are only the emotions that we choose to attach to each event.

Someone said this to me one day, and after chewing on this idea again and again, I believe there is a lot of truth to it, because an event can be perceived by ten individuals ten different ways, according to their perspective, background, culture, education, social status, and so on.

For example, let's take the subject of 'walking for exercise'. Take a single mother who, for whatever reasons, has a few extra kilos hanging around that she does not want. This single mum is constantly running around, chasing her tail all day long (from 6-10pm) doing things for the people she loves, but how do you think she might perceive getting up at 4.30am to do something for herself, like exercise? While a single woman who has all the time in the world to herself, has a good social life and enjoys her work (10-6pm) will have no problem fitting in a couple of hours exercise each morning, thereby loving the opportunity, thereby associating more positive thoughts about the event. The activity of walking is neither good nor bad, it is just what we think about the event that makes it appear positive or negative.

If the single mother thinks about getting up at 4.30 in the morning as just another thing to add to her to-do list, then I give her two weeks, a month tops. However, if she can think about the act of getting up early as something she is doing for herself and see it as me-time, then maybe that is enough of a motive to push her and keep it up, long term.

Now, you may not be anything like me or you may be exactly like me, I don't know. But, for the first couple of years of my new life (in a chair), my *thing* was fear. For some people theirs is blame, for others it is anger, yet for me it was fear. Fear of what others thought of me, fear about what other people saw when they looked at me, fear about being in the way, fear about being seen as useless, fear of not being pretty enough to attract a man, and just fear of not being good enough.

I cared way too much about what others thought about me, about how they saw me, and if they perceived me as a valuable member of the community. So, clearly it was my attitude, my thoughts and fears that were the problem for me – not the outside world! And I realised that the world would change only when I changed what was going on inside of my head.

One day (sometime in 2002) when I was living in Sydney, my personal trainer, my girlfriend (let's call her Miss Café Breva), and I drove to a small beach inlet to have some fun in the sun. (I was trying my hand at match-making my best friend and my trainer, unsuccessfully). Even though I was very excited about the chance to get back into the actual ocean, I had my concerns and they must have been obvious to Miss Café Breva because she asked if I was ok. I replied 'yep', but she knew that I wasn't, so she enquired more. It was then that I told her that I was nervous and scared about what everyone sitting around the inlet would be thinking about me. I feared that they might be wondering what I am doing near water, I thought they might see me as silly or something. Then Miss Café Breva said something to me that day that I have never forgotten. She asked me, 'Do you honestly think that other people will be sitting there criticising and condemning you, when you are out there giving it a go?' When I didn't respond, Miss Café Breva went on to say that she thought, that if anything, 'people' would be saying to themselves, 'that girl is out there giving it a go!' Miss Café Breva reminded me that I am probably more critical of myself than anyone else, that people support others when they are 'having a go', and that there was another way to look at the situation. In that moment, Miss Café Breva taught me to be less concerned about what others thought and that having a go is more important than any concerns and fears. Thank Miss Café Breva for the person you are and what you bring to my world.

Now that I was becoming more aware of my thoughts, I realised that I could change them if I didn't like them or they were out-dated, and that I could replace them with whatever I wanted.

The exciting part is that I can choose the type of woman that I want to be in the future, and it is my new thoughts and beliefs about myself that will make it happen for me. Sure, there may be moments when I slip-up, however, then I can take a new, deep breath and re-commit to 'myself' again. 'Not reaching your dream is not failing, rather, giving up on your dream is failing'.

It's not that I'm so smart, it's just that I stay with problems longer ~ Albert Einstein

bit six – Healing

Like any cut or wound that we get when we take a fall or hit, before the skin can mend, the fluid from the damaged layers underneath must be expelled. And usually, the healing happens from the inside out, with the scab on top being the most evident sign that our injury is almost healed. I want to say that it does not matter how big or small the event, it is the same with emotional and spiritual damage too – whether it be the break-up of a relationship, the loss of a sibling, or something that has caused you trauma. We have to release all of the shit (technical term for emotions, feelings and thoughts) first, that is inside of us, before any sort of healing can take place – otherwise we are just suppressing it, and you know what happens if we do that? At some point, sooner or later, the cork will fly right off that bottle and there will be an explosion! And all the stuff that you have not allowed yourself to feel, comes bubbling and exploding up to the surface of your reality.

Not only does your body need time to heal, yet also the real you – your core, spirit, essence, whatever term you feel comfortable with, needs time to heal as well. Even though our mind and body are two different entities, they are interconnected, they are entwined and cannot be separated. Something cannot happen to your body without it affecting you (and registering on some level) through your mind and vice versa. So, if something happens to one part of you, you can bet other parts will be impacted to some degree.

It is obvious that there is damage when people experience anything that causes pain or harm, such as a loss, an accident or a disease. The damage that I am talking about is not merely physical, the scarring that happens on the emotional plane can, in fact, cut far deeper and require significantly more healing. It is my belief that the degree of emotional damage that is caused depends largely upon two aspects, (1) the person and (2) the degree of physical injury experienced. But that's just my un-educated, un-qualified guess (Smiles).

However there is no hope for healing when us humans, spend our days and nights criticising, berating, condemning, judging and blaming ourselves on so many levels. You might be blaming yourself for getting behind the wheel when you had too many drinks, you might be berating yourself for making a poor decision, you might have condemned yourself for falling asleep when you were driving, you might have criticised yourself for getting on the back of the motorbike…. If you are doing this to yourself, you are only hurting yourself. Perhaps that is your goal, because you feel that is what you deserve. I don't know, that is your business. Regardless, I want to say it loud and clear, so that I am certain you hear me - *You are abusing yourself!* And this does not do you any good. I know this because I have done it too.

This sort of thinking is pointless, because, if we are truly living in the present, then we need to accept, manage, come-to-terms-with (whatever phrase you like) what has happened, and deal with what is real for us, in the present. Only when we are living in the present, can some sort of healing commence.

First thing is first - give yourself permission to go through the experience, whatever that entails. What I mean by this is really allow yourself to feel whatever it is that is stirred up inside of you, be that heartache, pain, loneliness, fear, anger, guilt………. I don't know. What you experience is unique to you. Usually, you will know when it is the right time for you to leave that place of healing and return to the real world, you will get a nudge of some kind from inside you and the grey clouds around you will start to clear-up, what is going on in the world will start to be interesting again, and step by step, you will slowly feel that you want to be a part of life again.

Have you heard of proverbs like, 'you can lead a horse to water but you can't make it drink', or 'you can show people how to do things but the people must help themselves'? Yes, they are old and worn, but they exist because they have been proven to be true. You are the only one who can pick yourself up and dust yourself off and start again.

Like yours, my world was turned on its head in less than a split second, a blink of an eye or a snap of our fingers. The details of what happened are not relevant here, but the crux is that there were two people in the accident, one survived and one did not.

So, let us fast forward one, two, three years on, and I was still holding on to those past memories so tightly, for if I let them go maybe they would cease to exist. We cease to exist, he ceases to exist. I don't know if it was because I was afraid of forgetting those precious people and times, but, for whatever the reason, there was zero chance of any healing because I was not permitting it.

It took me weeks, months and years before I came to the conclusion that I had to purge any pain, guilt, anger, resentment, or fear that I had, so that there would be space enough for the healing to happen – and I am passing this knowledge onto you because I don't want it to take that long for you, I don't want you to waste any more time than you need to before you can start to live again.

You need to decide for yourself *if and when* you want to move forward. Notice I used the word *want* instead of *can*! You can buy an ice cream, you can buy a gold sequined dress, but, it is the wanting, that makes you do something.... You get what I am trying to say? The desire has to come from within you, in order for you to take action!

TOOL – LOVE WHO YOU ARE

I want to tell you about an author I stumbled upon years ago, through my friend's sister.

Louise L. Hay – internationally respected leader in all things metaphysical says, 'When people come to me with a problem, I don't care what it is – poor health, lack of money, unfulfilling relationships – there is only one thing I ever work on and that is LOVING THE SELF'.

For me, loving who I am means seeing my worth, giving myself respect, not judging, and believing in myself and my capabilities.

I challenge you, 'What does really loving who you are, mean for you?'

Think about it, if you dare (Smiles).

In 2004 I was coming up to my 34th birthday and feeling pretty sorry for myself I saw a movie advertised that I thought I might be interested in, that movie was *Under the Tuscan sun*.

In this movie the lead character, a female, finds her life turned upside down when the lies her husband has been living start to unravel. So in the middle of her life when things should be coming together they are literally falling apart as she finds herself divorced, living week to week in a 1 bedroom apartment, and almost frozen in time. She is fearful of making any decision – be it good or bad. After being given a flight and tour to Tuscany, she finds herself bidding on a villa for sale as she realises she can't go back to where she came from.

As the movie unfolds we see that things she wished for became a reality, just differently to how she had imagined - I adored it!

Life may not unfold the way you planned, hoped or dreamed, but it can still be spectacularly beautiful!

bit seven – Your choice!

In the morning we choose if we are going to hit the snooze button or not (in my case it is how many times will I hit it!) We choose what to have for breakfast, we choose how to wear our hair, what colour lipstick, we choose what time to leave for work, and we can even choose our mood for the day. Every decision or choice that we make will impact the direction of our path, both on a day-to-day basis and in the big picture of our life.

I can honestly sit here and tell you that every choice that I have made has led me here to the very spot that I am in at this very moment (which is in a house high up in Mudgeeraba, sitting on my bed, writing a book). When you take time to ponder that whole concept, it can be pretty scary – because, then we are faced with taking responsibility for everything that we do or choose.

Even when we choose not to make a choice or decision, we are still picking a path to follow, it is still a choice! (Big grin).

When we fail to 'do' – we just fail.

At this moment, I am waving a gi-normous (combination of giant and enormous), bright yellow flag in front of you and letting you know that it is decision time again, right now! Your choices are as follows -

TOOL – WHAT WILL YOU CHOOSE?

1 – You can lay around in bed all day long, not care for your body, never leave your house, never invite friends over, never brush your hair or teeth, and sit around watching television all day long, basically just taking up oxygen and space on this planet. You can give-up on yourself, your family and friends, and basically life in general – that is one choice.

Or

2 – You can say "Ok, if life is going to throw rocks at me, I'm going to catch them, scrub them up, and see if any of them are diamonds?"

We will all get things thrown at us, through-out our life. Sometimes it will be small, like a tennis ball, other times it might be more like a basketball, while other moments we might get hit by what seems like a car. That is life, and it is not going to change. The only difference is how we respond, what we do about it and the outcome.

Can we use what we have experienced to better the lives of others in the same boat or the community in general? Which, in turn ultimately help us too? Or will we just moan and complain, over and over, about what has happened to poor, little old us.

The bottom line is that we have nobody to hold responsible, except ourselves.

And, I can hear you asking me, *but don't you miss dancing, walking hand –in-hand, driving a manual car, running, and just doing whatever it is that you want to do?* In all honesty, I have to answer, of course I do. But I am also extremely grateful for the function and freedom that

I still have right now. Things have happened and I have to accept that and enjoy what I have, which I do!

Yes, I remember how it felt to have the sand between my toes, the thrill of changing gears in a manual car, the fun I used to have doing step aerobic classes, the excitement of feeling someone press their whole body up against yours when you're dancing. Those moments in my life are dear and beautiful memories that will always be with me, yet, in order to be happy now – I have to make myself happy on a day-to-day basis. Meaning, I had to get out of my head space and back into life.

TOOL - GRATITUDE

This may not be an easy task in the beginning, because you are trying to de-code what has been re-playing in your head over and over, for who knows how long.

On day One - you need to start by finding one thing to be grateful for. I don't care if it is being able to make a cup of tea yourself or being able to enjoy a sunset, perhaps you are grateful for being able to see the people you love and care about, or being able to feel when someone touches your shoulder or face. I don't want to hear that you can't find one thing to be grateful for – I know there is at least one thing, so find it.

- Then, I want you to 'thank the universe' (or whatever you call it), verbally, for that what you are grateful about.

- Now, you need to write it down somewhere and stick it to your mirror, fridge, or next to the toilet. It is important that it is somewhere you can see it every day.

- This is the important bit – you need to write your gratitude sentence six times. Why? Because, I have

---

found that the first few times the sentence is just words, then each extra time we write it or say it, we actually get closer to really meaning it.

On day Two, I want you to find a different 'thing' that you are grateful for and follow the above steps again. Every day I want you to stick up your new 'gratitude', so that at the end of the week you have seven reasons why you want to be here.

This technique is something that got me through the early stages, and if you can commit yourself, you will find it can work for you too. Some people claim it takes 21 days to break habits, I believe it depends on the person. Commit yourself for 21 days, it is only three weeks out of your entire life! Are you worth 5 minutes a day for 21 days?

I think you are, but do you?

You need to be committed to yourself – that means re-committing every day or every time you don't do it. This is not for anyone else, this is just for you.

Warning: I am going to get in your face here!

Our life is our choice – it is that simple!

Our life does not depend upon anyone else except us. Whether we become a nurse or a fashion designer, has nothing to do with the fact that we use a wheelchair, if we travel overseas or not has nothing to do with sitting down all the time, if we fall pregnant and become mothers has nothing to do with the fact that we use a wheelchair..... I want to say that if you desire something so dearly, I encourage you not to give-up. If you get a 'no', go somewhere else. I say we are the Captain of our vessel and we chart our own journey.

bit eight – Don't play small!

When I started thinking about my employment options I began to freak out a little because I knew I could not perform all the duties involved in my previous role as a computer support person.

Some of the things I actually enjoyed about that role were that I got to chase wires under desks and physically install new computer points and all of that hands-on stuff. I loved it. Then I started thinking about positions that were desk bound, like receptionists, administration, book keeper and the like. These are good jobs that suit some people down to a 'T', but I am not one of them.

While I was in hospital, the Education Unit asked some people in chairs to come in and talk to us about their lives, and I recall one was a successful computer person and the other was a Paralympic athlete in wheelchair basketball. These people were successful and loved what they did now, I just wasn't sure if I would enjoy those roles. Then I put it in the too hard basket because I felt somewhat dismayed at the lack of options.

However, one day I sat myself down and said to myself "Enough is enough, what are some jobs that require people to sit down?" and as I started naming a few, the list kept growing. Then my mind started expanding and I thought about not just having a job, but doing something for myself. Now I was talking. And the looming grey clouds started to lift.

Playing small time, putting myself into a box does not serve me in any way, shape or form, and that was exactly what I was about to do. In no way is it honouring me as a whole person. It is not honouring what I've learnt through my life experiences, it does not recognise my skills and abilities that I had gained from life. What it does is squash them, making them null and void.

When I made contact with an organisation that provides services for people with a disability, I also discovered that they tried their damndest to get people back into jobs that they used to do or would really love to do. I cannot speak highly enough of that team of employment professionals at Spinal Injuries Association in Brisbane, Australia. They told me how they helped one man get back to truck driving after his accident. Can you imagine it? A person who lost the function of his legs driving a semi-trailer – awesome! Another man became a horse trainer and another re-claimed his real love - farming. So, there are like-minded professionals out there that will help you achieve what you actually want – not just shove you into any old job (you can find their website at the rear of this book).

bit nine – Is this the total of me?

Are you just your body? I want you to move your derriere over to a mirror and sit there and ask yourself the following question, right now please – 'Is this the total of me?'

I know the answer and so do you, but I want you to really feel it inside you - so that when you have a down day, you are strong enough to pull yourself back up.

So, answer me this question too – 'Are you just your mind?' If you are honest with yourself and brave enough to look inside, you will see that you are not the total of these aspects of your package.

For all of the airbrushed and perfectly proportioned Barbies in the magazines and on television, thank God there are those people who love themselves enough that they don't try to fit into this ridiculously twisted and tormented, sutured and superficial box that the world is growing more infatuated with every day. A person is more than what looks back at them from the mirror. Did you hear that? I'll say it again, a person is more than what looks back at them from the mirror! Just stop here for a moment and let that really sink down into your being, ok...........

I also want you to stop! Stop comparing yourself to every other woman who can still walk, and while I'm at it, I want you to stop comparing what you look like now to what you used to look like (in your previous life)..... the past is the past, it is gone, it is dead and buried. Right here, right now is our new reality.

You are more than the package or box that you inhabit right now! If you are Christian/Catholic/Anglican/Baptist/Jew or Muslim, you will know that you were 'made in the image of God', and if you are Buddhist, you will believe that we are a spirit here to learn and grow from the lessons of the various lives that we live. But, regardless from whatever angle you look at life, you have to acknowledge that we are more than this package that we inhabit!

I am certain most of you have heard this before, but I will say it anyway – when our lungs do stop taking in breath and our heart stops beating, the package in which we live will wither and die – kind of like if you could stop a plant from taking in air. But that is just what happens to the package or vessel, so to speak. I will leave it up to the philosophers to debate what happens next, but you get my drift, right?

So, what I am trying to say is what makes us, us, is not the outside, but it is the inside, the unseen, the untouchable part of us. That is what really separates us from every other person on the planet, not our hair, or our smile, or the way we walk.

bit ten - It is now up to you what happens next.

Regardless of how much you have or don't have, regardless of how you grew up, regardless of how many parents you had, how much love you had or didn't have, regardless of your height, your education, your age, your ethnicity, your ability or disability - it is now up to you what happens next.

I want to take a moment to say that I have the utmost respect for our grandparents, because they endured events and times that I will never truly be capable of conceiving. For example, my dad was born in 1919, one year post World War I. At a very young age his father passed away leaving his mother to care and provide for twelve children. Yes, that is right, not one, not two, not three or four, but count them, twelve children!

My father was quite the entrepreneur. He started making money from nine years old, selling milk to the workers at quarries for their coffee. Being born just after World War I he lived through both the great Depression and World War II, so he knew only too well what it was like to struggle and not have money his pocket. The point I am getting at here is that despite the lack of money, education, and general hardships of the times, my father put 100% energy into making his life what he wanted it to be, and making darn sure that he had enough money for today, next week, and of course the 'rainy day'.

I am trying to show you that there is no event, scarcity, lack, loss, disability, or pain big enough that you cannot live through and triumph. You are bigger than any story that you have to tell! You are the inventor, the painter, captain, the architect, and the master of your life, no one else, just you.

What kind of life will you create for yourself?

Warm Regards,
Violet

Chapter eight

Personal management

bit one - the Bathroom

The first topic that I want to touch on in this particular chapter is the public bathroom.

First up I want to say a very sincere thank you to McDonald's!

I can hear you, 'why on earth is she thanking McDonald's?' Well, it could be the fact that they offer drive-thru service, which is absolutely fabulous for those of us who are time restricted, or perhaps it is their charity work? But, maybe it is their luscious McFlurrys? It could be, but not this time.

For me, it is the fact that no matter where I am in the world, be it Australia, England, USA, Germany or France, I am a-l-m-o-s-t guaranteed that if there is a McDonald's around, I can be pretty certain that it will have a bathroom I can access. And, if that isn't reason enough to jump-for-joy, then I don't know what is! Because, if you aren't aware of it, you soon will discover that wheelchair-friendly bathrooms can be somewhat difficult to find. Europe in general is a tad more of a challenge than most countries in the world, but at least McDonald's try. So, once again I want to give a 'shout out' to McDonald's for including 'everyone' in your small portion of the world.

Just before I move on – I really want to give credit where credit is due. I love the fact that in the US bathrooms for people in chairs are included within the respective gender, unlike in Australia and the United Kingdom, where 'people with a disability' seem to be a whole new gender altogether! So does that mean that (in Australia) I am not really a woman because I utilise a wheelchair – I am just a wheelchair person, as some people often describe us. You get that I am taking the piss here, right. However seriously, it can impact how we see ourselves, and also how the community sees us too. Sort of like segregation, but that is a whole other book (Heehee).

Getting back to locating bathrooms.

Apart from the ever trusty McDonald's, you might find some bathrooms at service stations. I have also discovered that service stations sometimes only have one central toilet, which we might be able to use - depending on the size of your chair. Of course large shopping centres are a definite, while the smaller ones may or may not have wheelchair-friendly bathrooms. In my experience, the older the shopping centre looks, the less chance there is of finding one. Some libraries have wheelchair accessible bathrooms, particularly the new ones and if all else fails, look out for a hotel, RSM/RSL or bowling club in the area – thank God for large numbers of older people.

Oh, that is right. It almost slipped my mind. There are some public toilets that include us and are accessible for people who use wheelchairs. Warning: If you do use public toilets, remember to take in some sterilizing gel and hand wipes, because they do not provide any hand soap or hand towels. The sterilizing gel comes in a pen-sized quantity which is handy for the glove box or your chair pouch. In my experience, I found that toilets in the UK were a heck of a lot cleaner than most of the countries I have been to, I think it has something to do with the fact that only people with a disability can access them (with a special key - RADAR). Shame Australia doesn't get on board with that idea! (Huge hint).

When we do locate an accessible bathroom there will be times when it may be empty and times when it may not. From my personal experience, there are a plethora of people who like to use the 'disabled toilets', be it to have a smoke in a shopping centre, change into clothes they have just purchased, for privacy, or simply because that is the toilet of their choice.

I recall one time going to a local cinema with my friends and having to stand outside of the accessible bathroom for almost ten minutes.... I sat waiting there wondering who was going to walk out this time? Then to my total surprise, out walked a young girl followed by a boy. Looking at them, they only looked about 16 or 17 years old. At that age, they are mostly in their own world, so I didn't bother saying anything to them and they would have seen me sitting there as they walked passed me. I don't do the whole angry thing, I just want them to respect my rights as much as they want respect. But again, that is an entirely new topic all of its own.

So getting back to the story - I just made my way inside and locked the door. After washing my hands I went to transfer onto the toilet when I noticed a condom and packet floating in the bowl – so now there was another reason why people would use our toilets instead of their own. Great!

You can choose to get all worked up about those people in our community that use the 'disabled' bathrooms for their own pleasures. And, if you do a really good job of it, you can let it ruin the rest of your day too. Or perhaps you might think of something to say to them as they exit that might cause them to think of other people's rights. But, at some point, you will need to just let it go. Gosh, can you imagine the sort of people we would be if we stored up all of the frustration and feelings that we experience on a weekly basis? We'd be a right old sour puss, I think.

I am going to tell you now that more often than not I find the bathrooms are used by those who do not physically require them, but I can also tell you that I am not going to let them ruin the rest of my day or change my mood. I choose to be happy and I choose to have fun, and so can you.

There will of course be times when there **are not any wheelchair-accessible bathrooms in sight.**

Be warned: below are a few different ways that I have accessed inaccessible bathrooms. Now, I am definitely not encouraging you to try what I am telling you (below), but I know so many of us chicks in chairs that have had to do some unusual things in a moment of urgency! I hope these scenarios give you a giggle at least (Grins).

1. Ask your girlfriend to come with you and stand guard outside your cubicle (because the cubicle is way too small).

2. Squeeze into the cubicle, transfer onto the seat and then allow your friend to take the chair away and hold the door closed while you're otherwise occupied.

3. Take off one wheel to fit the chair into the cubicle and put it back on once inside. This one is a bit tricky and you need a friend to do it.

4. Get your girlfriend to stand inside the cubicle first. Now, you get your wheelchair as close to the door as possible. Of course, apply your brakes. Then, with all her might ask your girlfriend to grab and lift you from your chair to the toilet seat. No, there will be nothing for you to hold onto except for your girlfriend. And unless your girlfriend is built like Sylvester Stallone, she will need to do the lift as quickly as possible so that you get as close as you can to the toilet seat. My girlfriend (Miss Mint Tea) and I already had a bit of dutch-courage inside of us, and who knows if that helped or hindered. All I know is that I got to use the toilet and have a fun memory to enjoy and share.

bit two - Asking for directions.

Don't ask me why, but almost every single time I ask for a bathroom when I'm out and about, I get directions, but usually to the able-bodied bathrooms, not a wheelchair accessible lavatory. I don't know why, but I have found that I need to actually spell it out to the person I am asking, God knows why! Now the only reason why I am bringing this up, is because this has happened to me on more than one occasion and it just baffles me. I don't know why, or what on earth they are thinking, but it happens. Perhaps, they assume that I can walk, or perhaps they are blinded by my gorgeousness (Naa, not likely).

I'm giggling as I write this because I just don't get it. The people I ask for directions don't know if I can walk or not, but they can clearly see that I am sitting in a wheelchair in front of them, asking for a bathroom. So thanks to those people for the laugh, your memory will live on!

Now, I don't know why, but on occasion, I have found that the nearest wheelchair accessible bathroom is up steps – hilarious! Yet, I guess the excuse might have something to do with the fact that most people in chairs don't socialise that often, meaning that the majority of people with a disability years ago were people that could still use their legs. If you see this situation, please, please make a note of it and contact your local council (regardless of the country you live in), because it will help the next person. And who knows, I could be the next person needing to use that bathroom and I would be truly grateful to you (Huge cheesy smile).

Next, I want to mention that on my expeditions around the country (Australia), I have found that there are some public bathrooms that have a big serious-looking lock on it that prevents access unless you possess *that* key. As I did my rehabilitation overseas, I did not know about this 'system' that exists in Australia until I stumbled across it. I don't know how many other people have been caught out like this, but I will give you the information that I have discovered and hope that you are not inconvenienced as I have been.

The Master Locksmiths Access Key (MLAK) is a system that enables people with disabilities to gain 24 hour access to a network of public facilities around Australia. Anyone with a disability is able to purchase an MLAK master key which will open these toilets. It can also be used on the Liberty Swing, which is a swing designed for children who use a wheelchair.

When I found the website about this Master Locksmith key, it said I could call 1800-810-698 and so, I did. They then gave me another number which I called, only to be given another number to someone who knew little about this special key. Fortunately for us, the person I spoke to was proactive and made all the calls necessary to find out about this key and find out how his company could cut it. Anyway, long story short, I have saved you the drama and have the name and number of where you can get an MLAK key for yourself.

Surfers Paradise Locksmiths (07)5588-8111 at 101 Ashmore Road, Bundall can organise a key for you without you going into their office. I spoke to Josh who said that they can take payment over the phone and post the key out to you. The key cost me $15 (2010), however, it will save a load of headaches, as this facility becomes more and more widely used. This is their link too, www.splsecurity.com.au

The organization Spinal Cord Injuries Australia also maintains a directory of MLAK-enabled facilities across Australia. To view this directory, please follow the link below and then, download the associated file. www.scia.org.au/public-toilets

I also want to make certain that you are aware of something that might just solve a lot of our bladder concerns as well as ease the hassle of travelling. And this is a website (Australia-wide) which lists all public and private bathroom facilities for males/females, parents, and wheelchair users alike. **The National Public Toilet Map** (the Toilet Map) shows the location of more than 14,000 lavatories providing details of location, opening hours, provision of change rooms, and wheelchair accessibility. I have checked this website for its content in areas that I know very well, and it seems they have reliable information, even if it might be missing one or two here and there. This is an enormous task though and I applaud them for even attempting it. Job – well done.
www.toiletmap.gov.au

I am grateful that the MLAK lock system is being introduced at public toilets in some towns, but perhaps this system needs to go Australia-wide. And when I say Australia-wide, I mean on every single wheelchair-friendly bathroom – public and private. Only then can we be certain that people with needs are using them!! (This is a big HINT to government).

Note: The Continence Foundation of Australia also provides a National Help Line with an interpreter service for those of us in chairs with hearing challenges.
Call 1800 33 00 66

I believe I have mentioned that the United Kingdom have a great system when it comes to accessing wheelchair friendly facilities, yet I'll say it again. The only reason I am aware of this system is due to the fact that I did my rehabilitation in England.

The National Key Scheme, provided by RADAR (Royal Association for Disability and Rehabilitation) offers people with a disability independent access to around 7,000 locked public toilets across the country. That is 7000 toilets that are just for people with a disability! Isn't that wonderful? Anyway, RADAR is the UK's leading disability charity working to represent the need of over 10.8 million people (with a disability) throughout the UK. Holiday-makers to the UK can purchase this key, and I would definitely recommend it as it only costs about $10, and they will send them anywhere in the world. This is the website for RADAR key. www.radar-shop.org.uk

bit three – Bladder management

Now that we've had a bit of a giggle it is time for the big B&M. No, I'm not talking about intimate positions in bed with vinyl, leather and lace – I am talking about bladder management of course!

Over the years a lot of people have said to me if they could just feel and control their toileting aspects, their life in a chair would be a walk in the park, so to speak (Heehee). And I, for one, would have to agree with this. When you have grown up and lived a life with the ability to completely control your bodily functions, and then in one foul swoop that capability and power is taken away from you, well, how do I describe how that feels? Hmmm. I could say that it feels something like when a friend gives you a birthday present and then a few years later when you are playing with it, they take it back, yet even that would be an understatement. Maybe it feels like a death of a loved one – yes, I think that might be the closest analogy I can make.

This particular aspect of the disability (bladder management) could consume us, if we let it! Yet, I know you won't let that happen, will you? But, in all seriousness, it is probably the first question that comes to mind when I want to do something. Why would it, you ask? Well if I want to go out for dinner, I want to know if I am able to enjoy a drink with my friends/partner. If I want to go swimming, I don't want a full bladder, if I am travelling by car I want to know where I can access a bathroom, should I have the need. If I am shopping, I want to know that I can keep my fluids up during the day, and if I want to do that, then I need to know where the nearest accessible bathroom is located.

I don't know if you believe we came from monkeys or God, yet regardless, I am speechless at the internal wiring of this organism (our body). We really are a piece of work, a piece of walking, talking, 3 dimensional art! When we consider the fact that a tonne of processes and functions occur in our body and we don't even know they're happening, considering each and every single thing (technical term) in our body has a unique and specific purpose, considering that the body is self-regulating and self-healing, it just blows me away. Could you imagine if we had to remind ourselves to breathe on a minute-to-minute basis? The point I am trying to make is that when something changes in your body, like the ability to breath, use your fingers, legs or control your bladder – it will cause some form of distress on at least one, if not, multiple levels – emotionally, physically and spiritually. Regardless if this loss occurred at birth or through life, via some developing condition or near-fatal accident, you are missing the function of something you were born with.

It is only natural that we would have some sort of reaction or emotions about losing something that was previously a big part of our lives, or something that should be a big part of our lives. Let's face it, we live amongst people who use their legs, arms, hands, bladder and bowel constantly, and at free will. And, we also live in a world that is primarily designed for, and by, people who have four fully-functioning limbs, reminding us of what we no longer have. Yet, dwelling on this fact does not change, improve or help the world, it does not change or help our lives, and it does not help us as a person!!!! So stop it right now.... please, stop the torment.

Some of us might be able to feel when we are hungry, which is wonderful.

Some of us might be able to feel when we need to go to the toilet, which is marvellous. And, some of us might be able to actually control the action of going to the toilet (of which I am extremely envious). All of this really does not matter, as the point I am attempting to make here is the fact that everyone who uses a chair is still individual. We were all different and unique before our injury/ incident in our likes/dislikes, personalities, talents and more, but now, if it is at all possible, we are even more unique than we were before! And, when it comes to discussing this topic I know that I will not be able to cover the diverse spectrum of disabilities (and I would not try as I am not a nurse or doctor). All I can do is give you what I have learnt and experienced as a woman with paraplegia, and hope that some of it might be of help to you (hold on, just crossing my fingers).

Now, I want to talk to those of us who find they need a chair temporarily, for whatever reason. I want to say to you 'lucky you'! You will regain some, if not most of what has been taken away, and your life will resume its normality again. I am not saying that while you use a chair you won't experience the various emotions that are associated with using a wheelchair, such as frustration, despair and possibly depression. What I am saying to you is that you need to look at the big picture of life, because, even if you are in a chair for ten months – it is just a minute percentage of your entire life. And I know at least a dozen people who would die to be told that, yes, including myself. What you gain from your experience is the gift of seeing life from a different angle, you get to see how some people in this world are not included as much as they could be, and you have the opportunity to do something with that knowledge and experience to make a difference in the world. How good would you feel about making a difference to the world?

On the other hand, if some of you received a more serious injury and find yourself using a wheelchair for a slightly more extended period of time (like life), I say to you – *it is neither good, nor bad.* It just is!

Of course, whether we need a wheelchair for six months or for life, we can make it a lot worse by dwelling on all of the things that we can no longer have, do, or experience - which will take us down a very long and scary path, to a place where there is no light or hope. On the other side of the coin, we can choose to be grateful for those things that we still have, still can do and experience – which will mean that we are in control of our life and that we can create whatever we want in our life. It is as simple as a choice.

Louise Hay explains,

> The thoughts we have held and the words we have repeatedly used have created our life and experiences up to this point. Yet, that is past thinking, we have already done that.
>
> What we are choosing to think and say, today, this moment, will create tomorrow and the next day, and the next week and the next month and the next year, etc. The point of power is always in the present moment.

Yes, we will need time to come to terms with what has happened and what is now. It may be overnight, it may take a few months or even longer, however, at some point, we need to, for lack of a better word – surrender to what is now. Once we surrender, we can then start to move forward and create the new life that we want and deserve!

I want you to know that our bladder can be managed so that moments of incontinence are few and far between. Even though I say that, there will be moments throughout the course of our life when this is not the case and we lose that false sense of control, we feel humiliated and embarrassed and basically, feel like a baby again. Allow yourself to shed the tears that come from the pain you're feeling inside, but don't dwell there too long my friends. For surely, the longer you do, the harder it is to come back. Release your pain, grief and anger, pull yourself up and dust yourself off.

TOOL – BELIEVE IN YOU

Sit in front of a mirror and say something to this effect -

**I am a strong, independent and sexy woman and I love you....
I deserve all the good that the Universe has to offer and I
accept it with joy and gratitude. I love you, thank you!'**

You don't have to memorise this, yet it won't do much if you just say this once! Rather, I would like you to say it until you feel it inside you, in your core.

Now, I am not a religious person, however, I do often find myself saying the following phrase -

*"God grant me the serenity to accept the things I cannot
change, the courage to change the things I can,
and the wisdom to know the difference."*
~ Reinhold Niebuhr

The accident which resulted in my circumstance, and the time I spent in hospital was not just about giving me skills to live with my disability, it educated me about the things I never knew occurred in my body. For instance, I had no idea about the quantity of liquid my bladder could hold, whereas over the years I have learnt that I need to be conscious of what I am consuming (eg: coffee/water/alcohol) and how much I am consuming, as both of these aspects impact my bladder and life. Medical research states our bladder can hold approximately 400 millilitres.

I also learnt that as a result of our spinal injury, our bladder can be either a Flaccid or Reflex type. What this means is that if your injury is T12 or above you will probably have a reflex bladder like I do, that is, our bladder can automatically and involuntarily act without our permission to do so = we have zero control. However, if your injury is T12 and below, this means that you are one of the lucky ones (and I hate you! Not really), and you have a flaccid bladder that will not leak of its own will, yet you will still need to catheterise to empty the bladder. The owner of a flaccid bladder might even feel when they need to visit the lavatory, depending of course on the extent of damage to your spinal cord.

FLASHBACK

In hospital the staff tried to get 'things' (number 1 & 2s) working properly as best they could, and at that time 'things' were working ok for me. 'Accidents' (number 1 & 2s) will happen in and out of hospital, until you find out how your body really operates, and that is different for everyone, so unfortunately I can't give you an exact list of what to do to keep you out of trouble. But let me tell you a little story.

I had been out of hospital for about two months when all of a sudden things were not working how they were supposed to be working. What I mean by that is that, for no apparent reason I was having bladder leaks all over the place. You name it, in the chair, in the bed and in the car – everywhere. I have to say that it was absolutely freaking me out. No matter what I was drinking or not drinking, my bladder was still leaking. No set time, no set quantity. No predictability whatsoever. So, I decided to dehydrate myself deliberately for days, yet still I was experiencing incontinence. After going to my local GP, I started taking a medication that relaxed the bladder muscles, other people I have discovered get Botox injected into their bladder. Anyway, the reason that I am mentioning this experience is because, when I returned to the out-patient clinic at Stoke Mandeville Spinal Unit, (in the UK) I was informed that the doctors had received several reports from other ex-female patients with similar stories – that they had started experiencing bladder incontinence post discharge. The whole point being that - it might have been helpful for the doctors to mention that there is a possibility of things changing post discharge.   At least then, mentally, I could have been prepared for it and not freak out as much as I did, because I thought something serious was wrong with me.

We all know how important it is that we aspire to drink two (2) litres of water a day, well I believe this is even more important for us now, because, it helps the organs and muscles, it helps give moisture to our skin, and it also benefits the entire digestive system – if you know what I mean (bowel movement).   Now, if we are aiming to drink that amount of water every day, it is vital that we know we can access a bathroom anytime we need it.   Before I move on to the next point, there are a couple of aspects that we need to talk about here.   And that is, what we drink will affect us.

Below is just an outline of what I have discovered about my body and what works for me:

- Coffee, Tea, Hot Chocolate = Bathroom break in one hours time and possibly again in 30-40 minutes post the first bathroom visit to ensure it is all out of your system.

- Alcohol = Bathroom break in one hours time and continue this until two hours post consumption.

- Fruit Juice = Goes through the body quicker, and therefore I need a bathroom break around 30-40 minutes time after consuming.   Smoothies are approximately the same time frame.

- I don't have coffee after 8pm at night, if I am going to

bed at about 10pm. That way I can sleep through the night (I sleep from 10pm -5.30am). Actually, I do not drink anything after 8pm unless I am staying up.

- Before you finish your No.1, sit as upright as possible and wait for any remaining fluid to drain. It is my experience that when I do this, there is often more to come. The risk of having an inadequate drainage is that we have the risk of developing kidney stones and UTIs.

- I personally, have decided to drink water at room temperature, because I read somewhere that it is better for the digestive system. Also in the colder months I often substitute a cup of coffee for a cup of plain hot water – if the Chinese do it, it is good enough for me.

- Be conscious of the colour and odour of your No.1 as it will be a tell-tale sign for any infections, but the nurses will teach you this.

- I have a 1 litre bottle of water with me each day and I am the only one who drinks from it, that way I can see how much I am consuming. I found that I drink more when I have a large bottle to get through than I do when I just have a cup at a time. It is probably a psychological thing, but this is what works for me. You find out what works for you.

I want to tell you about one of the first things I noticed when I was first in a wheelchair, as it is pertinent to the subject at hand. What stood out the most about being in a chair was not the blisters appearing all over my hands, not the callus either, nor was it the numerous cuts I had acquired, but it was the amount of dirt I picked up on my hands from pushing around everywhere. I really want to point out that whenever there are hands involved with anything (now that we are in a chair) there is an increased chance of infection.

Yes, I am probably a little bit fastidious about washing my hands, but

I'd rather be pro-active than reactive to something that has happened to me that I could have prevented; that just means more hassle. Now back to bladder stuff...

Side track

I wash my hands before I eat or do anything related to my mouth, and I wash before I am doing anything concerned with toileting. And the stupid thing is that we have to think about what we are touching beforehand so that 'it' doesn't get all over our wheels, eg: watermelon or mangoes. Of course when someone washes their hands that much, there is a down side, and that is the amount of moisture that is lost, which is why during the colder months you might notice your hands looking dry or cracking. One idea is to keep a bottle of moisturiser next to the taps in the bathroom so that you don't have any excuses. Although, I have found that the moisturiser doesn't always soak in thoroughly

When I was mentoring at a spinal unit one of the ladies couldn't quite get the knack of intermittent catheters, and that is totally understandable as it is a tad tricky in the beginning. But, this is why I am now going to talk more in depth about the whole toileting experience for those of us who don't have the ability to wee at will.

I might have mentioned before, that there were a few of us girls in the spinal unit at the same time, which was great as we became good friends and bounced ideas off of each other – two minds are better than one! And I thank God that today I still have a strong friendship with one of these beautiful women (Miss Iced latte), because we share something that our other friendships don't. So, when it came to the bladder management topic, I think the only idea we came up with was using our fingers to guide us to the right spot. Later in this chapter I take you on a step-by-step journey on how one woman self-catheterises.

If you don't find the right spot the first time and end up somewhere else, please discard that catheter and start again with a fresh one. This might happen a bit when you are first learning, yet that is to be expected, right? Some of us acquired this skill easily, others take a bit longer, however the point is that it is not impossible. Just don't give up!

I know that I am going into details here, however us girls have to be even more careful when it comes to hygiene, than the boys, because we have more chances to get infections, due to the design of our body.

So when I am going to the toilet for two (2) reasons (eg: tampon and catheter) this would be the process:

- Wash my hands thoroughly and dry
- Move to the toilet (using the palms of my hands to push the tyres),
- Transfer and undress
- Catheter first and
- Insert the tampon last
- You can also use hand wipes (or baby wipes) as an in-between step after the catheter and before the tampon. Some people use gloves when inserting a tampon.

There are three primary items that aide bladder management for people with a spinal cord injury and these are -

1. Supra Pubic Catheter
2. Indwelling Catheter
3. Intermittent Catheter

I myself have never had a Supra Pubic Catheter, however one of my friends did in the spinal unit during my rehabilitation. She was a kick-ass woman who acquired Tetraplegia/Quadriplegia and seemed to prefer the Supra Pubic more than the Indwelling Catheter (IDC). Although, I do recall there was at least one infection while she was in the unit. At least with Supra Pubics the user doesn't need to worry about sitting on it or getting any kinks in it, like the indwelling catheter.

> Supra pubic catheters are surgically inserted through the abdominal wall into the bladder thereby diverting urine from the urethra. There is a slightly reduced risk of infection than with an IDC (Indwelling Catheter), and some people may be more comfortable with a supra pubic catheter. Disadvantages of supra pubic catheters include the risk of cellulitis, leakage, hematoma at the insertion site, and prolapse through the urethra. After they have been inserted, supra pubic catheters should be managed the same as IDCs. The skin area around the catheter insertion site should be washed with soap and water daily and the area kept dry. Avoid the use of powder or creams around the catheter site.
> www.nwmdgp.org.au/pages/after_hours/GPRAC-CIS-09.html

> An indwelling urinary catheter is a tube that drains urine from the bladder into a bag. The tube is placed into the urethra (the part of the body that drains the bladder) and up into the bladder.

> A common type of indwelling catheter is a Foley catheter. A Foley catheter has a balloon attachment at one end. After the Foley catheter is inserted, the balloon is filled with sterile water. The filled balloon prevents the catheter from leaving the bladder.
> www.mdconsult.com/das/patient/body/101471361-2/0/10002/14043.html

I can tell you that I have used an indwelling catheter a couple of times over the years but not for some time now and it was a Foley catheter. I recall it being a bit of a nuisance really, because I transfer a fair bit on and off toilets, on and off lounges, and on and off the bed, and into and out of the car, and the more transfers we do, the more careful we need to be as it increases the likely hood of something going wrong. I recall being bothered because I couldn't just wear what I wanted to wear, as I had to hide it, and I also remember that I was always scared about the tap flicking the other way and litres of my urine gushing out onto the floor – of course this never happened, yet... Apparently now though, I think the tap system for them has been improved, making it more difficult for your worst night mares to come true. Thank God.

> Intermittent catheters are hollow tubes used to drain urine from the bladder. They are inserted at intervals throughout the day, or when you feel the need to go to the toilet. Once the urine has drained out, the catheter is removed." Intermittent catheters can be either non-lubricated plastic, lubricated disposable plastic or non-disposable metal catheters. It has been noted from a number of medical reports that intermittent catheterisation reduces the risk of a Urinary Tract Infection (UTI) – which in itself is one enormous bonus. These infections are not pleasant, but are avoidable and can be reduced by high standards of hygiene.
> www.spinal.co.uk/pdf/bladdermanagement.pdf

Mitrofanoff Appendicovesicostomy

Basically, a canal is created using the appendix so that a catheter can be inserted to empty urine directly from the abdomen, instead of the urethra because there are blockages or such. The Mitrofanoff procedure allows the individual to self-catheterise so that he or she is not dependent on a family member or a medical professional to catheterise him/her. Documents show this procedure is useful for people with either paraplegia or spina bifida.

www.wikidoc.org/index.php/Mitrofanoff_appendicovesicostomy
www.apparelyzed.com/bladder-care.html

Bladder Augmentation

Bladder augmentation, also known as augmentation cystoplasty, is a technique which increases the bladder's storage capacity, lengthening the time periods between catheter use. The procedure involves tissue grafts (anastomosis) from a section of the small intestine (ileum), stomach, or bowel, and the grafts are attached to the urinary bladder by sewing or stapling to create a pouch or wider wall for the bladder in order to enhance its reservoir capacity.

www.apparelyzed.com/bladder-care.html

Yes, in the beginning intermittent catheterisation is tricky and as frustrating as trying to fit a sultana through the eye of a needle, however, if you persist and stick with it, you will re-gain your freedom, independence and self-dignity. So, for me it was worth it, yet it is your life, your choice! Oh, a tip - I choose one of the smallest type of catheter, (FG10), firstly, so that I cause the least amount of damage inside me and secondly, to ease the insertion process as much as possible. Now, I don't know if this tiny hole that we insert the catheter into will stretch with age, but in the last eleven years, I have not found any change regarding this area and I have not found any evidence to support this fear either

Sidetrack

I don't know if they do this anymore in rehabilitation, yet, in the beginning we had to learn how to catheterise on the bed first, before progressing to an actual toilet. That was an interesting moment, let me tell you! My nurse gave me a catheter, gloves, gel, a mirror and a bottle and said, 'knock yourself out'. Actually, she was lovely but there was little she could say – it was all down to 'practice makes perfect'.

However, I think this is a good way to start for two reasons: (1) If I can't find a toilet anywhere, I know that I can do it into a bottle in the car, and (2) By using a mirror you can get a mental picture of where things are down there, so that when it comes to progressing to the toilet it won't be as difficult. All I can say is, practice does actually make the difference between getting it right and not.

Ok, so now I am going to talk you through step-by-step what I do, so you have at least one woman's take on it. I am not a nurse, I am just telling you what works for me. It is up to you to discover what works for you.

<u>Toileting process</u> -

1. Clean the toilet seat with hand wipes (this minimizes risk of infection).

2. Unzip trousers or skirt.

3. Wash and dry hands thoroughly.

4. I use the palms of my hands to move my chair from the basin to the toilet.

5. Transfer from your chair to the toilet.

6. Pull down skirt (if you have one on – you can do this rocking from side to side and simultaneously pulling down the skirt by the waistband).

7. Un-wrap the Catheter at the end of the funnel. Take hold of the funnel and place the funnel between your teeth and the packet on the seat of your chair.

8. Get out your KY Gel and immerse the catheter tip in it. (Holding only the funnel).

9. You can slide your panties to one side without having to take them off if they are not too tight.

10. Place one finger at the top of the clitoris.

11. Hold the catheter in the other hand, and guide it to the urethra opening just beneath the tip of your finger. If you get the catheter in the wrong section, no urine will be expressed.

12. Ensuring that your bladder is completely empty will reduce the risk of developing problems later in life, eg: kidney stones.

Please take a look at the anatomy of the bladder.

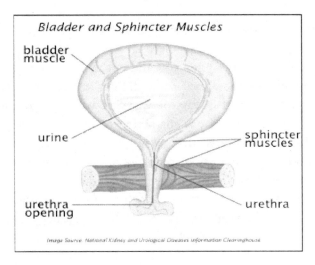

www.womenshealthzone.net/bladder/urinary-incontinence/anatomy-physiology

<u>Websites that provide healthcare products within Australia:</u>

NSW:www.paraquad.org.au/CommunityServices/
ParaQuadSpecialistHealthcareProducts.aspx

Victoria: www.independencesolutions.com.au

WA: www.sunmedical.com.au/default.asp?ID=02&catID=1954&paget
ype=productlist

SA: www.pqasa.asn.au/index.php

TAS: www.paraquadtas.org.au

QLD: www.spinal.com.au/index.php?option=com_content&view=fron
tpage&Itemid=1

QLD: www.intouchdirect.com.au

bit four – Bowel management

Now, for the really riveting portion of this chapter!!!

As most people, prior to my injury, I did not monitor or make note of any of my bodily functions as it really did not concern me. The most I knew about this aspect of my life was that whatever goes in, must come out. Now I was not one for taking note of what happened in the toilet, I only really cared that something did happen, like a lot of people, I think. I did not care if it floated or sank, what colour it was, the shape, or even how many times it happened a day for that matter. I can proudly say that I put more thought and consideration into the pair of shoes I would wear to work rather than what happened when I went for a number two! (Heehee).

Doing a number two is merely a bodily function, it is not something that I look forward to, it is not something that I plan for, it is not something that excites me, and it is not something that makes me feel proud or special – well, perhaps when it is over with, right? But, doing a bowel movement is not something that changes our lives, it just happens, like breathing.

Now that that is out of the way, I want to tell you what this sub-section (pertaining to our bowels) will include and will not include. Firstly, I will remind you that I am not a nurse or a medical professional of any sort, so I will not be going into detail about what you "should" do or "should not" do, or use for that matter. I will chat to you about our bodies and some of the possible changes that we might experience concerning our bowels (post injury), however, I will not be going into detail about my own personal routine. After all, I don't want to get into any strife here (Heehee). I will be talking about the fact that "accidents" will happen, but I will not be advising you on what you what to do (medically) to stop them. I will give you some tips that I have found to be true for myself over the years, and of course, I will be assuring you that we (you, me and every other woman in a chair) are beautiful, regardless of the side-effects of having a spinal injury.

So, let's get into it then......

If you do have a spinal injury let me say this straight up, because there is no kind way of saying it - *our bodies will never be the same*, this is just a fact as when there is damage to the spinal cord, things change. You might be one of the lucky ones that has a damage way down low and still have a lot of functions – of you I am totally jealous! (But only in a good way, of course). Or you might be like me, stuck somewhere in the middle - which is not utterly horrible or limiting. And then, you could be someone who has an injury at the top end of the scale, which means that you have people who will deal with all of the shit in your life – literally. Heehee and I don't see that as a completely horrible thing really! In all seriousness, I have utter respect for you and your circumstances, but I guess, I always try to see the positives in any situation.

Now, we don't know if in ten years or two years there will be a medical breakthrough or not, yet if there is something, anything that you can do that might improve your functions and situation in general I encourage you to grab hold of it. Yet, right now this is what we have to work with, so let's get on with it....

According to most articles, programs and websites (pertaining to spinal cord injury) our bowel capabilities will alter depending on where the damage was caused to our spinal cord, as is the case with the bladder. Remember how I explained a few pages ago about the bladder and it being either a Reflex (T12 or above) or a Flaccid bladder (T12 or below), well it is not dissimilar to the bowels. I want to point out that the same levels for bladder management also apply to bowel management too. But, the people with a Reflexic bowel cannot feel when it is full and have zero control over when and where the anal sphincter muscle opens and functions. While those with a Flaccid bowel may be able to feel if their rectum is full in some way, they may not have the defecation capability because of the relaxing of the anal sphincter muscle, meaning more attempts may be required before complete emptying of the bowel is achieved for people with a Flaccid bowel.

Whichever side of the coin you are on, a bowel management program is something that will encourage routine to your digestive system, produce successful results in the bathroom, and thereby minimise potential "accidents", which means, as a direct result, you and I can be more confident and less stressed as we move through our day-to-day activities and interactions.

Yet, lurking in the background, there is always a possibility that things will not go according to how they should. I call those times 'accidents' because as hard as we try, accidents will happen. The fact is that accidents can happen in our chair, the sofa, our car (or worse, our friend's car) and yes, even our bed. They may happen on the way to work, on a date, on holidays and God forbid, even in the middle of love-making. But I want to give you some really good news - *it is not the end of the world, just because you have had an 'accident'!*

For some people, it may very well and truly feel like the world is crumbling down on them or that they are useless, disgusting, and embarrassing. And it may well feel like that the time it happens, and the next time and the next, but I will encourage you that all of these things are not true! Yet, only you can change the way you see, feel and think about these moments.

Believe it or not, you are still the same person. Yes, you now have a second part to your life that is new and has some not-so-wonderful aspects to it, but hear me loud and clear when I say to you that *'You are bigger than this!'*

You are more than just the colour of your hair or the shape of your face. You are more than the clothes that you wear. You are not the job that you do. You are not the total of what others can see, and You are not your disability!!

Yes 'accidents' are humiliating and embarrassing. Yes, you will probably feel like a child when this happens, and no, we probably won't have 100% control in this area anymore, but this is not the end of your life, and it does not change the intelligent, fun, sexy and caring woman you are! (Yes, I'm talking to all of you women!)

If necessary, I will ask you to write this down, stick it on your wall, say it out loud when you are looking in the mirror, but please, don't just give up on life because you might have an accident or two. Sometimes there are things we can learn about our bodies from what happens, sometimes there is no rhyme or reason, and sometimes shit just happens, literally. Pardon the language, yet it does not have to change or rule us.

> *If life throws things at you – catch them, polish them*
> *and see if there are any gems!*

Take the lemons, squeeze as much out of them as possible (learnings, information and knowledge that is) and turn it into something interesting and tasty!

Events or experiences are not good or bad, they just are. Being human though, means that we will often attach meaning to these incidents which makes them seem either good or bad to us. What I want to offer is that we can also see them as opportunities to learn and grow from. Sometimes the growth is uncomfortable, other times it is painful, or simply horrible and unfair, however, on the flip side of the coin – if we never had any experiences or events in life that didn't stretch us or require us to look outside our own world, gain new skills/tools, then we would probably be stagnant, ignorant and uninteresting adults who never move on from their child-like life.

As soon as you can (after you've had an accident) it would be beneficial if you could stop and try to discover why you had this accident? Was it something you drank, ate, some activity you did, note the time of day/night, when was the last time you emptied your bowels, consider every aspect of it, and write it up in a journal specifically for bowel management. If you do this every time, you may start to see some patterns forming and you might get some insight into how your particular body operates. Then, when all is back to normal, you need to lift your head up and sit tall because nobody else will know what you have to deal with, but, you are dealing with and managing something that most people could not cope with!

I don't know if many of you have been to university or not but I am just using this as an anecdote. When a person goes to university, rarely do they go straight into the job they trained for with full pay, because they don't have the experience to do that as yet. University does not offer life experience, that is usually gained post graduation, and then they will have both the knowledge and experience to get the sort of wage they were aiming for. What I am trying to get at here, is that when we are in rehabilitation the nursing staff give us a lot of training and knowledge, and then we go out into the world and apply that to our lives, but sometimes it is not enough – sometimes it is not until we have the life experience to add to the formal training that we begin to know what we are really doing. Allow me to explain.

During rehabilitation, the nurses encouraged us inpatients to perform our bowel management routines in the am part of the day and it was usually done every second day. After leaving hospital though, I found that for me it was more effective to do this on a day-to-day basis as it decreased the chance of accidents for me. This was not something that I was told or advised, I just worked it out. And, that is often how it goes in life, that is, we get the knowledge and information and then have to work out how best to apply it to us, our lives, our bodies. In life, rarely do things "go by the book".

In my experience nursing staff can only do so much when it comes to the topic of bowel management, because each person, injury and body are so very different to the next, that standard treatments only go so far. I was reassured when this exact claim was stated in a patient-care manual for people with spinal injuries that I found on the internet (from the USA). No two people with the exact spinal injuries are the same, and no two bowel management programs can therefore be exactly the same either. Take me, I have 13 yrs of personal experience of conducting my own bowel therapy management, yet there is no way I would feel I have the knowledge or experience necessary to tell another person with a disability how to manage their bowels – there are just too many indefinites.

The best advice I will give to you is to always check resources every couple of years or so just to make sure that what you are still doing is still current, to make certain we are not missing out on some new methods or products that have been released since. And, make sure that you are in contact with a community nurse through your local disability service providers, because, they are required to keep up to date on research, techniques and products. Yet, one of the best pieces of advice that I was given and would like to share with you is - 'only change one thing at a time'.

Making more than one change at a time will mean that the impact of that change will be lost to you, and that we don't want. Only when we can clearly comprehend and observe the outcome of a change, can we discern if the change should be permanent or disregarded. Let me give you an example; let's consider changing your bowel routine from am to pm. Now, let's also change our diet at the same time because we want to eat healthier – so from now on we're going to juice some fruit and vegetables for breakfast and stick to salad for dinner, so that our biggest meal of the day will be at lunch. Now, let's also start exercising four times a week, it doesn't matter what type, eg: a gym work out. In this one example, we have changed three things so there could be three reasons why we would have a bowel accident when normally we wouldn't, and we would not have the slightest idea what was the cause.

FLASHBACK

Seeing that we are talking about the times we perform our bowel routine, I will share with you my story. Now, pre-accident I was definitely not what is known as a morning person, I just adored sleeping-in regardless what day of the week it was. And now that I have said that, it will probably come as no surprise that one day I had the brilliant idea of changing my morning bowel routine to the evening - brilliant in theory, not-so-brilliant in reality. When you consider making a change like this, you need to allow a certain amount of transition time for the body, for accidents, for the dust to settle so to speak. Another handy hint is to record, record and record, as this will give you a means to see any patterns or recurrent problems.

Personally, I would allow a month for the body to settle before making any sort of judgement. But for me, doing this routine at night time proved inconvenient and interfering as I had to plan my outings around being home by a certain time and could no longer go to bed early. So, I just went back to my previous habit of a morning routine.

Every individual is different, and while I have reluctantly altered my lifestyle, you may not be so easily swayed. Think about the pros and think about the cons to both options of what it is you are choosing between, consider how it will positively and negatively impact your life and your lifestyle, consult people who are professionals in the topic, talk to others in chairs, yet ultimately, it is never a life or death situation, and I guess the worst case scenario is that you change it back – no big deal really, is it?

These are a few tips that I have picked-up along the way – take what you like, leave what you do not, and work it out for yourself:

- The sorts of items that are a good idea to store near your bed and in your car are garbage bags, towels, latex gloves, hand wipes, gel and some smelly stuff for the air.

- You will have been given a contact number in order to obtain the necessary supplies for bowel and bladder management. I would also source a local chemist that can order some of your products, in the event that something goes wrong or is not available.

- You will probably need to wash and dry the upholstery on your chair some day, yet I warn you to beware of dryers; I have found that they can sometimes melt the glue that holds the upholstery together. So, perhaps a spare piece of upholstery for your chair is a good idea.

- Some people like to include prune juice in their diet to aid the digestive process. Others recommend pear juice as it is high in fibre, and I have also found that a hot lemon drink beforehand awakens the whole system.

- In my experience, not everything is usually excreted in the 'accident', so I get on to the toilet to finish the job so that there are no more surprises later on in the day/night.

- In some instances I have found that if I am holding off going to the bathroom for too long (and my bladder is full) I wind up having a No.2 accident as well as a No.1 accident – As I am not a nurse I cannot say how or why this happens, perhaps the bladder presses onto the bowel? What I do know is that this does happen.

- Be sure to empty your bladder before getting intimate with your partner.

- In my experience, a high intake of food with a lot of water content (such as soups, fruit), may make it necessary to empty the bladder more frequently, in order to avoid accidents.

- Over the years I have discovered (for me) that a high consumption of peanut butter or chocolate may lead to an accident. I don't know why, it just does.

- Try not to have sex prior to your bowel routine, it has been known to expedite the matter, quite literally.

- Keeping strictly to your routine will ensure things don't go haywire in the middle of the day. Be religious about taking your medication (to help you go to the toilet) at the correct time, and make certain you get on to the toilet at the correct time (12 hours later).

- If you have not had a good result from your bowel routine, beware, it may be a sign of things to come later in the day. I have no problem staying a little longer in the bathroom in order to prevent accidents happening later on in the day.

- If you keep a daily journal you can watch and learn how your body responds to fluids and foods (quantities and types) and watch your energy levels. It was also a good space for me to release some of the pent up feelings that might be rattling around in there.

- If you are travelling overseas, stick to your times (in Australia) or else change them at least 1-2 months in advance to make sure that your body clock has really got the new routine down pat, so to speak. Be aware that you might experience an accident or two during the transitional time.

- Watch what time you finish drinking of a night time, you may need to get up during the night in order to avoid having an accident in your bed.

- In your car, it might be handy to have the type of seat covers that you can wash in your own washing machine. It would not hurt to have some of those waterproof sheets between your seat cover and the chair too, just in case.

- Sard Wonder Soap really is wonderful at removing stains and odours. It is efficient and economical, we just need to add a little elbow grease. And apparently, popping some white vinegar into the washing machine is an age old method of sterilising, thanks Mum No.2.

- Mattress protectors are not always waterproof. When choosing a waterproof mattress protector, there are two types (a) one that makes a plastic sheet sound when you move and make you feel like you're still in a hospital and (b) the one that doesn't. (b) Is easily recognised by the cotton cover it has.

- I personally have noticed that flatulence (a fart) will usually precede a bowel accident, however the scent seems to have more substance to it, for example: it would be more of an Eau de Parfum than an Eau de toilet – if you know what I mean (Wink, wink)?

- When you are heading into the bathroom after you discover you've had a bowel accident, you will need to get a couple of garbage bags for soiled garments and garbage, a couple of towels for your chair or a spare chair, clean garments, sard wonder soap and scrubbing sponge (to clean cushion and cover), and of course, all your everyday items that would probably be near your toilet ordinarily (such as gloves, gel, suppositories, hand wipes, catheters).

TOOL - MEDICINE

Being *able to laugh*, at life, yourself and anything in general, is by far the best medicine ever prescribed regardless what comes your way – be it extra body weight, short-sightedness, diabetes, blockage of an artery, epilepsy, quadriplegia or the big C (Cancer).

There will never be a time when there are no obstacles, they are a part of life, as much as the sun and the moon. Some challenges may be like freckles, some like mole hills, others might be like a small mountain, while there will be some that are likened to Mount Everest. However, unlike those people who train to physically climb Mount Everest, there is no training for the challenges or obstacles in life, and if there were, it would be different for every one of us because everyone faces, deals, and manages situations uniquely (Yes, I do agree there are standard generalisations that are true though).

Yet, I know that we all have the resources already inside of us to manage whatever it is that comes our way.

You'd be surprised what you can do, when faced with no other options, like I was. Maybe you will need to learn how to laugh again. Did you actually know that there are therapy groups based on laughter? Go and rent the dvd, *Patch Adams,* played by Robin Williams. The movie is actually about a real life doctor, Hunter Doherty, M.D. (born May 28, 1945 in Washington, D.C.), who uses laughter as an important and integrated piece of a holistic treatment of patients.

Pre-accident, I was one of those people who had said, 'just let me die if I end up not able to function'........ But when you come face-to-face with that moment, it is really hard to actually do it. Yes, your world has turned upside down and inside out, and it seems like something that you can't do! It did for me too. Yet, like most tasks/goals, by breaking it down and taking baby steps, it too is surmountable. I am not saying that there won't be days when you are frustrated, emotionally exhausted, or just hate it, but what I am saying, is that your new life can still be fun, full of life, love and all of the fantastic things that this world and its people have to offer.

Now, I don't particularly like this quote, "what doesn't break you, makes you stronger", regardless, I do believe that it has some truth to it. Everyone in the world faces challenges – your neighbour might be trying to get pregnant (for 3 years now) without success, your mother might be diagnosed with diabetes, your sister might all of a sudden become gluten-intolerant, the lady down the road loses her lifetime partner of 46 years, your girlfriend's sister becomes bankrupt, women in Ethiopia face starvation every day of their life, women lose unborn babies every week of the year. There are some things in the world that I don't understand and don't think I would be able to face.

However, I do know that there is no point to ask, 'why me?', because, there is no answer to that question. What I do know is that, everyday that you don't give-up – you win, and you can be proud of the person that you are!

Look at what you have (not what you don't), and everyday appreciate one thing in your life. Truly love yourself, and through this you will create the life that you desire!

Love and respect,
Violet

Chapter nine

Relationships

bit one - Friends (New and Old)

After returning from a visit to the USA, I thought that Sydney might be the most practical spot for me to live, as it had staged the Paralympics in 2000, and was probably more wheelchair-accessible than most cities. So I made the decision to relocate there even though I did not know a solitary soul in the city or anything about it. Actually, I had only been there once before in my life and that was with a high school girlfriend and her family when I was 16 years old.

I know, I know, you can call me brave or stupid, but whatever you think, I did it anyway. My intention was to join the women's wheelchair basketball team, if they would have me, and see what that was like. After playing basketball for a while and getting a job, I made some nice friends in Sydney, but twice a year I would hop in my car and make the 12 hour drive back to the Gold Coast. I liked going back there because it was familiar territory for me as I had previously spent about 10 years there, on and off between travels. There is nothing like visiting familiar territory to be with people that I have known for decades. And sure enough, as the years passed, I began to wonder what I was doing in Sydney anymore, so I packed up my things and left the cascading concrete towers and headed back to the friendly face of the Gold Coast. There are only two things I would miss about Sydney – and they are my second Mum and Dad who lived in the unit right next door to mine - two very special people who have had more than their fair share of hardship, but regardless, continue to have a positive outlook on life and people, Mr and Mrs Latte.

I had two very good reasons why I wanted to move back to the Coast and they were Miss Earl Grey and Mrs Vienna Coffee.

Miss Earl Grey, I met in 1992 at work, we lived together in Japan for a bit, then we were in England together as well. We sort of followed each other around the world a bit. And I am so grateful that Miss Earl Grey was with me in England when my life very literally turned inside-out and upside down. I don't know what it was like for her to go through that with me, I imagine it was painful and life changing for her too, but gees, I am so very thankful that I had her around me.

The second reason was Mrs Vienna Coffee, a woman I had known since I was 3 years and she was 2 years old. Our mothers met on the way to pre-school and became best buddies, and so, Mrs Vienna Coffee and I naturally grew-up like sisters. It is a wonderful feeling to have such a history with someone, because there is nothing that they don't know about you. It is because of these bonds that I was very excited about being more involved in Miss Earl Grey's and Mrs Vienna Coffee's lives again.

Your true friends will really not give two hoots if you need a wheelchair or not, so long as you are the same person post injury that they knew before. And just to prove it, all of my girlfriends (Miss Earl Grey, Miss Double Shot, Mrs Vienna Coffee) that I knew before my accident have all mentioned time and time again that they actually forget the fact that I sit in a wheelchair now. I know that what they say must be true, because often, when we go out somewhere they will do something funny like park in a regular car parking space and I will have to remind them that we need one that fits my wheelchair - which makes us both giggle, however, it proves that perhaps they really just see 'me' and nothing else.

The point I am trying to make is that if my friends (who have known me for decades, pre and post injury) forget that I am in a chair, then it only proves that what is significant for us – may not necessarily be the case for other people. I want to say upfront, the world is made up of a whole mishmash of personalities and you know that.

We have those who love the arts and think the world would die without the various forms of art, and then, there are those who think that everything should be censored so that children are not exposed to potentially harmful music or movies. And we've also got people who think that science should rule the world while there are those people who are opposed to using discarded embryos to help paraplegics walk again. There are those who seem to have a problem with everything, and those that are so laid back that no job would ever be completed. There are those who wear 'blinkers' like horses, because that is how they like to see and think about the world, and then there are those who think that people who use chairs are *useless* and *good for nothing*.

Now, I will be the first to jump up and get in the face of a person who tells me or someone I know (in a wheelchair) that I or they can't do something, because of our disability. And, because I have been in a chair for twelve years now, I know our disability touches every facet of our world and life. What I am trying to say is that our disability doesn't need to be the focus.... all the time, because if it is, I think we can tend to make it far bigger than it needs to be. Sometimes, everything can get a bit foggy and appear distorted, and I guess, I just want to let you know that this can happen – so that you don't bump into as many things as I have.

The greatest griefs are those we cause ourselves ~Sophocles

Let me say up front, that your accident and new situation might catch some people off-guard, because they either didn't know you had been involved in an accident, or perhaps, they just have to get their mind around it. But that's perfectly normal though, because, I think if the situation were reversed we might need a second or two to adjust as well...

But, if some of your friends don't want to spend time with you anymore, then perhaps they weren't that much of a friend anyway. And that is fine, as it is their loss, right? If the girl who lives next door to you has longer legs, is she better than you? I don't think so. The girl who goes to a Catholic school down the road, is she smarter than you? Not necessarily. Is the child who can speak five different languages going to have a better life than you? Maybe, maybe not. Is the woman who has had her breasts removed any less of a woman than a stripper? Hell NO! Different is not good or bad - it is just different.

Nobody can make you feel inferior without your consent
~Eleanor Roosevelt

What you will need to do, regardless if they are old or new friends, is share with them your attitude toward living with a wheelchair, so that they are not left confused and out in the dark. When people have never spent time with people who use chairs, of course, they don't know when to offer help and when to pull back, they have never stopped to think about topics that are a part of our everyday life. But, that is not so ignorant or strange – have you stopped to really consider the challenges for those who have Motor Neuron Disease. No? Hhmm.... Come on, you know we're a minority, just like the Australian natives, and just like people who are gay. And, the only way we can make a difference in our world is to get out there and do tonnes of stuff and talk to tonnes of people.

So, to start with, I would suggest you to talk to your friends about being carried up stairs to a restaurant, share what you think about shops that don't provide access, share your thoughts and feelings about able-bodied people who use disabled parking, or discuss what you do in the shops when you can't reach something. Basically, just open the lines of communication. And, because I have talked with my friends about sharing a drink with them, they only look at restaurants with an accessible 'ladies room' inside or nearby. They know this because we have talked about topics like this, and I've been open about my needs and opinions on things. By talking with my friends, I have left little room for confusion and awkward moments, and that makes for smooth sailing all around. This is my choice, you need to decide and work out what works for you and your friends.

bit two - Need-to-know basis

Every single person, other than myself and my partner, are on a need to know basis. When I say need to know, I am talking about keeping all personal information personal. And just as a side-note, even in the beginning of a relationship my partner is on a need-to-know basis too.

When I say 'need-to-know basis', I am talking about overviews or big picture concepts, not graphical step by step processes about intimate parts of your life. Others do not need to know what happens behind closed doors, how it happens, why it happens, and when it happens.

After all, you have no idea what they do in the bathroom, how, when and what they use, do you? That is because it is personal. Just because you have a disability, doesn't mean that you have no privacy now.

Why? You ask.

Well, it is kind of like watching the 'making of *Mission Impossible*', before watching the actual movie! It might take away all of the enchantment, fascination and thrill of the actual movie, as the 'making of the movie' unearths all of the behind-the-scenes methods, madness and realism... possibly deflating any sense of magic or atmosphere. So, to me it only makes sense that if this is the case for movies, it may well be true in relationships too - especially when it comes to anything concerning personal care. For me, I like to keep my relationship and my personal care management, well and truly separate. This is easy for me though, as I am paraplegic and have an income. I also want to add that my partner agrees with this decision. Some people in chairs think differently and their partner in life also does their personal management (eg: bowels), and that seems to work for them, which is fantastic! Look, I just care. I care about you and I care about your relationships. So, please consider the implications before making any decisions.

bit three - Friendship is about Valuing

It is inconsequential whether you are in a chair or not, we all have things in life that challenge us, frustrate and annoy us, people and events that we like or don't like, things that we prefer and things that we dislike completely, and each and everyone has that right – that's what makes us individuals.

When your friends call to cry on your shoulder, or moan about something that is causing them pain (physical or emotional), let them, because that is the basis of a friendship. And we both know that a friendship must involve both give and take. It needs to provide empathy and support and it needs to lay on a non-judgemental foundation, if it is to survive and flourish.

We all want to be validated, we all need to be heard, and by just being there for our friends – we are showing them love! What our friends experience is just as real as our experiences, is just as painful, and is just as important as ours!

Side track

More times than I care to remember, strangers have said 'hi', and then proceeded to tell me about how they have spent three, six or nine months in a wheelchair too. Ring any bells? Now, at that point, part of me wants to say something like 'yes, but your spinal cord was not severed and you could still feel your entire body!' And, if I am completely honest, a few expletives come to mind as well. But then, I tell myself to take a deep breath, shut your mouth and think about why these people are telling you about their story... That's when I realise that it is not about the story they are telling me – it is about letting me know that they have had a glimpse of what it is like to be 'in one of those things'.

These people are trying to connect with me, trying to let me know that I'm not alone and that they know that it is.... s!#t!

Let's look at a different sort of story that removes our disability from the equation, like a broken leg. Pre-accident, I had never broken a bone, and maybe you haven't either, however let's pretend we have for this purpose. And we are out doing our shopping when we see a person on crutches with one leg in a cast, and they are struggling with a door. Now, being the nice people we are, we decide to go over and get the door for them. At that point, we might mention that we once had our leg in a cast as well, and there it is! I am certain that when we say that to the person in the cast, our intention was not to be be-littling, rude or hurtful in any way..... And that is exactly how we need to take it from the general public, because it only comes from a good place and nothing else.

Okay, so let's get back to the point.

Let's face it, unfortunately us humans can't help but compare and contrast. We compare how smart we are to our friends, how well we do our job compared to work colleagues, we compare how pretty we are to the waitress, how clean our house is to another's, we compare our cooking to our mothers and so on. We all do it. I get that comparing helps us to learn and comprehend how things work, however as an adult, I think it does more harm than good. For isn't comparing a big contributor to anorexia, others max out their credit card because they are comparing their assets to others. Magazines invite women to compare themselves to celebrities, and television adverts ask men to compare their sexual performance with other men, so they can sell them a pill. It is entrenched in our work today, and nothing is thought of it. I want to ask you what about when we compare our friend's experiences to ours, how does that impact on our relationship?

Everybody in the world has a story – some are not nice, some are horrible, and then there are some stories that I can't even fathom – like children being treated as animals. There's always someone who has gone through something worse than you or I. But, just because another person's story or experience is not similar to ours does not mean that it is not worthy or of value. At that point in their life, that was the worst thing that has happened to them, and it was obviously pretty painful for them because it stuck in their memory. Yes, you or I could rate the stories and claim that 'what happened to me was way more terrible than what happened to them'. However, it is all inconsequential really.... as each individual's experience, or story, will always be more painful, challenging, or scarring because it is theirs! Do you get what I am trying to say here? Regardless of what happened, or the outcome, another person's experience was horrible for them, it was something that affected and probably changed their life – which makes it very real!

This one point took up a bit of my time when I reconnected with an old friend who had had some challenges in life over the past years, as she saw her struggles were in the same vicinity as mine. Now, being honest, I had to chew it all over for a while before I could realise that life is not about who has the worst experience or the most amount of pain or the greatest loss. Human beings, all of us, are made up differently, we come from different backgrounds, we view things differently, hear things differently, and feel things differently. One person's definition of 'pain' can be worlds apart from another person's definition of 'pain' – but that does not make it any less real or hurtful!

I asked myself two questions, 'What gives me the right to compare what she goes through to what I go through'? 'Who made me judge and jury of her pain, her life?' Then, it was very plain to me.

So, I am grateful for this event, as I gained and grew to learn that 'life is about recognising, acknowledging and valuing another person's life experiences, no matter how big or small'.

So, I give my friends a sincere ear when they want to b!#ch and moan about something, yet most importantly, I let my friends know that their experiences are just as important as mine. I truly believe in *doing unto others, as I would have them do unto me*. Dale Carnegie, an American famous for lecturing on the topics of public speaking, self-improvement and interpersonal skills, says that every single person on this planet only wants one thing in life, which is 'to feel important'. He goes on to explain in depth in his book, *How to Win Friends and Influence People*, that, if you can help make a person feel important – you will never be short of friends.

You may actually find though, that some of your friends, the ones that have a good idea of what you deal with, might actually avoid talking to you about their problems altogether. This has happened to me twice, with two different friends, but I sorted it out quick smart when I understood what was going on. When I confronted them about it, they explained they didn't have the right to moan about their menial troubles. Now, while this is very sweet of them, it creates a one-sided relationship, and ultimately a break down in the relationship. So, I chatted to my friends and told them that because they were not sharing their woes, they were in fact cutting me out of their life. I asked, 'Don't you think I feel better when you tell me that you have worries too?' And my friend realised what I was trying to tell her and agreed, adding, 'Well, I guess it takes your mind off your concerns for a bit.' And we both giggled.

I have also found that when I make fun of being in a chair or something silly that happens with the whole disabled thing, it shows others that (a) I have a sense of humour and am still human, (b) can still laugh at life, and (c) it lightens the atmosphere - which then makes them feel relaxed and more comfortable about the whole chair thing – which comes full circle and helps me too (Smiles).

Talking about this reminds me when my girlfriend and I were out one day shopping and she said to me that her feet were killing her, and she asked if we could sit down for a cup of coffee for a while. I smiled and looked at her and said, 'Can I have them?' She asked, 'Have what?' I replied, 'Your feet of course. I said, if you don't want them, I'll have them?' And we both laughed ourselves silly. I want to make it clear here that it was my intention only to have a laugh with her, not to make her feel bad for saying something like that in front of me. I don't want to make others watch what they say around me and feel like they are always walking on egg-shells..... (Heehee, another funny one). Gees, if I was actually serious about watching what my friends said in front of me, well I don't know how many people would want to be around me.

People say things all the time without thinking it through – I know, because I do too. And, because we are mere humans, I am aware that it will continue to happen until the end of time. The point is not what is said or done, but how we react or respond.

Side track

We can choose how we react to or respond to a person's comments or behaviour – it is not something that is involuntary. And, more often than not, a few well chosen words can result in more of a positive outcome than a loud, irrational and emotional outburst. However, that is just my experience, perhaps it is different for you. Actually, while we're on the topic of things that will happen out there in the big, wide world – I will tell you that the only point I enforce these days is how we are perceived and referred to. I have to tell you that I have had some doozies, generally, I have just been called the 'wheelchair'. It is at that point that I excuse myself and correct them, and explain how firstly, I am a person, and secondly, yes, I use a wheelchair. The chair is not me/ us and I/we are not the chair – it is merely a replacement for a part that no longer functions as it used to.

But, back to the point.

It took me a while to understand that there is more than one way to see a situation, I guess because I was so stuck in *my view* of the world. In the beginning, when my life first changed, I would see mothers pulling their children close whenever I was walking by, and because I was so stuck in my negative perspective I could not see another way to look at it. Can you imagine, I seriously thought these mothers were pulling their children to their side because they were so scared that I would run over their children. It wasn't until a couple of years later that I could see a different perspective - that mothers were just trying to keep their children out of my way. Silly isn't it, how many different angles there are to one situation. But, the lesson I learnt from that was - I was so focused on my disability being a problem to others that I could not see any other perspectives. In the beginning it is easy to see why this happens.

When we personalise too many things, life all of a sudden becomes a lot of hard work, and life has enough challenges without us piling more on top. So, why not just try to laugh things off. I mean, that good old phrase, *Laughter is the best medicine,* must have some truth behind it, right? Otherwise, why would comedians actually get paid to make people laugh?

I heard someone once say that, 'life is actually very simple, yet so many people complicate the heck out of it!' And, I have to say that I could not agree more with this perception, because I know that there have been times when I have done this. What I am talking about is thinking we 'should' do this, or we 'should' be that. It is not being able to say 'no', yet regretting the ten million things we have to do before we go to bed. It is about wanting everyone else to live by our expectations, and the mountain that we create when they don't. It is not being able to walk in another person's shoes, and it is all the insignificant mole hills that could become mountains, if we let them. Bottom line - it is our choice.

I have also heard someone say that, 'Life is as simple as a smile'. Now, this was something that I not only knew, but it was something that I had actually proven to be true myself! Funnily enough, I only became aware of the power of my smile after I had my accident. Beforehand, I was completely oblivious and it was just another thing I took for granted.

Yet, now... I am a believer!

I believe that a smile has so much power that it can even make an entire wheelchair vanish into thin air. Yes girlfriend, I said vanish! And I mean it. A smile can make your wheelchair seem utterly invisible, so that the only thing people see when they look at you, is your smile! But, let's consider what a smile can do - a smile can break the ice, a smile can grab a person's attention, a smile can change your mood, it lets others know you come in peace, it can strengthen your own confidence, it can show approval, it can brighten everybody else's day, and I believe, a smile can even stop an argument. But don't take my word, pick a day to test it and go out and see what happens! Go on, I dare ya (Big cheesy smile).

Side track

My dear friend, Mrs Iced Coffee, just absolutely adores roses. She always has. I think she inherited that love from her mother. Her Mom grew them behind the white picket fence in her front garden, and now Mrs Iced Coffee grows them in the front garden of her house too. I used to go to Mrs Iced Coffee's house to pick her up on the way to school, and since childhood I have always thought that roses were both romantic and exquisite. They are the Queen of the flora world, and rightly so, for no other flower is so highly revered, prized or purchased in such quantities, as the rose. Roses are given in moments of love and lust, hurt and happiness, respect and regret, peace-making and passing. But all of us know that with their beauty, comes the thorns. And that is life - life has happiness and hate, love and pain, exhilaration and despair! Without the pain, the heartache and despair, we might not appreciate the utter beauty that could come from all of those other moments. And, we might just let them pass us by without truly appreciating them for what they really are!

Now, we all know that having friendships or being a part of a relationship means that we own 50 per cent of the enjoyment, 50 per cent of the growth, 50 per cent of the involvement, 50 per cent of the communication and everything else that makes up a healthy bond. So, we know that we play a big part in how successful or unsuccessful a relationship is, now let's consider how we play our part. There are probably many ways that people participate in relationships, however right now I would like to consider just two of them – reactive and pro-active.

Most of us have responded or reacted to events and people in a certain way our entire life, and those responses become habits – just like smoking is part habit and part addiction. Changing a habit is not impossible, however changing lifelong habits are not going to happen overnight (Grins). That makes sense, right.

Life will present loads of opportunities (every single week) that could boil your blood, my question is – what do you do then?

Do you moan about it till you get sick of talking about it, do you let it all out at whomever is in front of you at the time, or do you push your feelings and emotions down so that no-one could ever tell how hurt or frustrated you really are, because that would be inappropriate. Hey, life is full of moments that could annoy, frustrate, bother or anger you, every week if you let them. In these instances, you have the choice to moan about them, or let it go.

Reacting to people or experiences is as natural as a knee-jerk response. We know that when someone hits our knee with a ruler, our leg just kicks up without a thought or feeling at all. Our knee does not stop to ponder what to do now, it does not take into consideration what hit it, there is no free will or choice because our knee does not have the capability. The knee has no brain itself, it does not have the power to deliberate or analyse, it cannot reason or rationalise, it merely reacts, involuntarily.

While actually being in charge of our emotions and choosing our behaviour takes time, patience and perseverance – it is a whole lot more deliberate and demanding. And, let me say right now that talking about it is 1 million times easier than actually doing it! Why? Let's think about it.

Being fully present is about being witness to our emotions, and deliberately choosing how we want to respond to circumstances and people. In my experience, stopping to listen to my brain, my emotions, or just stopping my mouth (more importantly) in the middle of a given situation is neither easy, nor natural. Being in control of my emotions and state of mind are two of the most challenging goals.... because, it means that I need to be constantly in the moment and that requires effort and energy. And this is not something that can be mastered in a few hours, days or even weeks, however, that does not mean that it is an impossible task and that we should give up before we even try.

Mastering our state of mind and our emotions would mean endless benefits in all aspects of every single sort of relationship we have in this life. Could you imagine a world where the majority of people lived like this? I can (Big smile).

Stop being an emotional reaction to things, be a human being
~ Author unknown

bit four – Acquaintances from a previous life....

When I was considering relocating back to the Gold Coast I realised there would be a good chance that I would inevitably run into people that I knew from Part 1 of my life. And yes, that was a scary thought, because part of me feared being seen like this.... in a wheelchair (Allow me remind you that at this point, I had only been out of hospital one year and two months). And I will admit that I looked for faces that I recognised when I walked into shops, restaurants or supermarkets. Then slowly, it started to happen, here and there. The first few times I was able to make a get-away and let out a huge sigh of relief. It was difficult to pin-point what I feared the most, because there were a few different thoughts running around inside my mind at that time. So let me dig deep for a bit here and see what we come up with hey?

Ok, firstly, I think there is the fear of being judged for whatever reason – whether it is comparing what we are now to what we were before, comparing what we look like now to what we looked like before, or perhaps being judged just for being disabled now.

Side track

In the beginning, part of me had a very clear sense of who I was, yet part of me fell into the trap of identifying with my chair – basically, thinking that is all I was now. And, while society may not judge us in our chair, I know that I did, and maybe you do too.... it is only natural. But I want to ask you to stop asking that horrible question 'why me?' It gives no hope, no encouragement and nothing positive. Rather, I encourage you to ask, 'what can I still do?', 'what can I get out of this?' or 'how can this help me?'

Secondly, there are the feelings of failure because, well, let's face it - no one considers being in a wheelchair a sign of success do they? I know that at some point you might feel like you have less of a life and might be less of a person compared to everyone else - It is an easy trap to fall into, yet the truth is actually the complete opposite! We (us people in chairs) are more of a person for deciding to go through what we did, surviving it and doing what we do on a day-to-day basis. That is what winners do - they just get on with it!

Thirdly, there is the pity party, which will pretty much get anyone's back up when it is dished up, 'poor girl, look at her now', 'her life must be so horrible'.

These were the top three reasons for not wanting to cross paths with people that I had known prior to my accident. And now, outlining these fears, I can understand why I felt that way, however, that is just one way to look at it. Another approach is, 'so what, they can like it or lump it'. The old, ever faithful love yourself regardless, and tough titties to anyone that doesn't! (No offence intended). I've been to hell and back and I am still here sort of attitude – which is one of my personal favourites. It is your choice how you view the world, why don't you try a couple of different ones and see what works best for you? :-)

I best get back to the story though........

Suddenly, as if something was testing me, I started bumping into people at places I had been a hundred times before. But what shocked me was that while I was nervous talking to these acquaintances, perhaps this was an opportunity for them too.

FLASHBACK

In 1989 I graduated High School and started my first serious job with a decent pay cheque. Now, within this organisation was a husband and wife team who had decided to move from rainy England, and even though they worked in separate departments, it was easy to see that these two were a top duo.

Anyways, in between leaving that company in 1994, I had travelled the world, had various work opportunities, and started a whole new phase of my life before I ran into them again, in about 2007. So they only knew me as the shy, naive and inexperienced 20 year old that

I was at that time of my life. And as usual, they were curious about 'what had happened and why I was now in a wheelchair', so I satisfied their curiosity and gave them a brief overview, updating them on what I had been doing with myself since.

I don't believe I would be exaggerating when I say that I think they were very surprised for a number of reasons - at what they were looking at in front of them, by how well I looked (in my new situation), by the type of woman that I had blossomed into, and perhaps, how well I was doing for myself. Seeing them again was great for me too, because in their eyes I saw the person that I had grown from, and into. I will say that I don't believe that I saw or heard any of the things I had feared. Talking with them also reinforced how happy I was with the person I had become, and my attitude to life – that I don't let a little thing like a wheelchair dictate my life (Cheesy grin).

Now, it is important that you understand that all of those fears I have previously outlined, existed primarily in my mind. While I have heard a couple of people say some things like that, I refuse to believe that the general population thinks like that! But, regardless, I was pretending that I knew what everyone thought about people in wheelchairs, and that is both flawed and dangerous.

It is wrong because (join in with me here) *to assume makes an ass out of you and me*, and I am not God! I am not omni-present or omni-powerful and therefore, cannot mind-reads nor should I imagine what goes on inside a person's mind, let alone a group of people, like society in general. And making assumptions is dangerous because no-one wants to be told what they're thinking and it might cause a whole stack of trouble and arguments.

Permit me to demonstrate what assuming can do, for eg: let's say that Harry has always thought that only bums lie in the gutter. Naturally, when he arrives at the bus stop and there is a man lying in the gutter, Harry just assumes he is a bum. Now imagine Harry arrives at the bus stop 3 minutes earlier to see this man fall off his seat (at the bus stop) and roll into the gutter because he is suffering a heart attack. Does Harry know all of the details? No. Was he making an assumption based on what he believed to be the truth? Yes, Harry was. Would Harry feel horrible if he knew what actually happened? Undoubtedly, yes.

If you only remember these two points from the whole book, I will be over the moon, (1) the general population **needs to be educated about people who use wheelchairs** and (2) **we are the educators.**

When you look in the mirror to see yourself – whether you have survived a huge change to your life, or you were born with your challenges, please hold your head high and be proud of the type of person you are –

> You are not a quitter – You are a survivor,
> You don't let anything stop you,
> You live outside the square (instead of in it),
> Every day You are making this world a better place,
> And that makes You a Winner in my book!

bit five - 'Them and Us'

I know that when I go out into the world and go through my day-to-day activities, the man-made world I live in is not as inclusive as it could be and other times 'inclusiveness' just doesn't exist at all. But, love it or hate it, perfect or not, this is the world that I live in at this moment, right now, today.

I can't help but agree with Mahatma Gandhi, when he says:
Be the change you want to see in the World!

Maybe when you look in the mirror there are very obvious differences between you and the person who lives next to you. Maybe your disability is very easy for others to see, or perhaps, you wish your disability was more visual so that people wouldn't give you dirty looks. I know that I have to stop myself when I see someone parked in a 'disabled parking space' that appears healthy, because I think, 'so what's your disability, intellectual???' And, I know that is wrong, because I'm jumping to assumptions and judging a book by its cover.... bad, bad, bad girl! I of all people should know better, allow me to explain!

When other people see my good friend, Mrs Turkish Coffee, I am certain that what they see is a woman in her late 30s, with five beautiful children and a good husband. None of her health challenges or their consequences are evident when you see Mrs Turkish Coffee walking around Woolworths doing her grocery shopping, because on the outside she looks like most people - healthy.

There are no visual indications of her chronic epilepsy, her asthma or even her food intolerances and, it is not until you became friends with her, that you would find out that her husband has had a motorbike accident and numerous forearm reconstructions. Since Mrs Turkish Coffee was nine years old, the family have been working with and around her epilepsy so that she has a life almost like the person next door. Unless you have had something to do with epilepsy, you won't know that people with this disability could be at risk just by using the iron, cooking dinner or giving their children a bath. Should Mrs Turkish Coffee experience a seizure when she is cooking, then apart from hitting furniture around her as she falls, she could also be hurt by the utensils she is using at that time, making it very dangerous for Mrs Turkish Coffee to perform these functions, even though she does anyway. The most horrible aspects about epilepsy are the lack of warning signs before a seizure and the consequences of the out-dated medication that is the only source of relief for people with epilepsy.

So, I want to take a moment to talk about joining 'clubs' for a couple of seconds, because like it or not, we are all members now, of the 'persons with a disability' club. I have not done a census, however I think, I can safely say that at least 90 per cent of us would prefer not to be a member of this club. None of us have had the chance to object, to state our case or even say 'no, I don't want to join this club'. There usually isn't a choice, just like we don't have a choice about the colour of our hair, eyes or skin – it just is.

Now, I understand that when any other person decides to join a tennis club, chess club or line-dancing group, it is an intentional choice because they love the tennis or chess and get a kick out of it. Secondly, when someone plays tennis or chess, it is just one piece of the pie – one aspect of who they are. Tennis does not change how people look at them, it does not change how others think about them, or impact their day-to-day lives. Unless of course, they are a member of a sci-fi group and have sci-fi parties at which they proceed to dress-up as a character like Chewbacca (Heehee). I'm just kidding (Just thought it was time for a bit of comic relief).

I know that when I was training in ballroom dancing and competing with my partner as a teen, I copped some flack, yet was mostly left alone. However when you have an interest like ballroom dancing, tennis, even scrapbooking, you can walk away from classes/competitions and return to your job and your colleagues would be none the wiser, unless you are practicing routines on your lunch breaks (Heehee).

However, when it comes to joining the club of people with a disability, it is a whole new ball game. It probably has something to do with the fact that people with a disability don't have a choice, probably wouldn't want to join the group if they did have a choice, don't enjoy being a part of this group, and are often defined by their disability. I know that I have and maybe you have too, to some degree.

Now that I have said these points out loud, for me, it is the last point that causes the most angst – 'we are often defined by our disability'. Talking plainly, having a disability means that we have something that limits us, in some way or to some degree. And, yes, I have physical limitations that mean that I can't change light bulbs, won't be able to reach some power points no matter how resourceful I am and won't be able to whipper-snipper the side of our hill in front of our house.... yet, I don't want to live like that. I want to live thinking about what I can do or how I can achieve my goals. Yes, I have been on the receiving end of people who see and define me by my limitations, but I, like you probably, don't spend much time with them. There are some people in society that are amazed I can drive a car, some people think that people in wheelchairs always need a carer with them, some people in the community tell me I can't go up escalators, some people in society tell people in wheelchairs they can't be pilots, or telling amputees they can't be a doctor, or a blind person they can't be a lawyer.

Side track

A lot of people are familiar with tennis, chess or volleyball, they may not like it, play it, or even follow it, but they have some sort of knowledge of it - which I think takes away a lot of the apprehension and uncertainty. Whereas disabilities in general, have a lot of 'unknowns', and I think that is enough to cause outsiders to become anxious, feel uncertain or seem awkward. Right or wrong, that's my hypothesis (Grins).

Despite the lack of positive information concerning people with a disability in society, and in spite of the negative advertisements attempting to lower road accident numbers through fear (advertisements that show car crashes and then have a person in a wheelchair tell you how horrible their life is), positive change has, can and does happen.

We know that change primarily happens through education, and education happens through the day-to-day activities we experience, whether it is television shows like Glee, working with someone with a disability, seeing someone with a disability out doing their grocery shopping or friend's stories. Positive change, (as with other minorities such as homosexuals) occurs steadily, via every day people and everyday interactions. And, the best way I can help is by simply getting out there and living a full life.

Now, I also want to ask if you have ever defined yourself by your disability, without knowing it. I know that I have, especially when the house looks like it needs a vacuum (Big grin). At that time, I have no problem saying 'but I can't use a vacuum'. And if you can ever recall thinking something like, 'I can't do that'.... then you're just like

Side track

When I met Marty for the second time in my life, twenty years later, he came with two extra benefits – his gorgeous girl and sweet boy – and I am so glad that he did. We get the opportunity to be a family once every three weeks (or thereabouts), and I love it. I have never seen myself as a mum, or had a strong urge inside of me to be one, yet I enjoy and cherish these moments. However, what I want to share with you is one of the sweetest moments I have had so far.

Because Marty's boy (Mr Milo) and I have been in each other's lives on a regular basis, he recognises what it means to have a spinal cord injury and the changes and implications that are part of having a wheelchair in your life.

I think Mr Milo saw the wheelchair as just another thing to play with – which I think is fabulous! Why? Well, if a wheelchair can be categorised with items like Xbox and mountain bikes, it means that the chair (and the person in it) loses the truck-load of redundant connotations and stale stigma that usually trail behind a wheelchair like the stench from an old pair of socks.

Marty's boy, Mr Milo, loved popping into my chair anytime I was not using it. When he first started, it was five minutes here and ten minutes there. Then, next thing I know he was asking if he could use my old chair I still have. Of course I was nervous and anxious about the possibility of him tipping over, yet those fears quickly vanished as he was showing off his capabilities. He would go up ramps, down ramps, up the corridor, round and round the lounge room, up and down the verandah and do it all time and time again.

Then, as time went on Mr Milo wanted to experiment more with the chair, with every day activities that he had saw me do like getting the butter from the fridge, carrying his cup of Milo from the kitchen to the table or making his lunch. He even tried doing transfers the way that I do them!

Then one day when the family was going out to a shopping centre, Mr Milo asked if he could go in the wheelchair like me? My first thought was, 'I don't think so'. But, then I thought about it some more...... hang on, here was a 12 yr old boy wanting to go out in a wheelchair to a big shopping centre in front of everyone... 'wow', I thought. I didn't want other people to think Mr Milo was being disrespectful or just playing around so I thought I would give him some rules and see how he responded. So, I said (1) you can't move your feet, (2) you can't use your legs and (3) you have to stay in the wheelchair the whole time, and you know what? Strangely, he seemed more determined to do it. Secretly, I was impressed by him, and thrilled for us as a family.

For Mr Milo, I was excited that he would really get to see and learn more about what it means to live with a disability, and specifically a wheelchair. This opportunity would expand his mind, knowledge, skills and life experiences beyond his years, as he experiences first-hand what life is like from my point of view. The family of course would benefit from everything that Mr Milo took from the moment. Miss Café Bombon, his sister grew from being there by his side and going through it with him, and the family became closer as a unit. Actually, as we made our way around the shopping centre something that Marty did notice was the looks on people's faces as they saw the family with me and Mr Milo both in wheelchairs, followed by Marty and Miss Café Bombon walking behind us. I could imagine the thoughts possibly going through their minds, but, Marty wasn't sure if it was shock or sadness that he perceived in their faces.

Yet, I could not be more proud of Mr Milo for having the interest, guts and fortitude for wanting to experience the outside world in a wheelchair, and for actually doing it. It is awesome that Mr Milo wanted to step outside of his comfort zone, that he respected the parameters Marty and I outlined, and that he didn't just do it for fun but learnt and grew from the experience as a human being. And what a wonderful human being he is growing into.

me. Able-bodied people define and limit themselves all the time, for eg: how many people have you heard say that they can't dance or what about another all-time favourite, public speaking. How many people have you heard say they can't stand up in front of others and talk about a topic? I've heard it a lot (Heehee). I try to be aware of that though, because I don't want it to take over my life, and I don't want that to happen for you either. Oh, and I vacuum the house nowadays (Smirks).

I don't know if I am just imagining it, however, I have noticed that during the moments when the world comes together for one purpose, like the Olympics, or a natural disaster, it really feels as if the world is one, if only for a fleeting moment in time. At that moment, it gives me goose bumps on my arms, and I feel what the world could be like – when people unite it is a powerful thing. When the world is divided, fighting and attacking each other, nothing beautiful or powerful can come from it; it is destructive and self-serving. When we separate the world into able-bodied and 'disabled', nothing beautiful or positive can come from it, as we are discriminating against another for what we have lost. Yet, it is not their fault that we are now in chairs, just like if the roles were reversed and our neighbour was the one in the chair and we were walking, that would not be our fault at all.

I understand how, some days, it really can seem like there are two populations existing on this one planet. No, I'm not talking about men and women, I am talking about Population A – are the people who can access anything and physically design the man-made structures of this world, and Population B – the people who can't access everything because of their physical challenges. Yet, breaking the world into 'them' and 'us' is just one way of looking at the world, and I fear that if we adopt that prerogative - it can't help but spill over into our entire life, influencing thoughts, words, attitudes, interactions and relationships.

I say this with love - blame does not turn back time and change what happened to you or me, anger does not improve our predicament, resentment does not make us feel better, only we can do that, and you know what I am saying is true. The facts are what they are, and nothing can change what has happened. Regardless of my predicament, there was and always is something to be thankful for, and if it's true for me, then it is true for you also. Work with what you have right now, maximise what you have, and find one thing every single day to be grateful for.

bit six – Relationships are a two-way street

Now, I know that I am not a psychologist, a psychoanalyst, a psychiatrist or any other psych-o-sorta professional, and while I may not have studied psychology to any real depth, I do know that the everyday person does not have to have an IQ above 120 in order to sustain successful relationships with their friends, family or work colleagues. I know that some people are fantastic at creating and sustaining relationships, while others can create them yet not sustain them. I know that some people choose their career around being in and amongst people, while other people choose their career around minimal human contact. I know that some of us enjoy every aspect of relating to another human being, while other people loath and avoid it at all costs... but, regardless of our own preferences, I do know that we have all been having relationships since before we could talk, and like it or not, they are a part of this world.

Seeing how I am just your average Joe (or actually Jane), the only thing I know about relationships is what I have experienced for myself. I could list my personal ideas on what it takes to have a healthy relationship with another human being, and while those ideas might hit the mark with some experts, that is not my intention in this chapter. What I would like to do now is discuss two particular points here concerning relationships, (1) it takes two people, and (2) if we abuse our relationships, they will die.

So, let us get into it then.

We all know that anyone can talk to a brick wall, it won't respond but we can still do it. We could also go out to lunch with our dolls or teddy bears, but we also won't get too much interaction from them either. We can go and sit on a see-saw, but if there is no-one on the other end, it is never going to move from where it is. So, from our mighty powers of deduction, we know that it takes at least two people to create a relationship, not just one. It takes two people communicating, not just one. It takes two people respecting the other and their beliefs, choices and rights. This means that it is not up to your friend to make you feel good about yourself, to get you out of bed, to get you out of the house, to make sure you go along to events and be involved in the many activities that friends share, just like a two-way street. A two-way street can carry two vehicles, giving equal room to each vehicle, and allowing each vehicle to go their own way, just as in a relationship. Yet, a one-way street cannot carry two cars simultaneously, just as one person cannot carry a relationship on their shoulders alone. So, needless to say, a relationship that is one-sided will most surely de-hydrate and wither.

Of course, we all know that not all relationships are the same, of course they aren't – they are as individual as the people in them! They have their own dimensions, feel, purpose, characteristics and lifespan. What is that phrase....?

People come into our lives for a season, a reason or a lifetime....

My girlfriend told me this phrase about a decade ago, and still today, it is relevant and that is – because it is true. Some relationships or friendships come with a job and finish with a job, while other relationships come with a job and last a lifetime. We all know there is no blueprint for a relationship or manual we can buy, and so they are, what they are. Which leads me to my second point, (2) if we abuse our relationships, they will die.

The Macquarie concise dictionary (2001), describes abuse as –

1. To *use wrongly*, 2. To do *wrong* to, 3. To *revile*, 4. *Wrong or improper use*, 5. *Insulting language* and 6. *Ill treatment of person.*

When most people consider the term, abuse, there are certain images, words and stories that will flood your mind, without any effort whatsoever. They might be images of physical assault, rape, or bullying, or it might be stories of neglect, prostitution, pornography, or theft, or perhaps you know people who have been harassed at work, verbally abused on the road.

So, my question to you is this: *when person A consistently and deliberately takes advantage of another, ignoring their own capabilities, is this the frame for a healthy relationship, or is this at the edge of abuse?*

Let's look at an example for some clarity, shall we? Let's say that my friend and I share a house together, and after work each day we mostly just chill in the lounge room doing our own thing. If I (a paraplegic) ask my friend to stop what she is doing, get up and make me a cuppa just because I would have to get back into my wheelchair and she doesn't... isn't that taking advantage of another person, and using them?

Since my accident, I have noticed that there are some people in the world (both walkers and rollers) that have fallen under the misconception that the world does in fact owe them. Perhaps, they have felt like they have been hard done by, constantly behind the eight ball, or that life has treated them unfairly, compared to others. Yet, we all know, that the bottom line is that life is not perfect, most of us will have things that we have to overcome, every single person experiences their ups and downs, most of us will get their heart broken at least once, everyone will at some point lose the ones they love, and everyone will experience both joy and despair. I know I have said this before once or twice, *it is not the stories in our life, it is what we make of them.*

When I was a part of the wheelchair basketball scene in Sydney, I don't recall a single person of either the women's or men's teams exploiting their disability, or acting like the world owed them. Everybody in that community had a reason to moan as they lived with their own challenges, on a day-to-day basis. For some, it was cerebral palsy, others amputation and a large number of people had paraplegia, and yet in spite of their limitations, this group of people had accepted where they were – physically and mentally. These sports people didn't aim to be independent, they just were! They had come to terms with the hand they had been dealt, and basically, just got on with life - grabbing it with both hands. And because they just got on with it, they were making their life something that they enjoyed and gave them satisfaction. These basketball players amplified their capabilities, ignored their limitations (as much as is possible), and that is what I want to highlight here, because this is what counts the most. When push comes to shove, everyone could moan about something that is stopping them from reaching their dreams, but my point is – if you want it bad enough, you will work out how to get it! Their collective unspoken attitude corresponded with what I regard to be true – *We are only as 'disabled' as we permit ourselves to be!*

Yes, some of us start off in life with more challenges than others, however, I truly believe that despite our background or upbringing, where we grew up, how long we stayed in school and the grades we got, our jobs and income, experiences and events or ups and downs - our life is greatly influenced by how we look at it, our choices, our effort and our determination.

Most of us know that walking around (or pushing, limping, or whatever) with a chip on our shoulder does not really help us make friends, get invites to parties, encourage others to help us, or benefit us at all.

TOOL – TRY EVERYTHING!

I know what I am about to ask you might sound a bit funny, but just give it a go. Do it in the privacy of your own bedroom, so that you don't feel like a dill.

I want you to go and sit in front of a mirror and open up to yourself.

Yes, I want you to sit in front of your own mirror and I want you to talk to yourself out loud. No one else is there, so there is nothing to be embarrassed about. Go on. Talk about everything that has happened to you, share how you really feel with yourself out loud, cry, scream, feel whatever comes up for you, then talk about what you want for your life.

I have found that sometimes talking to myself, like this, is when solutions become obvious and life gets put back into perspective. Perhaps that is just me. Who knows? What I do know is that this is not going to kill you and it might just help.

Now, there are two sides to every coin of course, and while there may be people who take advantage of every situation, there are also those people who find it almost unbearable to ask for help. To those people who see this in themselves, I say, *I hear you* because this was me.

Independence, I have discovered is more of a masculine trait, than a female one, so it is no surprise that this is a large part of who I am, considering my mother passed away when I was ten. Now, apparently asking for and receiving help is a feminine trait - at which I am utterly horrible at. Well, I used to be utterly horrible, yet now I would just say that I am okay with it. While I will be the first one to help another person, I am conscious of the internal battle that exists when I force myself to ask for assistance. Of course, being in a chair, I know that from time to time I will require some sort of aid, whether it is getting help to transport my groceries from the supermarket to my car, getting my favourite coffee down from the top shelf, or moving furniture around in a store so that I am able to navigate and shop, just like other customers.

I heard someone say that there is such a thing as being too independent for our own good, and yes, okay, it was my best friend, Miss Cinnamon Spice Mocha, who told me this. I know that she is just a friend wanting to help another friend, and that her intentions are nothing but pure and loving. Yet Miss Cinnamon Spice Mocha also understands my fears, my feelings and my position concerning my independence, because I have shared them with her. I believe that because she knew me pre-accident and knew that I have always been self-reliant, it was easy for her to understand that I still needed to feel as self-reliant as possible, post-accident too. I also opened-up to Miss Cinnamon Spice Mocha about the moments when being in a chair, I feel like I don't have a lot of control in life and feel somewhat dependent and vulnerable as well. And, I am sure that your closest loved ones know how you feel too.

I think it is not until someone can walk in your shoes, or at least beside you, that they can see things, how we see them! Now, before when I talked about *protecting my independence*, I was talking about holding onto what I can do, rather than giving it up to someone else, just because it is easier for them. I just think that if I can work out how to do something for myself, then it is another resource that I have up my sleeve.

Because I was aware that I had difficulties asking for help, I was curious as to why I had such a problem. So, I put the question to myself asking again, and again, and again, and again.... when it finally came to me. I was just looking at it from one angle, when there was, in fact, another angle to look from. And, that angle was *the feel-good factor.*

I tried to recall a moment, pre-accident, that a person had asked me for assistance and I was able to help. This is when I remembered that, it makes a person feel good when they are able to help another human being. And there it was – I had to change the way I thought about asking for help, so that I did not associate feelings of powerlessness and vulnerability with asking for assistance. Instead, by *asking for help*, I would be giving an individual an opportunity to feel good by providing me with assistance – I think psychologists call this re-framing.

Below is a snippet of information I found on reframing, there are only two types and these are – content and context.

Content *reframing is simply changing the meaning of a situation - that is, the situation or behaviour stays the same, but the meaning is changed. For instance, a famous army general reframed a distressful situation for his troops by telling them that "We're not retreating, we're just advancing in another direction."*

Context *reframing is taking an experience that seems to be negative, not useful, and distressing and showing the gems in it! Children's stories are full of reframes designed to show children what might seem a liability, can be useful in another context.*

TOOL – WHERE DO YOU SIT?

Ask yourself where you sit in on the spectrum between taking advantage of those around you, and being defiantly independent to the extreme?

Do you always ask your friends to get up and make you a cuppa even when they're sitting on the lounge? Or do you only ask them when they themselves are heading to the kitchen? Do you ask passer-bys for assistance if you can't reach the brand of sundried tomatoes you like in the grocery store? Or do you insist on doing everything yourself because you don't want to be seen as weak, incapable or useless?

And lastly, think about the opportunity you are giving others when you ask them to assist you every now and then.

I don't know how useful it is to sit at either end of this spectrum, I have decided to sit somewhere in the middle, and I try to be very conscious of not abusing the kindness of my friends or those around me, just because I use a chair – because, frankly, that reason is not good enough.

bit seven - Family

The family, its members, values, traditions, behaviours, background, and culture in general, is so diverse across each city, region and country, it is easy to see that the concept of the family is becoming more and more complex, with each year and generation that passes.

It is generally accepted that in the 1950s the family was seen as more of a simple, yet precisely structured unit, predominantly consisting of a husband, a wife and their children. In this era, each component of the unit owned and performed their specific roles and duties as according to the unspoken code, effectively and devoutly. While in the 21st Century, never before has there been such determination for distinction and individuality amongst each family member and in society in general. Neither the man nor the woman want to slot into the out-dated, one-dimensional roles of 'the breadwinner' or 'the housewife', no longer do we want to be solely defined by our traditional family roles, and it seems that people in general are biding their time before taking the big plunge into the big M (Marriage).

When we consider the modern day family in all its complexity, I believe it is an understatement to say that it always will be an ever-changing, continuously growing and evolving organism with each new generation and era. And, due to the mere scope, magnitude, and significance of this topic, it is not a subject that I want to probe too deeply. However, if I want to be of any use at all, I realise I must consider some aspects of this topic. So, here goes.

First of all, I want to remind you that I have not studied families, family relationships, or even relationships in any academic depth whatsoever, and I will advise you that the information I will be including here comes from my very own experiences, events, observations, musings and mull-ings.

Ever since the age of 10, I am, and always have been curious of families. That was when my mother passed away and our family unit changed forever. You see, I grew up in a family that had a traditional mother figure – one that performed every task and duty inside the house, while my father took care of everything outside the house. After my mother passed away, I was virtually left to my own devices. Yes, I had a father figure, but he was a father in title only. I did all of the grocery shopping, clothes washing, ironing, most of the cooking and the general domestic duties. You could say that I basically stepped out of my shoes (as a kid) and straight into an adult's shoes, these being my mother's.

Yes, dad was around, but prior to my mother's passing, however, I only saw him in the evenings and on the weekends when he was doing things around the home. It wasn't really until it was just the two of us left that there was more interaction between us. But even then, it was mostly purposeful, rather than personal. He would tell me what he wanted for dinner, I would ask him how to do the tasks he set me, he would tell me to do the clothes washing before going out and so on. I got a hug and a kiss on my birthday, any gifts I was given were prizes that he had won at card games or from raffles at the local club.

In complete honesty, there was zero father-daughter relationship, unlike other relationships that I had seen amongst my girlfriends. I saw my friends get hugs, affection and attention, I wasn't jealous, just curious and unsure why my family was not like theirs. I guess I didn't really understand it or accept it until I was much older. But, then again, my father was a whole lot older than those of my girlfriends, and from a completely different era because, at the time I was born my father was already 52 years old and my mum, 44.

The information I just shared with you is really very personal and private for me. But I think I had to share it with you to let you inside my world, so that you might understand why I was so curious of people's families, and why the interactions between the members were so important and interesting to me. Each and every family is precious, has its own culture and its own essence. In reality, each family is its own mini universe.

But before we start, I think it is a good idea to get a clear picture, such as a definition, of the topic, so that we are starting from a similar stand-point.

When I was in school, in the 1980s, the family was defined as 'a father, a mother and 2.3 children'. Today, the Family Law definition claims that a family is -

    a. A group of individuals who share ties of blood, marriage, or adoption;

b. A group residing together and consisting of parents, children, and other relatives by blood or marriage;

c. A group of individuals residing together, who have consented to an arrangement similar to ties of blood or marriage.'

As society changes, adapts and grows, I think it is necessary for our definitions to also grow in conjunction to reflect what is happening in the world.

Way before my mother, father, and only brother had passed away, leaving me the sole survivor of my blood family, I had begun creating a family of my very own. And today, I am surrounded by a delightful array of warm and wonderful people that I am proud to call 'family'.

It is my opinion that there is nothing in life that is totally independent to anything else, meaning that when A happens, it will undoubtedly impact B, C and maybe even D. Everything that occurs has an impact or a footprint, if you will – be it physical, financial or psychological. It has been generally recognised by psychologists the world over, that when an individual is involved in a traumatic event, such as a spinal cord injury, the injury and consequences of that event not only affect the person involved, but in fact ripple out beyond their family, to their friends, to their work environment, and into the society at large.

Such as we have seen in recent years with the environment, we humans cannot continue to think it does not matter how much toxic waste we release into the air, earth or water because at some point, be it 5, 10 or 150 years down the track the impact will be seen and felt by those who are still present, our future flesh and blood. What we must remember, is that the reaction may not always be immediate, and may not be evident for some time, but the impact always occurs.

Let me lay some ground work here.

England and Australia has a reciprocal agreement, meaning that I was fortunate enough to stay at one of the largest and oldest spinal units in the world for my treatment and rehabilitation. History notes that the first ever treatment of spinal injury at Stoke Mandeville was in 1944 as soldiers returned injured in WWII. Stoke Mandeville is also credited with the birth of the Paralympics, as it held the first ever competition between female and male paraplegics, coinciding with the Olympics in London in 1948.

Stoke Mandeville Spinal Unit consists of four wards unselfishly dedicated to treat people with spinal injuries, it boasts approximately 100 beds. Three of the four wards are filled with newly injured people, ranging in ages from 15 – 65 years, mothers and daughters, fathers and sons, there's no discrimination when it comes to disability. The fourth ward is solely occupied by people who have to return for surgery or treatment of their spinal injury. I am extremely grateful for the attention, care, respect, and treatment that I received from all of team, and that is probably why they have received international acknowledgement of the quality of the services they provide.

During the seven months in rehabilitation, I saw a wide variety of families come and visit inmates, oops I mean inpatients, in my ward. There were the families that were represented mainly by one figure head that would turn up religiously every day (usually the mother). The next most frequent were the brother/sister, grandmother and the like. There were some male visitors, usually for the male patients. However, most families would try to make the journey 2 hours north of London by train on the weekends, that's when mine did too.

My family members at this point in time were Miss Chamomile Tea and Miss Short Black (my girls), Miss White Choc Mocha (Mile's sister) and her mum and dad, Mr and Mrs Cappuccino. They were all such a God-send to me. Miss Chamomile Tea and Miss Short Black would generally come up for a whole day (or if I was lucky), sometimes they would stay overnight, this usually occurred on the weekends. When I saw their faces my whole world became a little bit brighter, as you may have experienced yourselves. Hospital is not exactly the place you look forward to visiting, and when you are there longer than a week, time almost stands still.

Miss White Choc Mocha, her mum and dad, also took it in turns to visit me every week. The moment they walked into the room, tears would automatically well in my eyes and as much as I tried I could not stop them.

Side track

Miles was the spitting image of his father, something that I am sure causes pain when Mr Cappuccino looks in to the mirror. I want to take a moment here to let Mr & Mrs Cappuccino know that never before in my life had I experienced such unconditional warmth and acceptance from a family. I had only been dating Miles for six months & met them only a handful of times. But they just took me in so readily. Mr and Mrs Cappuccino – thank you for having hearts of pure Gold.

When we consider the 'family' in general, I could be wrong, yet I don't think that anyone's family is 'perfect', or the relationships between family members 'perfect' either. Personally, I think that the word 'perfect' should be removed from the dictionary because I think it conjures unrealistic and unreasonable expectations in our heads because they will remain unmet. But that is just my personal prerogative.

Back, to the point.

In fact, I think that every single one of us has inherent 'short-comings', 'imperfections', or whatever you want to call them, because we are human. Which is why I think, it is impossible for us to be 'perfect' or have 'perfect' relationships - just like there will always be unbalanced aspects to our lives as we endeavour to juggle all of our human wants, needs and dreams to fit within the parameters of the twenty-four hour day or the seven day week. Don't get me wrong, I believe it is wonderful and necessary to aspire to have great relationships with everyone in our lives, because having that aspiration will encourage us to have better relationships than if we didn't have that goal. What I am hoping to point out here, is the unreal pressure and self-criticism that we set ourselves up for when we don't allow ourselves to be anything less than 'perfect'.

Now, it would be arrogant of me to think that I can somehow, someway foretell, how your particular family and its individuals will respond, react, behave, and cope with everything that has happened to you. We all know that everyone responds differently to an event or an experience, if they didn't, there would only be one form of therapy to apply when someone experiences trauma. You can have twins experience the same event and still they can see it, experience it and respond to it in totally individual ways.

Side track

I heard this one story about twin boys who grew up in a low income family, without a lot of 'things' and without a lot given to them. As they grew up one of the twins decided he wanted to change his situation and went on to university to become a lawyer. The other twin stayed in the same town and walked in his father's footsteps, living much the same life. The twins had the same background and upbringing, the same opportunities, the same challenges, and yet, ended up taking two completely different paths. My point here is not that one twin had a better life than the other, they are neither good or bad. However, the point I am attempting to show you is that life is an individual choice.

Right now, I want to remind you that the world is made up of a great mix of people. Sort of like a box of chocolates, as our old friend Forest Gump would say. And while some people might pick up a chocolate and bite into it and relish the flavour of a Turkish delight centre, there are others in this world that most definitely will not, and will want to spit it out of their mouths. It is not the chocolates fault, it doesn't mean to be pungent to some of the population, that is just how it has been made.

So too, there are families that might not change one iota when something happens in their life, they will simply sit back, look at the facts and move forward with life from there. I have seen other families become even closer when one of their members ended up in a wheelchair, then there were other families that just did not know how to 'handle' the change to the person, and then there were the families that went into 'protection' mode out of pure fear. In general, I can say that I don't think families change who they are, yet, I think it is possible for other families to tilt to the 'extreme' end of the stick. I've seen some families that have gone to the extreme left, where they become radically protective, or there is the extreme right, where families don't offer any assistance, because they believe in tough love and the old Australian slogan, 'she'll be right mate'. However, generally, people remain true to their essence. Like I said, there is no way of predicting how people are going to respond and react, and I won't endeavour to chat with you about every single possibility, but I will share with you a couple of interesting stories that I have.

One stereotypical family could be nick-named the **'Don't Care' Family** – meaning exactly that, this family does not really have a strong connection or perform the traditional family roles of caring and supporting.

This girl's family was an interesting scenario, a real assorted mix of chocolates!

The father of this girl was previously married, and from the first marriage came five children. One day the first wife just up and ran away to a hospital, taking the youngest child with her, and for unknown reasons left the baby girl at the hospital. Putting the father in an awkward and unfair position, as he had to cope single-handedly with the other four children, make an income and all of this during the years of the Great Depression. Barely making ends meet, the father had no way of getting to the hospital to pick the baby up that was left, and with enormous regret and guilt, the baby was adopted out. At a different period of time, a few of the children spent some time in an orphanage while the father was looking for work and trying to sort things out. Several years later the father found another woman, this woman was the mother of the girl who told me this story. With his new woman, he added two more children to his party of four, the youngest of which was the girl. By the time the girl in this story came along, the first bunch of children had children of their own. The girl's only brother was already 21 years old and lived on his own. Even though the second wife/partner tried to meld the two families into one, it was a mission that was never realised.

This girl's father was born in the year 1919, it was the year after WWI had drawn to a close, but, by the time he was just 10 years old (in the 1930s) the Great Depression had hit every country around the world, particularly Australia, with 32 per cent unemployment. The Depression lasted until WWII hit, in 1939, and by the time this young boy had turned 19 years old, he had lost his father and had the responsibility of helping his mother care for his eleven siblings. Growing up through such harsh and scarce times, it was no wonder that this man's primary purpose was to make and store as much money as possible. It is no wonder he put little time or effort into his family, and it is no wonder he valued money above everything else.

Now that I have laid the background regarding this family, I want to tell you about how this family reacted and responded when this girl found herself laying in a hospital bed overseas with her spinal cord eighty percent severed.

It took time for the word to reach her family, and so it was about a week before she received a call from her father. The girl was unfamiliar with the emotion she heard in her father's voice. The girl had witnessed her father cry only three times during her thirty years on the planet, all at times of personal loss. The conversation was disconnected and impersonal, yet it was the uneven pitch and wavering that gave his feelings away. He asked how she was and what had happened and he listened to her story. The girl understood that her father was not going to start being all supportive and telling her how he felt when he heard that his little girl had almost died. She knew, without him saying a word, that he would not be flying over to see her, hold her hand or just be with her. He was far too old and frail himself, and she was too far away. She reminded herself that all she really needed to know, was that he cared about his little girl.

She received two phone calls from her father during the seven months of hospitalisation, one in the beginning, and the other to ask her to come home.

As for her father's first family of children, the girl was hopeful that the kin blood would be enough to motivate concern and care, especially considering the severity of the accident. A couple of these children had done quite well financially, and she wondered if they might fly over to see her, even just briefly. She also had wondered if they might send flowers, but no-one arrived and nothing came.

Over the weeks following her accident, the girl received some cards from her father's other children – three in total. That's it. Three cards over the seven months. There was nothing from their children, her nieces and nephews that were closer to her age. There were no cards from her father's brothers or sisters. There were no stuffed toys from family members. Nothing, zip, zero, nada! Meanwhile patients around her had dozens upon dozens of cards tacked to their walls, in front and around their beds. Other patients also had daily and weekend visits from loved ones and friends. And, there was a constant smell of flowers in the air, as new bunches arrived every week. These items are an expression of love, care and support – something that she had never received from her blood ties.

Yet, interestingly, over the course of time that she was on bed rest, which was eight weeks, she had received more cards and well wishes from the people she worked with than those who were supposed to be her blood relatives. So many people from her work gave up their own time to take the two hour drive north to sit and visit her. People from all levels came to spend time with her - her team mates, other colleagues, supervisors, right up to top level management. She had never experienced such support before in her life. Some of the company staff got together to give her something big enough to cuddle at night, a chocolate-brown teddy. If it weren't for the kindness and support of her colleagues, her friends, she would have had no-one and nothing!

Toward the end of her rehabilitation she received the second phone call from her father in which she was informed that he was of ill health and requesting her to return home. She reluctantly consented, even though this meant that she was giving up her job (which had been kept for her), and giving up the love and support of her close friends that surrounded her there. Leaving the United Kingdom meant leaving everyone that loved her and leaving everyone that she loved.

Her father asked her to move back to the town in which he lived and where she had grown up, a small country town of only 12,000 people. He said that he could renovate one of his units so that she could move into it – which is probably the sweetest thing that he has ever said to her. Small towns are always gossiping about someone, and she did not want to be the centre of that gossip.

As if this girl needed some more proof that her blood ties could not care any less than what they have proven so far, she decided to move to the town where they lived. One of them organised a room for her, not at their house, but, at a hostel. Can you imagine??? She left the love and warmth of her friends in England, as well as her job to come back to live amongst complete strangers in a setting that could not be any less supportive and homely. I guess, if the girl was not happy, then she could have done something about it. And you know what - she did. I know this because this is my story, 'this girl' is me.

The moral to this story is that regardless of the events, experiences, ups or downs – people don't change. The core of who they are does not alter, you might find that they become a more or less intense version of themselves, but their essence does not change shape. Sure, you may find that certain moments might draw out specific attributes or traits of a person's character, but I believe that they would have always been there in some degree anyway. Just as doctors claim that every individual already possess the potential for diabetes within their body, it just needs a trigger to stimulate the diabetes into action.

Next, I would like to take a look at what happens when a family member's traits are intensified, how that might be expressed, and how that impacts the person with the disability within the family.

This form of love could be coined the **Bubble-Wrap effect**.

The title of this sub-topic is precisely what it suggests - the family will want protect you, defend you, wrap you in bubble-wrap, cotton wool, or whatever soft-cushioning material they can to keep you safe from now on in.

Now, of course, I have realised that this is not for selfish or negative reasons, they have no ill intent. The truth is that they just love you, and because they love you, they are now terrified of anything that could harm you.

This bubble-wrap effect stems from the fear of the unknown I guess, because the family/member once came so very close to losing you, they are not prepared to take that risk again. Yet, that is the essence of life. Life is literally full of 'unknowns' - some of them are surprise birthdays, some of them are pregnancies, some of them are changes as we grow, some of them are lovely people who come into our life, some of them are engagement proposals, some of them are losses, and some of them are just twists and turns in the road. However, if life was not full of these 'unknowns', then how boring would that be? That is part of the fun of life, the fact that we do not know what is down the road, around the corner or over the hill. If everything was a known, I don't think there would be a point to us being here, because then, the opportunities for challenge, learnings and growth would disappear as well. I think that 'unknowns' are a necessary and more often than not, fun part of this life. But then again, maybe I have it all wrong, what do you think?

If you are able to take a step back from where you are, you will be able to see that your family members have just escaped a huge loss –You. You have possibly had a near death experience (whether that be by accident or illness), and you have lived to see another day. So, it is easy to see what might be at the forefront of their minds right now, and that is 'protection and prevention'. As you can imagine, if there was a slight hint of motherly instinct there before, you can bet it will be magnified now. I can virtually guarantee that she will do anything she has to in order to keep you safe. I mean, even though we are highly developed, hopefully civilised and rational-thinkers, we still have instincts and bottom line, we are still creatures.

Sort of like the spectrum of chocolate lovers.

Not everyone enjoys chocolate to the same degree. There are those who can buy a family block at the shops and it may actually take them the entire year before they get around to finishing it. Then there are those who will have a little something sweet in the cupboard and maybe treat themselves a couple of times a week, like biscuits with tea or ice cream after dinner. Finally, at the other extreme, there are those people who will blissfully indulge at any moment, regardless of the consequences, because it gives them what they need – whether that is comfort, pleasure or a 'hit'. They might enjoy something sweet each day or each hour.

You also need to be aware that the Bubble-Wrap Family may even start to think that they know what is best for you and your new situation. With this particular set of traits, this family may want to know everything about you in great detail eg: what medication you are taking, your bowel routines, your toileting techniques, how much water you are drinking, are you eating enough fibre, bla bla bla. They may not see that what they are doing is intrusive, because all they will know is that they care about you. Should something go 'wrong' once or twice, they may feel the need to step in and sort things out for you. Living this way does not serve you, it does not serve them, and it won't serve the family unit either.

When someone cares for you, there is nothing more comforting, yet when someone is controlling, there is nothing more crippling.

Before we finish on this topic, I would just like to share a word about your doctor with you. GP stands for General Practitioner, and therefore, must have a general knowledge on every aspect of the body. However, when things escalate past their general knowledge, they must refer you onto a specialist. The majority of doctors in practice won't have in-depth knowledge to deal with the specific issues that you and I have, and will face, with our varying challenges. You might find the odd doctor that has extensive knowledge of disability, such as a doctor I had in Sydney who had several patients who used chairs. It always pays to do your research before you make your choice, because it is nice to be able to put your trust in someone who knows precisely what you are talking about.

Other than your local GP, you will find assistance by calling the spinal injuries unit where you did your rehabilitation, or call an organisation that provides services to people with spinal injuries, or lastly, an in-home nursing/care organisation.

bit eight - the General Public

Now, I would like to chat about an event that has only really occurred a couple of times over the last twelve years for me, and perhaps may never happen to you. So, I guess, this is more like a..... *just in case-* topic really.

I am just going to tell you that having handles on your chair will only encourage people to use them, which is why I no longer have handles on my chair. While generally, most people will ask if we need help, there are those who will not.

There are some people who might just take charge of the situation, and push you up that hill that you are climbing, or they might just move you out of their path. It is not my intention here to discuss whether it is right for them to do this, or outline how they could do it better. What is my primary concern here is *us* - how we react, and respond.

I am going to repeat myself yet again, but it is unavoidable because it is true - how I react/respond won't affect just me, it ripples out to all persons in a chair.

Men used to open doors for women for decades. It was a part of their role as a man, it was a part of their identity, and it was an expectation. Then, things changed when some women saw this act as a negative thing towards women. So, more and more women said they preferred that men didn't open doors for them anymore. We can't interview thousands of men who went through this change, yet it seems commonsense that men felt some rejection about this, and nowadays, I can count (on my hands) the number of men that open doors for me.

The common denominator between you and me is our chair, so that when we reject an offer, it will be a rejection by a *person in a wheelchair*. I know, I know, we are people first and wheelchair users second – I know that, yet, the wider population won't categorise us that way. Which is why I ask you to stop and think about all those other PWAD, who might need assistance navigating through a shop, getting up a step, or making their way up a ramp.

Actually, in my experience a lot of the public have informed me that they are afraid to offer help because of past experiences. Some of the public have told me that they have been told off by the person in a chair. Others simply don't know what to do, and are nervous about doing something wrong. And, then there are other members of the public that don't want to help because we, PWAD, want to be totally independent, even if it kills us (Heehee)!

So what are you are going to say when help is offered to you? I have decided to -

1. acknowledge their kindness,
2. choose to **accept** or **not**, and
3. thank the person.

Please think about other people.

Now, this next story actually happened to me, and might well happen to you too.

Ok, my girlie and I had a window of opportunity to catch up in between all of her classes and assignments at university, so we grabbed the chance. We met up at the shopping centre, but decided to go somewhere else for lunch. So, she popped into my car and we took off. We had a good gas bag, enjoyed lunch and then, I took her back to her car and we went our own way. It wasn't until I was 10 minutes down the road, wondering what I have to do next, when I look over to the passenger seat and immediately scream 'Shit!' My chair is not there. Then I look into my rear vision mirror and see my chair behind me in the boot.

I had left my chair assembled because it was quicker for my friend to put into the back of the car, I just forgot that we would be going our own way. So there was a huge sigh of relief when I saw it, but quickly came another *shit*. Firstly, I am relieved that I didn't forget my chair altogether, as I have almost lost my cushion about five times. But, then there was a second *shit* because now I had to work out how to get it from the back of the car, to the front passenger seat next to me.

As my mind was rattling through the various places I could pull into to get assistance, I drove past a service station and I thought 'that is exactly what I need'. So I drove to the next one, pulled in and parked next to the entry of the shop and waited for someone to walk by. I needed someone to pull the chair out of the back, and put it on the ground next to me, so that I could do the rest. Oh, and shut the car boot too. The first person to come past me was kind enough to come to my rescue, which puts my faith back in humankind. I'm very happy to say that this has not happened to me again (touch wood). And, of course, nothing like this would ever happen to you all (Wink wink).

I used to get my knickers in a knot about the general population over little silly things, like the person in front of me stopping when we are going up a ramp, or someone popping out of a shop when I'm coming down a ramp. Then I remembered that the general population have little interaction with people who use chairs, making it only natural for them to be unfamiliar with our world, and its challenges. Just like truck drivers who probably get annoyed when other road users pull in front of them, as they are trying to speed up for a hill. It is not that the other road users are stupid, it is just that they have no idea about driving a truck and no concept of how difficult it is to get a truck up a hill.

There is no education or courses for the general public about people who use chairs, so, the only way that they learn about us is through speaking to us, or hearing about us from their work mates, friends or family. This is precisely why I say that part of our new life is about education. The government has limited resources, so too do non-government organisations – so, if you can spare a couple of minutes, we make the best possible teachers for the rest of the community.

bit nine - 'The' Question

I was talking to my girlfriend one day and something must have just happened to me because I don't usually moan to my friends about my problems, yet I must have this day. I told my girlfriend about how I am constantly asked (at least once a week) about what happened to me and why I am in a wheelchair. I assured her that I was not exaggerating. However, I think she hesitated to believe that society, as a whole, could have such poor judgement. That was, until she had holidays and saw that what I was saying, was true.

She was astounded by people's forthrightness and blatant rudeness. She actually became quite protective of me, sometimes stepping in and cutting the question off. Then, as we talked about this situation, we decided to start having some having fun with it, and so, we started making up hilarious, far-fetched stories about what I was doing when the accident happened. That way, we were in control and got a laugh out of the predicament.

I don't know if these people are trying to make some poor attempt at conversation, or perhaps it is just 'curiosity killing the cat', but, I have no doubt you will hear 'the Question' again and again and again and again. I have a theory on this, and it is that I believe the general public will only ask you 'the Question' if you appear to be coping well with your predicament. I have no facts, no hard evidence to prove this of course, it is just a theory, and nothing more than what I hear, and see, and feel.

Now that I have told you what you can expect, I want to chat with you about what you are going to do when it happens to you.

For me, in the beginning, I was stunned and shocked that the people could be so rude and blunt. It is not as if they were asking me how I made a casserole, they were asking me about the most painful and horrible event in my life, yet, that did not occur to them, obviously. And each time I answered their question, I noticed that I felt as if it had just happened to me all over again. As time has passed, the pain associated to the story waned, but it took years to get to that point. Someone told me that each time you re-tell something negative that has occurred in your life, your body actually re-experiences the event each time, and apparently, this has been researched and proven to be a fact. Instead, I now choose when, and with whom, I share my personal information.

Over the years, I have had my accident when I was jumping up and down on a trampoline, when I was on a ride at a fair, but my favourite is when I had the accident naked bungy jumping on holidays – guaranteed to silence even the rudest of people (Heehee). I only use this when I really don't like the person who asked.

You decide what feels right for you, because it is your life.

bit ten – Work Colleagues

As with friends, I have to say that work colleagues are also on a need-to-know basis. That said though, whether you are starting a new job or returning to your old one, you will find that there are parts of your role that might now be physically impossible for you to perform. That said, you might not be aware of what specific tasks need reviewing, until you are in the work environment again. It is quite obvious that you will no longer be able to run up the stairs to the lavatory, yet you might not be aware that making coffee for your boss and delivering it to him, is now out of the question. Yes, you can do it at home, however at home you don't have people coming in and out of rooms along the way, or people in their own world running around all over the place either. I just don't want you to end up with a coffee coloured blouse, rather than the pink it used to be.

Another aspect that might be worth mentioning is the fact that by now you have noticed that going to the bathroom takes considerably longer than what it used to. This is one part of my previous life that I really miss – only 3 minutes in a bathroom, Geeeees, what a difference that would make (Heehee).

We know that we may not have an 'accident' every week, month, or even every six months, however, I prefer to be upfront about the possibility of something happening so that *no-one is left out in the cold*, so to speak. You don't need to get into the messy details of what might happen, or what you will need to do when it does, but I have found people are understanding if they have a general idea. That way, they will know that when you tell them 'you need to go home right now', that you have a valid reason and you don't have a less-than-desirable work ethic. Having open communication will also limit unnecessary questions.

I would advise you to make a mental note of your coffee and water intake throughout the day so that you aren't bringing an 'accident' on yourself. Set the alarm on your mobile if you have to remind yourself when you need to go to the bathroom. I find that when I'm working I just get absorbed into what I am doing and forget what needs to happen and when.

Not everyone is going to be your best friend, not everyone is going to like you, and not everyone is going to agree you deserved the job.

When you have decided to return to employment, remember that there are all sorts of people in this world, and this will be reflected in your work environment too. There might be those who want to mother and protect you, or those who treat you like the invalid that they think you are. There might be others who want you to prove that you deserve the position, or the odd one or two colleagues that treat you like you are stupid. There might be some who are nervous around you or who just want to avoid you. But, I'm telling you right now – just give them a little time. Soon enough people will see you are independent, and only slightly challenged. Soon enough staff members will see that you deserve your position just as much as anyone else in the office. Be mindful that all new people take time to settle in to new jobs and to make friends, so why would this be different for us.

The bottom line is that there is only one person that you need to worry about - your boss. If your boss is happy, then you should be happy too.

That is all that comes to mind in regards to the work environment. So, 'That's all folks.'

Oh, P.S. I wanted to let you know of two books that I discovered (while looking for something else) that have to do with job searching and people with a disability.

At the website below you will find two books that acknowledge and discuss there are challenges and processes, for people with a disability who seek employment.

www.diversityworld.com/Disability/jobseek.htm

If you don't have access to a computer, the books are –
Ryan, D.J. *Job search handbook for people with disabilities* by Jist Publishing, 2011.

Bolles, Richard N. and Brown, Dale S. *Job-hunting for the so-called handicapped,* Ten Speed Press, 2001.

bit eleven - Socialising

It is a funny thing being hospitalised for a long period of time, those white walls really can start to become a twisted version of a sanctuary for its inmates, sort of like how I imagine a prison would become something similar for its residents.

Inside the hospital walls, people don't look at you strangely, people won't cross the street when you are coming their way, and people won't just stand there and stare at you. Inside those white walls, you are *normal*. You know that inside those white walls you can reach and do most things for yourself because of its purpose-built design (or if you can't, then the person who helps you knows exactly what you need). It doesn't matter if you have befriended any of your inmates, regardless, you all share a common denominator, and that is that you have had a life-changing event or injury. It is a weird sort of connection because none of you may have anything in common, and none of you may even like the others much, yet in the hospital, none of you stand out like the sore thumb - as you will in the real world. So, I understand that the possibility of leaving those four white walls may seem a little concerning, daunting, or even frightening. It is my experience though, that the longer you stay there, the harder it becomes to leave and actually slot back into your own life!

So, when you finally have been discharged and are back in your own space, sorting out services, and basically slotting back into your life again.... you know that your friends are going to start calling you to *get back on the horse again,* right? If they are solid friends, they will be showing up on your door or inviting you out for drinks and such, and that is awesome. But, even though you were keen to escape the hospital, perhaps you are getting the flutters at the thought of getting back out there again....? I did.

REGARDLESS of what you are feeling, thinking or fearing – you must GO! The capital letters and the exclamation mark means it is important (Big cheesy).

No matter how you are feeling!! Regardless what fears or thoughts you have running around that head of yours, you simply have to stop yourself from thinking.... and just say 'Yes'. Trust me! Why? Well, because if you don't, if you (God-forbid) start listening to those fears, concerns and worries doing laps in your head, you will undoubtedly turn yourself, unconsciously, into a hermit and a hobbit (Heehee). In all seriousness, I know this because I've been there, done it and probably should have printed a t-shirt. When we (us humans) have too much time on our hands and spend too many hours stuck at home, things can end up a bit twisted in our heads. So, in all sincerity, don't think at all, just say 'yes' and take every opportunity to get out of the house and into Life!

There is so much good stuff out there (in the community) for us to get stuck into, even if you don't know which direction you are headed right now, volunteer at a charity, if you are considering changing industries - volunteer to learn about the field, find a mentor doing what you want to do, join a club, take a road-trip with a couple of friends, fundraise money for a charity, take a cooking lesson, join a book club, learn a foreign language, take a sewing class, the list goes on. Ooh, let me add, that by just getting out there you will also do good for us people who live with a challenge. How? Well, hopefully people will stop parking in our spaces because they can see we actually exist and use them, others will learn from interacting with us and we will have more of a visible presence which supports our requests for access etc, and thereby result in improved conditions and opportunities. Let's face it, if we just stay at home and do nothing, why should the government enforce the law to provide access or accessible bathrooms for our community, or anything else for that matter?

Are you a Dr Phil fan? Well I am, and I recall him saying this one phrase again and again, which is *we teach others how to treat us*. This could not be more true or important for the community that we are a part of now.

Being a minority, 'we' stand out from the crowd, and I believe that people remember us more so than other people, which means that how we act, behave and interact stand out more as well - thereby making us involuntary educators. So, maybe we need to stop for a second to think about what we want them to get out of it, each time we go out into the real world.

One of my girlfriends (able-bodied) was doing some placement during one of her degrees, and it happened to be with an organisation that provided services to people with a disability, and I have to say that I was so proud of her when she told me this story.

The group was being instructed 'how' a person with paraplegia performs tasks such as getting into a car. After the instructor showed them the process, she asked if the group had any questions about what they had just seen. Someone in the group asked if that was the only way of getting into a car and my friend spoke up and said that she has seen her best friend (me) use several different methods. When she finished the story I could see a big smile on her face and it was clear that she was proud to have that knowledge and experience to share with others. So was I. It was in that moment that I realised just how much she had picked up from just being around me, how much I had opened her mind and her world.

> *What we have done for ourselves alone dies with us; what we have done for others and the world remains, and is immortal*
> *~Albert Pike (1809-1891)*

Next, is the topic of going out with your friends. There are not really many things to worry about when you go out with your friends, in fact, the only two that come to my mind are accessing 'the little girls room' and being man-handled in order to get into somewhere.

Now, if you don't catheterise intermittently the 'ladies room' is not any sort of issue at all. Yet, because I know that I have covered this topic in another Chapter – Living in the real world, I will re-direct you there and move onto the last point, which is being 'man-handled'.

In regards to going places, we only have two choices! Of course we can continue to keep to our old haunts (because we just like them) regardless of the steps and lack of access to bathrooms, or we can discover some new spots that give us everything we need. Oh yes, and remember to talk this over with your friends (because they aren't inside your head) so that they know your preferences when they are organising things with others.

If you want to opt for going to the places that you have always been to, you will need to decide your attitude around asking for and receiving assistance, whether that be someone helping you up one huge sucker of a step or someone carrying you up a flight of fifteen steps. Some people see being carried as a negative, a weakness, an embarrassment, and focus on the staring of others, the humiliation, and the feelings of lack, and I am forced to acknowledge those feelings, I myself have experienced them. I don't know if those feelings went hand in hand with the newness of my circumstance, yet nowadays, I focus rather on the kindness of others, how I can help others (who use chairs) by doing something about the restaurant, cafe, or business, and lastly, I focus on being grateful for the people that surround me.

It really is as simple as changing our perspective.

When I can, I prefer to support places that do not discriminate against those of us who use chairs. However, if there is a particular place that I want to go to for a particular purpose, I will not limit myself because of a few steps, and so, will graciously accept a person's kindness and assistance. I would like to add that I am wary of getting help though, as there are so many different people in the world, and some of them would do anything if it meant that they could benefit financially.

That said, I believe I have covered the main points concerned with socialising.

And so, in this chapter we reach the last topic left to discuss. I have to say that I left this topic till the last not because I wanted to keep you dangling, or because I strategically designed the book that way – simply put, I knew it would be the hardest section to write. This topic is the most personal, the most trying and yet, probably the most important. I know what it is like to be a single female who suddenly finds herself in a chair and wonders if she will ever be loved again.

bit twelve - the Opposite sex – MEN!

(My apologies for not being able to provide information on every sort of partnership in this book, in no way do I mean to exclude anyone, but I can only share what I know).

Wow, where the heck do I start with this subject matter? There are so many angles, facets, aspects, and parts to this topic and relationships in general, that I find myself a bit over-awed just considering what I am attempting. Because, when you start talking about one thing, you find that you also need to talk about a load of other things as well! For example, when you talk about men – you end up talking about relationships, when you talk about relationships - you end up talking about 'kissing someone in a chair', then you find yourself talking about 'catching a guy', then you're onto flirting do's and don'ts, the ins and outs of disabled-dating, and then you can wind up talking about sex, positions, and gees - I'm exhausted just thinking about it all. I mean, this one subject on its own could in fact end up being an entire book unto itself!

Well, when you think about making a cake - you have to make sure you have the right ingredients, when you think about luring a fish – you need the right bait, when you are going to make a dress – you have to have the right colour cotton, buttons, and pattern and.... when I think about men – I think about starting with 'us' first.

Now, before you even conceive attracting the attention of a male and rush head-on into a relationship like a dear into headlights, I want you to make certain you are ready for it. Because, if there is uncertainty in your mind about if you are ready, then people might get hurt – like you, him, your family etc. I am sure that you don't want to mess around with people's hearts and lives, right. People's hearts are as precious as gemstones, and let me tell you, I have discovered that they are just as fragile as diamonds, sometimes. I don't know if you have ever broken a vase or something like it, well I have, and it is darn fiddley work trying to fit and stick all the bits back together again, in the right places. My advice, take things slowly when you are dealing with people - it is far easier to heal a crack, than it is to try to repair something that is completely shattered. We all know what happened to Mr Humpty Dumpty, right!

So first things first here, I knew that if I was anything less than utterly transparent in this book, that you would not get anything out of it at all.... and that, to me, is pointless! - Because, you and your future is the only thing pushing me to complete this endeavour. Unfortunately, what that means for me is that, I had to open my heart and my life to strangers. Complete strangers who might agree, disagree, like, hate, support or criticise me. As a result, while writing this chapter in particular, I have felt embarrassed, scared and vulnerable. But, in going through those emotions, being with them, and knowing that I am doing this so that hopefully you can get something, anything out of it, gives me strength to stand tall and say, 'yes, this is who I was and who I am – love me or hate me – this is Me'; which leads nicely into what I want to chat with you about now.

Have you ever heard the phrase,
> ***You have to love yourself first before anyone else can.***
> *~Unknown Author*

This particular topic (Men) did not even register in my consciousness until many years post-accident, because unlike other inpatients, I was the only one that had had a 'double whammy' – a spinal cord injury and the loss of a beloved.

Towards the end of my hospitalisation and rehabilitation, there were moments when the girls would sit around the unit hypothesising about men and their futures – questioning if we would still be attractive to men, if men would look at us now we were like this, and of course, if we would one day find Love. For me though, these thoughts were fleeting as my heart was still grieving.

Now, I know that my friends would whole-heartedly agree with me when I tell you that I am not a negative person. Yet, I will gladly admit that in the beginning of my new life there were a lot of dark clouds surrounding me, and it took me a while before I could see the good bits of my life again.

I could only see the steel
In the beginning of my new life I could not see Me,
I could no longer wear the clothes that I used to and when I looked in the mirror I saw a stranger,
What I did see was how all of my trousers sat short in the legs,
I could only see how my clothes were always dirty from rubbing on the wheels.

How my hands seemed constantly dirty from the chair,
I could only see that I was no longer the size 8 waist that I was pre-
accident,
I could only see my swollen ankles and legs,
I could not see Me – I could only see the steel and…. I could not see a
single reason why a man would look at me now.

I think a lot of us people, whose lives and bodies change dramatically,
put ourselves in a box (without even noticing it), by telling ourselves a
tonne of negative things that stop us from being the women that we
actually are! Why would we do that? Well, we do it because inside
a box, it is safe – nothing and no-one is going to hurt us and we
can control everything inside of it. And, let me say that for a brief
period of time, being inside a box is probably necessary, and dare I
say, beneficial. However, I also need to tell you that NOBODY CAN
LIVE INSIDE A BOX.

Life is not about building walls around us…. If you consider the way a
human is designed, it is obvious that life is not about being separate,
but being a part of.

Our skin is not made of steel, it is penetrable, it can be damaged by the
outside world, and it continues to change throughout our lifetime.
Our brain is not separate from our body, it is within our body and
communicates with all parts of our body. It has the capacity to learn and
grow, and does so throughout our lifetime. Our spirit (or soul) is not
separate from our body, yet lies within it… it listens, gains knowledge and
interfaces with our entire package, and the world around us.

Life is about connecting, life is about interacting, growing, and learning
- life is a result of the ingredients that mix together, how they react and
respond to each other, life is about change, growth, movement.

If I am honest, in the beginning, I know that instead of being grateful
for being alive, being thankful for what I still had, my mind was
primarily filled with a truck load of negative stuff. I know that I
focused on what I didn't have and the fears churned around inside my

head for a long time – especially, every time I considered leaving my house, and I don't want that to happen to You! But then, I decided to tell myself to 'stop being silly' – I did, I literally told myself out loud to 'stop being silly'. Sometimes you have to do that to be louder than the voices inside your head.

I don't know if one or any of these questions have crossed your mind or maybe none of them have? Yet, I know that when I spoke to my able-bodied friends about my worries, a lot of them admitted to having had similar fears to mine, despite the fact that they had nothing physically wrong with them. Of course, now that I have thought about it, pre-accident I remembered that I worried about being skinny enough, attractive enough.... and all the normal female dilemmas.

As I went about my day-to-day activities with these questions at the forefront of my mind, I noticed that on some days it was obvious that people had a problem with the chair, and on other days I noticed that people had no problem at all, and in fact, could not be more helpful. Which then made me ask myself.... could it be them as individuals, or shock horror, could I play some part in the equation? I wondered if it could be as simple as society reflecting the attitude I was sending out into the world that day. Or not?

So, after listening to those questions churning, I became frustrated enough to do something about it. While I wanted answers to my questions, I had no idea how to get them, without asking people bluntly. And I knew that if I sat in front of the general public and asked them how they felt, saw and looked at people in chairs, there was no way that I was going to get an honest, untainted response. They might tell someone else, but not someone sitting in front of them in a chair, asking those questions.

How can I find out if I am right, or if I am completely wrong?

It was then that I realised the only way that I could prove myself right or wrong was to test it. That was it, if I tested me and there was no change – it must be the general community. Yet, if I test me and there is a change – then the only person I have to change is me. Which is great news because it is way easier to change one person than it is to change an attitude of the majority of people. I hear you asking, 'well, what did you do then?'

Ok, I decided I would test both 'attitudes' for a month each, keeping notes on any events and experiences on a daily basis.

For the first month, I tested and recorded the same attitude that I had held since the injury. I didn't really have to work at keeping the same thoughts at the forefront of my mind, it was completely natural for me at that point. These thoughts were about me **not being** sexy, desirable, or attractive. I focused on the fact that I now felt a-sexual. During that month, I noted no looks from the male species, no advances, not even acknowledgement really. Overall, I experienced much as the same as I had before, whereas, the second month, was different. Way different, let me tell you – I'm excited to tell you.

At the beginning of each day, I put more effort into getting dressed (like I did pre-accident), I think I might have even bought a couple of new garments too. What I did differently was each day before I went out into the world I stood in front of the mirror and talked to myself. I told myself that I looked great and I said it until I was convinced, then I told myself that I am beautiful just the way that I am, then I told myself that I deserve only good experiences and lovely people in my life. Next, I thanked the Universe for all that I had been given, and I reminded myself that I am grateful for this gift of life and for the love that surrounds me. Each day I tried very hard to remain in that state of mind throughout the day, whatever I did, wherever I was and whatever happened. For that month, I changed how I looked at my life and the attitude that I carried inside me, out into the world. As a result of that change, I noted a lot more positive outcomes for me including more positive interactions with people in general, positive comments from people about how I looked, more positive outcomes from everyone and even a date proposition from a complete stranger (Cheesy smile).

Ok, I guess I have to tell you about it now –

FLASHBACK

I can't recall how far I was into this second month but it doesn't matter, so long as you hold your positive attitude. So this is how it went. I was just standing in line waiting to be served at the local Post Office and it was not exactly busy, yet not a quiet day either. And as you do when you stand in line, I was looking around just watching people do what they were doing. A guy who appeared to be some sort of labourer, because of his blue singlet and shorts, was addressing an envelope over at the customer counter and spoke up asking what the post code for the area was? There was no answer so I spoke up and gave it to him. Then after I was served and on my way out, he thanked me for helping him out and mentioned that he had finished work for the day and wondered if I might join him for a drink at a nearby bar? I was on my way to basketball training and was only rushing to the post office because it was urgent, but I literally had to run to get to training on time, so I declined his offer. After basketball had finished, I was telling the story to one of the girls and I cannot for the life of me understand why I said 'no' to him. It wasn't as if he was ugly to look at, or that missing one training session would make a whole lot of difference. Thinking about it now though, I recall being scared at the time. Anxious about access and stuff, scared of going out in public with a male for the first time, and scared about what other people might think. My self-esteem was shot to pieces, and I guess I didn't know how to react because I had never had such an offer before.

But, it was a beautiful and perfect example of what can happen when your attitude is facing the right direction, isn't it? From this little experiment I conducted, I learnt that we only receive what we give out – which is something numerous religions have been trying to tell us for centuries. Before I finish up here, I want to add that us people, disabled or not, experience and interact with the world on more than one level. Firstly, we are a physical being that has senses through our eyes, ears and skin, as well as having a spirit/essence, and a brain, meaning that we receive and process things not just intellectually, but emotionally and spiritually. So having said that, I think it is necessary to remind ourselves that it is not just important to be mindful of what we say to others, yet also what we feel and think, because you cannot have a puncture in one wheel of your car and still expect the car to function normally.

Guess I don't have to tell you how I decided to live after that (Grins).

Which brings me back to the point I am trying ever so hard to make here, and that is – regardless of what you have and don't have now – You have to truly love yourself, warts, wheels and all!

There is a movie, titled *Erin Brockovich*, starring Julia Roberts, that is based on the true life story about an out-of-work, single mum of three who manages to, despite her lack of legal qualifications, secure the biggest payout of a direct-action law suit in America. Well, I own it because I love it. If you have not yet seen it, get it.

Have you ever watched a movie that brings out more than one emotion at the one time? This was it for me. There is one scene that made me scream and cry at the same time, I guess it must have resonated somewhere deep inside.

Let me set the scene – the most outstanding aspect of Erin is that she actually feels for her clients pain and becomes very close to those people she represents, learning even the most private and painful parts of their life. This scene starts with the husband outside his house on dusk, picking up rocks that he throws in the direction of the PG&E plant across from his house. As he throws the last rock, he begins screaming out in pain and collapses to the ground facing his house. What I assume is the next day, we see Erin driving to visit these clients.

Erin sits facing the wife, on the side of her bed. The wife is sitting upright holding her body, with her arms across her chest. She then looks Erin in the eyes and asks - *do you think that if a woman has no uterus and no breasts that she is still technically a Woman?* Luckily I don't live in suburbia because I screamed at the television as the tears flooded my eyes. It was not difficult for me to empathise with how I imagined she felt, I guess, because my own body has changed so much from the accident, as I am sure yours has also. But right now, I want to ask you –

Q. When our body/appearance alters, are we any less of a person, or any less of a woman?

Before you give your answer, I want you to think about some of those truly horrible stories you've seen on television or read in the newspapers, like people getting 6 degree burns all over their body, yet still surviving somehow. I want you to ponder on people who have lost their breasts, uterus', parts of their face, had multiple appendages amputated, leaving them barely alive or recognisable. Then think about if they are any less of a human or a woman? Finally, I want you to put yourself in that picture, and then tell me if you are really any less of a person, or any less of a woman because you have some metal around you?

And if you answer anything other than No, please don't take it personally, however, please be warned.... I am about to scream at you. No!!!

Let me say it plainly - You are more than simply the sum of your parts!

We are not a Woman merely because we have breasts, a vagina, a utcrus, long hair and painted fingernails. What makes us a woman lays far deeper than the surface of our skin. The package that contains us is not who we truly are.... yes, it is a big part of how we are seen, and it defines us in terms of which public toilet we utilise, but it does not define us on a deeper level. And, I have to say, that I loathe that phrase, 'beauty is only skin deep'. This phrase undermines women, reduces them to merely what is visible when we greet each other, and completely overlooks the three other dimensions (social, emotional and spiritual) of who we are, as human beings. There are plenty of women, who may never be chosen to represent their country for Miss Universe, yet their beauty beams so brightly through their eyes and hearts, that they are so much more than anyone given that man-made superficial title could ever be.

I want to state that it is inconsequential if our skirts are a size 22 or 6. We may not like the extra skin we carry around our body, we may not care for the shape of our nose, or the way we look in bikinis yet, despite these superficial grievances, we are still Women. So let me hear you roar! (Remember that song, I am woman, by Helen Reddy?)

If you look for a dictionary definition of Woman, you will find this un-elaborate description - 'an adult female human' - no more, no less.

I wish I could sit in front of you right now, face to face, hold both of your hands in mine, look deep into your eyes and declare, 'You deserve to love yourself Warts, Wheels and all'. Regardless of your size, shape, sexuality, age, education, financial status, culture or beauty - all humans, no, scrap that, all living things deserve love. The trees in your street don't do anything to deserve to grow and sprout leaves, yet it happens. When a baby is born it has done nothing to deserve love, yet it is loved instantly and abundantly. There is nothing we need to do in order to deserve love – nothing – we are worthy of love because we 'are'.

I hope that I have convinced you that you are still a woman. Now, let's chat about maximising you!

This next lesson I learnt was from Miss Chai Latte.

There was one particular time Miss Chai Latte came down to Sydney and stayed with me that will stick in my memories forever, as it made such a powerful impact in my life.

I think we were getting ready to go out for lunch somewhere, and we were standing next to each other in front of the mirror, sharing it, as women do (which was easier as she was up high and I was down low). When I found myself looking at her and thinking, 'I used to be that gorgeous!', and then I realised that I was thinking that out loud! She looked at me and bent down and gave me a warm hug. We finished dressing, went out and had a lovely time together as we always do.

The next morning I recalled those days when we used to cause such a stir when we would go out together, pre-accident. And I started reminiscing with Miss Chai Latte about some of those moments. There were lots of giggles and stories filling the air. Then I thought, 'well, what is stopping me from causing a stir now?' Then the conversation (inside my head) followed like this, 'I guess I could if I wanted to'. That was all I needed.

So after thinking about it some, I knew that I needed to attack my femininity or rather, *not being myself* from 3 different angles – my weight, my clothes and my mind. In order for my efforts to be successful, I knew that I had to use all three senses, kinaesthetic (doing something), visual (how I looked) and auditory (using the power of self-talk and visualisation).

I considered what I was going to do in order to burn fat and reduce my fat intake, then I viciously sorted through my wardrobe, tossing everything and anything out that was not feminine or flattering (thinking, 'I'm going to have to go shopping'). I just wanted to feel more like the Violet I was before my life turned upside-down. Of course there wouldn't be any short skirts or any sex-kitten heels, yet I wasn't about to let that stop me from being me.

Then, there was the work I had to do with how I thought about myself, felt about myself and saw myself – image-wise, this obviously required the most amount of work and took the longest time to alter. However, bit by bit I started slowly to see the changes and then others started seeing them too. I'm not a superwoman and don't pretend that there are zero moments when I feel less than the person I want to be (like I did pre-accident), yet, now I know how to minimise those moments, so that I am in charge, not them.

There is a Goddess inside each and every woman on this planet, whether we believe it or not. And, whether we need a wheelchair, carry extra weight, are 4 foot nothing, aren't a math-wiz, I believe the difference between those women who seemingly have it all and those who don't is - truly loving every inch of who we are.

> *Sex appeal is fifty percent what you've got and fifty percent what people think you've got ~Sophia Loren*

I want to ask you, *How do you truly see yourself?* I don't want an instant response, I want you to write this down somewhere and chew on it for at least one day. Then, I want you to imagine asking your friends the same question about you (Q. How do you think your friends see you?) Then, think about the possible answers they might give. Let's see if you are surprised by what comes up.

Now, as outlined before, us humans are the most advanced creatures on this planet because we operate on many levels, which is why I think it is necessary for us to remember this when we get dressed to go out.

FLASHBACK

I want to tell you a story of another good friend of mine, let's call her Miss Espresso. I met Miss Espresso while working up in Brisbane at a fabulous organisation that provides services and resources for people with a spinal cord injury and Polio across Queensland – Spinal Injuries Association (website in the Resource section).

Oh, I probably need to mention that Miss Espresso uses a wheelchair too.

We would organise to meet up about once every couple of months. And every time we met up Miss Espresso would always complement me on something I was wearing. She's a sweetheart. In the early stages I think she felt limited with what she could wear yet, over the months that we met, I saw her confidence grow, and I saw her experiment more and more with fashion and her style. Personally, I

TOOL – YOU ARE A BEAUTIFUL WOMAN

As I told you before, there was a long period of time when I was not happy with my new life, or the new version of what I looked like in my wheelchair. I have said before that I talked to myself in front of the mirror, and that is what I am going to ask you to do, here and now.

All I am asking is that you give it a go for one week – if you do it for any less, you aren't really giving it a chance! Hey, it can't hurt us, right?

You might like to start with simple stuff like, telling yourself that you are a 'Woman'. You could build on this by telling yourself that you are a 'beautiful woman', a 'sexy woman', or a 'sexy and intelligent woman'.

I would suggest that you let your heart guide you, so that each day you hear what your heart tells you is most poignant for that day. To ensure you really get the goodness of it, I ask that you really look into your eyes, not just at yourself on the whole.

So, go on, put yourself directly in front of the mirror and sit up straight, lift up your chin and give yourself a big smile from your heart. Now, please tell yourself something like 'Name, I love you just the way that you are!' I ask that you keep saying this until you feel it is really true for you.

If even reading this request puts you out of your comfort zone, I hope that you don't give-up so quickly….. because you are worth it! Perhaps you would like to try something else like my suggestions 2 or 3 instead?

Suggestion 2: the empty chair technique. You need to transfer out of your chair (onto a lounge or bed or other chair) so that your wheelchair is sitting empty in front of you. Now, I want you to think about what you would say to yourself if you could! What advice would you give to her? What do you see that you like or don't like? What are you happy about or would like to change? Basically, just open your mouth and start talking. It doesn't matter what it is about, because it might just be babble in the beginning but it might lead somewhere good.

Suggestion 3: get creative! Maybe it is writing to yourself, or perhaps it is cutting pictures out of newspapers/magazines to create a collage of who you are. It doesn't have to be enormous or complete, it could be something that you do over a month or something small enough to fit inside your purse. All I ask, is that it is real and personable, because what is the point otherwise?

Again, you are worth the time and effort you will be putting into these activities, because you are going to have to live with yourself for a long time yet. And, I want it to be absolutely fabulous!!!

love fabric, textures, style and fashion so even though in the beginning of my new life I felt ugly and awkward, it didn't take long before I acquired the fundamentals about living in a wheelchair. I learnt what fabrics sat best in a chair, what to look for in clothing styles and generally, how to look good even in a chair.

I remember one day we were having coffee and I saw her noticing the shoes that I had on. I recall I was wearing my black witchy flats (pointy toe shoes). During our chat, she complimented me on them and asked how they stayed on my footplate. We finished our chat, said our 'goodbyes' and went our own ways. It was probably less than 10 minutes when I bumped into her in the shoe section at David Jones department store. It wasn't until this point that she told me that the shoes I was wearing were one of her favourites, pre-accident. Miss Espresso informed me that it had been 10 years since she had worn pointy shoes. She said she wanted to give it a go and see if she could wear them again. I was very excited about helping her do something that she loves and get closer to being the real 'Miss Espresso'. So of course, I stayed and helped her get her own pair of points. I think it was a little less than a week later that Miss Espresso sent me a text message saying that she had worn them to a corporate event, and she also said that she had received so many compliments that night. I could hear the huge smile on her face over the telephone, and that put a huge smile on my face, and in my heart.

So when you are going out, whether you are trying to attract the attention of a male, female, boss, colleague, service provider, or your postman, just make sure before you leave the house, you look in the mirror and that you are one hundred per cent happy with what you see. Yes, it might take some effort sorting through your wardrobe, shopping for new garments, getting alterations, updating your hairstyle or make-up, but you will feel good for it, and you'll be surprised how it will influence other parts of your life. After all, when you meet someone for the first time, whether you are going for a job interview, joining a new interest group, testifying in court, or doing your weekly grocery shopping – because people do not know you from a bar of soap, they have to trust what they see, hear and feel.

Yes, I'm talking about first impressions. It is important and it is influential! I don't know how many times I have been asked out on a date, from just doing my day-to-day things like getting my computer fixed to grocery shopping. Seriously.

Let me give you a scenario. Who would you trust to sell your house? A real estate agent who turns up in an unironed suit, holding his mobile and driving a Toyota, or an agent that showed up in an ironed suit carrying relevant paperwork and a Mercedes parked in your drive way? I hate it, yet because the second real estate agent cares about how he looks, puts in the effort and is serious about his career, it makes sense that if that is true about how he looks, then it probably is true for his work too. This is why that phrase about how we look is still around – *you never get a second chance to make a good first impression.*

So, when it comes to the whole 'dating' thing, finding a 'partner', or just meeting new people, you must remember that it is about what they see in front of them, because people need to like what they see, so that they stop to find out more about who you are!

Right now, you might be thinking – 'yes, but I've got baggage! I'm in a wheelchair'. And I would respond, 'but seriously, who hasn't got baggage?' I would find it very difficult to believe that someone can move through life without acquiring some sort, some degree, some form of 'baggage'. I dare you to tell me just one person you know, that does not have any hint of baggage! I dare you.

Life is about experiences and events, some of them positive, some of them negative and some are just neutral, yet we are constantly interacting with everything in life. And because of that, dings and dents are going to happen. Sometimes the damage is visual, sometimes it is not. Yes, we use a wheelchair to get around and it is a very visual part of our life, whereas, other people's baggage is not as blatant as ours. Like riding a bike, once you've learned the in's and out's of life in a chair – there's really not much to it, but we have no idea what lies inside of other people when we first meet them. So, I would say to you, 'don't worry so much about your metal legs'. As I've said in other chapters, the chair only has as much power as we choose to give it.

What is important to keep at the forefront of our minds, is that not all men will find all women attractive, and not all women will be attracted to all men either!

Some men are attracted to blondes, while others will have weaknesses for brunettes. Some men can't go past Asian women, while other men will crave the more fuller-figured woman. There are some women who are a sucker for a man who is a wealth of knowledge, and there are others who wouldn't want anything but a good ole country boy.

We all know that there is no rhyme, rule or reason why or who we are attracted to – it is as mysterious and individual as the grains of sand on the beach. And, we know that sometimes the men we crave – do not return that craving, sometimes the men we crave don't even know we exist, and sometimes that darn man we crave doesn't want *us*, just the sex thank you very much. However, despite our conviction, he really isn't *the one* for us, perhaps there really is someone better suited for you out there, just waiting for you to turn the corner and perhaps, it won't happen when it is convenient for us, or happen like we planned. That is life. I know that as much as I try to control my world, things are going to happen when they are meant to happen.

"The greatest griefs are those we cause ourselves." ~Sophocles

So, I say to you, forget that your wheelchair plays a part in the reason why you haven't found *the one* yet, actually, just try to forget that you're in a wheelchair and get on with your life. Have fun and make sure it is with a capital F!

There are so many men on this planet and all of them are their own 'nugget', so to speak, just like all of us women are our own individual 'diamonds'. Some men want something pretty to hang off their arm, some men want a career partner, some men like a motherly sort of woman, some men want a housekeeper with benefits, when other men just want the sex.... which means it is impossible to tell you whether or not that man you find appealing will return your feelings. And there are no 'signs' that I can give you to look out for, yet I can tell you to watch out for the aspects I have experienced -

    a. If your man does not give you any PDAs (public displays of affection)

    b. If you feel *isolated*

    c. If you feel like you need *saving*

    d. If you feel that you are not able to be *yourself*, or

    e. If you feel that your man is more *into* your wheelchair, than into he is into you.

Let's face it – we chicks-in-chairs are a minority, which means that most of the men out there will not have much experience at all with us. However, I want to tell you that just because men have not known any chicks in chairs, it doesn't mean that they can't/won't find you attractive... also, it doesn't mean that they will.

What I do want to share with you, is information I received from a word-of-mouth survey about this point (do men find chicks-in-chairs attractive or not?).

The odd one or two here and there said that they would not consider dating a person in a chair, while some said they had not thought about it before, and some more said, no problem!!! The biggest point that came from this survey, was that a lot of them said that it depends on the chick, and they didn't use the word chick, I did. Which really does prove my point, which is, it all comes down to you at the end of the day. It comes down to how much effort you put into yourself, your appearance, whether they are attracted to you, your confidence, your attitude to life, and just who you are as a *package*.

Sure, you might find that men might be a tad unsure about what to do, how to do it, and general 'stuff' about dating a chick-in-a-chair, yet the biggest thing to remember is that you are not a chair, You are You! Yes, you have a chair in your life and it will be a part of his too, because it is your legs, BUT it is not You.

Y*ou are the only one who can put yourself in a box!* ~ Me

And for those men that consider having a wheelchair an issue – I say, *to heck with them!*

It will be fairly obvious if they are superficial, and if they are, then why would we want someone like that anyway? Can you imagine the quality of the relationship with someone like that? Can you imagine the depth of conversation and the stability of their love for you? That's not for me, no thanks. I want to be certain that when a female walks past us, that the man in my life only has eyes for me! (And that would be true for me, pre-accident as well).

While we're on this subject, let me share a little something with you. The Spinal Unit, at Stoke Mandeville, held weekly sessions on 'Life with Spinal Cord Injury' that lasted for about six weeks I think. One of the sessions was titled 'Sex and Spinal Injury', and us girls went in hoping to answer some of our questions. Let's just say that we walked out of there (or rather rolled out) rather discouraged, agreeing between us that, 'well obviously us girls can't have sex anymore'. I won't expound on the lack of information and research for women in chairs and sex, but suffice to say, that class that day was all about men. It was about what they can and can't do, potential problems and possible solutions. I know I was not alone when I say that as we, the girls, went back to our separate rooms that day, felt uncertain about that part of our future.

But, allow me to put your minds at rest, if you haven't already walked down this path yet, I want to tell you that WE CAN. And they do and yes, we can! Oops, perhaps I should have outlined the questions first – Can we still have sex? Will the men enjoy it? And, can we still orgasm? So, there you go. Yes, it will be different, but not necessarily bad. Um, what else can I tell you? Experiment, think outside the square and remember that there are no rules. I have included the name of a really good book on sex and disability, you will find it in the Book List I have included. Just relax, breath and have fun.

I hope you will allow me a couple of seconds to touch on the whole subject of the orgasm because I think it is important for us. The noun, Orgasm, brings all sorts of thoughts to my mind – mostly happy, positive and exciting ones. And, what I have discovered, post injury, is that this is something we can still experience, despite what doctors may tell you. I want to ask you, 'how the heck would they know anyway?' What I have learnt is that yes, the doctors learn about anatomy and the general body, however they can't know what we can/can't feel because they don't have a personal experience of having a disability. As I've said before, you can get two people together who have the exact same injury, and yet, they can experience different sensations, feelings and experiences. So, there is no 'general' rule that applies to us.

Yes, the experience of it will be different for us now, but I know that I still have the ability to have that heightened, sensual state of an orgasm and so do you. I don't know if you have ever had sex with someone over the phone or internet, but if you have, you know that the mind can get turned on just by what you hear and can imagine – which proves to me that the mind plays a very significant part in the whole orgasm experience. Yes, there has to be some sort of a physical connection and sensation, but I will reiterate that the mind is such a powerful tool, we cannot neglect its importance and contribution.

So, don't deny the physical aspect of yourself because of what others might think, don't deny your sexuality because you are afraid, and don't deny yourself pleasure because doctors or some peer has said that you can't have or enjoy sex now. Again, I will tell you that You are your own expert.

I want to quote a sexuality educator and researcher, Mitch Tepper, who happens to be a man with a spinal cord injury.

> *There is growing evidence that sexual knowledge, sexual self-esteem, and time since injury are related to the ability to experience sexual pleasure and orgasm. Orgasmic sex requires tuning in to our sensations – in the moment – and forgetting about quad bellies, atrophy, catheters and making embarrassing sounds. It means not worrying about performing up to some imagined standard. It means forgetting what we learned in the past about what is and isn't pleasurable.*

Oh, and if you want some proof that your wheelchair isn't the reason they (men) are not lining up outside your door – just remember this.

My dear friend, Miss Chamomile Tea, will confirm that what I am about to tell you is absolutely certain, maybe I should include her email address (Na, don't think she'd appreciate that too much).

Miss Chamomile Tea is a long-legged, sporty blonde with green eyes who has a fun personality and exercises daily. When I say exercises,

I mean serious exercise like 5km runs. So, she is pretty darn ugly to look at – NOT. She's gorgeous. And you know what? Little old me, a chick who uses a chair, has had just as many dates as she has had since my accident. Yep, that's right, and the honest to God truth. And I'm only telling you this because I want you to know for certain that the chair has absolutely NOTHING to do with your attract-ability! Not a darn thing.

Luckily for me, I am out of the dating game because my Mr Right came along and swept me off my feet... (Heehee). Love you sweetheart.

Marty's
two cents worth

Some people with a disability believe they are worthy of love, and some people with a disability don't believe, think or feel they are worthy of love.... and I am grateful for the gift of love every single day. Look, I know that I have a one-in-a-million kind-a-guy, and so do a couple of other women on this planet, yet, when it comes down to it, he was just a boy that fell in love with a girl! It really is that simple.

So, Marty and I thought it might be useful for the readers of this book to hear what he has to say about chicks-in-chairs, disability, and everything in between.

So, Marty, could you please tell the readers how we first met?

Well, it must've been about 22 years ago. A group of friends I was a part of went to a restaurant, and some friends of friends came as well. One of these "friends" was a young bubbly 18 year old. How can I put it? Well, she sort of reminded me of a bouncy fluffy little puppy...full of life and energy...and yes, the bubbly girl was you. We became friends, not really close, but we associated with a lot of the same people, and saw each other often over the next few years during different social outings. I must say, I did always admire you. You were fun and very beautiful, and it's hard to pinpoint the exact words, so I will just go with "interesting and unique", yes, that's it, I think they are the exact words actually - a uniquely interesting young woman. Then, after a few years, I ended up moving away to pursue my career and we lost contact.

When we met again, post-accident, could you please share what you noticed?

So fast-forward many years, I had left the area, and had a new life with new friends, and a new town, but, as things change, circumstances lead me back home, and through a series of events, I met up with you again. I hadn't seen you for about 15 years, I didn't know about the accident, as I said, we had lost contact.

By the time I met you in person again, I knew you were now in a chair, we had talked on the phone a couple of times where you had filled me in on some of the major things you had done and what had happened during the previous years. I was looking forward to seeing you again, to see what you were like - to see the similarities and the differences, and to see if you were still the Violet I remembered.

The idea of you being in a chair didn't really make me think too much, except maybe a little sad that someone who was so happy and bubbly had suffered so much to now be in a wheelchair. These were my initial thoughts, before I met you in person. Thoughts just fly around your head, so I didn't think too much about the chair, at this point I didn't know the circumstances that lead to your accident, I was just waiting to see you again. I wasn't meeting up with you to see Violet in the chair, nor to see you as a paraplegic, I was just excited about seeing Violet, the lady I knew from many years before. And, ever since that first enchilada, that's the way I have continued to see you, as Violet, not as Violet in a chair, not as Violet as a paraplegic, but just Violet.

I recall we had planned to meet for dinner at my favourite Mexican restaurant. As I walked in to the complex where the restaurant was, I spotted a woman looking in a window of a clothes shop, it was you. It wasn't the chair I first noticed, it was your hair and your face, but most of all your posture, the way you held yourself. Even with the first glance of you, it was obvious this was you - beautiful, confident and proud. Of course I saw the chair, but I didn't really notice it, I saw the same Violet I knew so long ago.

And, could you describe what attracted you to me?

Hmmm....why was I attracted to you? Well it's pretty simple, all the reasons I have already mentioned, of course. I had always found you attractive and very likable. You always had your very own personality, yes I know we all do, but you just had and have something about you that I fell for. It is a mixture of your confidence, your strength, your love for life, but at the same time you have this very interesting part of yourself that is so soft and caring. The perfect mixture I guess you could say.

So, was the chair an issue for you at all?

Ok, time for the chair questions. No, I don't think the chair did come into it. But, that said, if it did, it would have come into it as a part of your strength, here is Vi, the same woman she always has been, hopefully a bit wiser (hehehe), but now in a chair. During our meal that first night, you hardly mentioned the chair at all, you talked about the past, old friends, travel and your life in general. Yes, you are in a chair, and yes, it has a very significant impact on many aspects of your life, but, it is not your life. And that's the way I have seen it as well, we all have things in our lives, the proverbial thorn in our side, but, we get along don't we? Life doesn't really stop because of an obstacle, it may slow us down, sure, but you keep going, and that's what you have taught me as well, your strength is rubbing off on me and I am very grateful.

Did the chair/disability make you reconsider dating me?

I think I have pretty well answered this question, so no, it didn't. Of course I had thoughts about how you do your daily tasks. I had thoughts about catheters, mobility, diet, "accidents" (as you like to call them), general health, and whether there are other health issues associated with paraplegia. But, these things did not help nor deter my desire to get to know you on a deeper level. Like anyone you may be wishing to "date", you are not going to give up just because he or she has something in their life you haven't experienced before. I decided to just enjoy the journey, and the journey has led me to a very beautiful and fulfilling destination. Yes, of course, the journey continues, but that's what life is all about.

Have you known anyone in a chair before me?

Off the top of my head, three people come to mind.

The first person I had any real contact with who used a chair (paraplegia) was a teacher at my primary school. Mr M was never actually my teacher, he taught my brother, but I went to a small school and all the students knew all the teachers rather well. Mr M was one man who had a big impact on my life, it wasn't because of the fact he was in a chair (I don't think so anyway), but he was very encouraging to all of his students. He seemed to understand where we, as kids, were "coming from", and most of all, he genuinely cared about what he did, which was 'teach'.

He was very involved with everything that went on in the school from sport, to school plays and even school camps. At one camp, I remember a couple of the other teachers picking him up and carrying him down the water's edge and tossing him in, he seemed very happy with this. So maybe, Mr M using a chair had a little to do with my respect for him, and I think he helped me form some very early attitudes about people who use chairs. Anyway, all I can really say is that Mr M did influence me in various ways, he was one of those teachers who you think about now and again during your life with fond memories.

The second time was when I was a 23 years old I studying a prep year for university entrance at Tafe. There was a man around my age who was in a chair, as a result from an accident in his late teens, in my class. I got on rather well with him, but, I tended to stay away from the chair "issues". So, I never really learnt a lot about disability from him. I didn't have a lot to do with him but I did notice him a lot. One day, as he was breaking down his chair to put into his car, I asked him if he needed help, and he snapped back at me, "No, I can do it myself!" I wasn't offended, but I did feel as though I had offended him, big time. I tried to understand that he wanted and believed in his own independence as we all do. However, having been with you for some time now, and having met a lot of others who use chairs, I do not find that to be a common thing. Like anybody, if you need help and someone offers, you will accept it. As you say, "you get more with honey". I can understand my classmate's frustration though, and I know he hadn't been in the chair long. He may have been asserting his independence, but then again, he may have been snapping at people all his life, who knows?

And the third person was my mum. My mother became an amputee and used a chair for the last seven years of her life, but the comparison is not really there. My mum didn't like the prosthesis that was given, and so used the chair permanently. Yet, other than that she had little similarities with people who live with paraplegia.

Did you have any pre-conceptions about people in chairs?

We all have pre-conceptions about everything around us, it's how we make sense of the world. I remember when I was a little kid, my mum took me into Brisbane city for the day and there was this man doing a "wheelie" in his chair down the footpath, and I thought that was "pretty cool". My mum, my nursing work, my classmate, the biography I once read on Frida Kahlo, the documentary I once watched on wheelchair rugby, and even the film Notting Hill have all given me a view of life with a chair I guess. I view "people in chairs", just as people who happen to use a wheelchair. Some will be independent, some overly dependent, some very beautiful people, some not so beautiful, some kind, some unkind, some old, some young, some male, some female, in other words, people, that's about it.

I realised, I don't know when, but I did, and do know people in chairs have other areas in their lives that impact on them. That said, I don't think it ever made me think negatively, or sorry for anyone who uses a chair, just a realisation that a person's life is probably more difficult than mine in a lot of areas I take for granted.

And, did you think about the issue of sex?

As we got closer, the idea of sex (horrible word), let me say, the idea of lovemaking, entered my mind, of course it did. I'm male, and I was now getting close to a lady who is very beautiful on the inside and out. Of course, I'm not dead, and you are one gorgeous mama!!! After I got to know you a little, you let me know a lot about your life, your injury, and what sensations you have since the accident. I knew I was about to embark on a journey of discovery, I didn't know what I would discover, but that's what relationships are all about, discovery.

I thought about how lovemaking would "work", I kind of figured it wouldn't be much different just because of your disability, so I just went with it, it didn't matter to me. If it was different compared to what I had known in the past, that was ok, it never was a negative thing with me. I never thought, "oh no, what if the sex isn't any good", and this is probably because you let me know in your non-subtle way that sex was still possible, very, very possible.

What have you noticed about dating a chick in a chair?

Hhmmm... Again, I think much of this has been covered. Being with a woman in a chair isn't an issue, yes there are adaptations you need to make, in time management, lovemaking, where you go to (the need for accessible toilets for example, or lack of stairs), but, as I said, these are just parts of a whole relationship. There are some aspects that I have grown to dislike I guess, but nothing to do with you (as an individual), or the fact you use a wheelchair. It is usually the things "outside" of our relationship that bother me, like strangers who think they have a right to stare and ask stupid questions. And I have really grown to hate the word "disabled", as in "disabled parking" or "disabled toilets". You may have a disability, but to me, you are far from being disabled. Disabled to me, means, not being able, and you are very, very able in so many areas of your life. You can sew and I can't, does that make me disabled?

Do you find dating a chick that uses a wheelchair better/worse/ same as dating an AB (able-bodied person)?

You are my partner, my friend, my lover. So whether it is better, worse, or the same as dating an "AB", is really irrelevant. You are you, and have things in your life that just "are", exactly the same as I have things in my life that just "are".

There may be a lot of differences, little ones and big ones. We may take a little longer when we go to the shops because we get the chair in and out of the car, but what, maybe 5 minutes over the day? There may be "accidents" now and again, but that happened to me last week, with that stomach bug. Lovemaking may be more creative, hhmmm, is that a negative thing? I think not! There may be adjustments, but no more than when you are in any relationship. A new partner may have children, may have a chronic illness, mental health issues, a large and very close family, interfering and overbearing parents, problems with addiction, the list is endless, but, if you love your partner, all these things simply become a part of your life, of your partnership.

What advice would you give to a guy who is attracted to a chick in a chair?

What can I say? If you are attracted to her there is no difference I can see. Maybe, if you are a guy who likes rock climbing, skydiving or surfing, and desires a partner who will share these activities with you, there might be some challenges...but that could be worked out. There are some pretty active "Chicks in chairs" around, and you will discover that not a lot stops them! I have been a "fill in" now and again in a wheelchair basketball team, and let me tell you, yes, there are some very active "chicks in chairs" around. I am yet to meet a woman in a chair who doesn't just live her life like all of us.

So, my advice would be to give it a go, as you would for any woman you may wish to spend time with.

What advice would you give to a chick in a chair that is looking for a partner?

As I said, if you find someone you are attracted to, why not go for it? My advice would be exactly the same for the girls.

There are a few things I would mention, so I will address the readers now -

I don't think there is any need to be totally upfront with a guy in the very early stages, there is no need to tell him about bowel or bladder "accidents", or even what you do or do not "feel" in particular areas of your body. These things will come to be known by him, and if he is worth anything at all, these things won't matter to him. Yes, he may feel uncomfortable with particular areas, but aren't we all uncomfortable at first with things we know nothing about. You may need to let him find his way of understanding and dealing with "new" things, he may just need a little time adjusting, but, if you are honest and open with him, and he is honest and open with you, there shouldn't be a problem. For example, when Violet and I entered into our relationship, I came with two children. Violet adores them, but she had never been a mum before, and has never had little brothers or sisters, so she had a few "issues" to figure out in her own mind. She had to adjust her way of thinking in some areas, but, that's just normal. I gave her the space and the time to do this, it may have caused a few disruptions here and there, but that's life and that's relationships. Anything of value is worth working on.

I often wondered what it was like for Violet when we made love. I know it was, and is, very loving, fun, sexy and lusty, but, I was curious about what actual penetration was like for Violet. I knew she didn't "feel" it the same as she used to, so I asked her. And she said "let me show you". Violet gave me a portion of the doona (duvet) to hold and asked me to make a small opening with my hands, then she proceeded to push her fist into the blanket opening that I was holding - she said "that's what "it" feels like for me". I could feel the pressure, I could feel the push sensation, but I could not feel Violet's hand, or skin, and I thought it was a great explanation.

So in summary, do I find having a partner in a chair better, or worse, or the same? I would say the same! The same in that every relationship has, at different times, differences and challenges, beauty and mess. So the similarity is in the differences.

Rights, Research and Education

- www.hreoc.gov.au/disability_rights/links
  (Human Rights Commission, Worldwide)

- www.spinal .co.uk
  (United Kingdom)

- www.scrc.umanitoba.ca
  (Canada)

- www.ukdpc.net/
  (UK Disabled People's Council)

- www.nscisc.uab.edu
  (Facts and figures)

- www.christopherreeve.org

- www.spinalcord.org
  (USA)

- www.pva.org
  (Not just for Veterans)

- www.spinalcordsociety.com
  (Solely about Cure)

- www.unitedspinal.org
  (Americans with spinal cord impairment)

- www.makoa.org
  (Jim Lubin)

- www.thequadlink.webs.com
  (Links to help connect people with Quadriplegia)

- www.thescizone.com
  (Educational knowledge base)

- www.spinalinjury.net
  (Explains anatomy, physiology and complications)

- www.sci-info-pages.com
  (Educational with a tone of links)

- www.ninds.nih.gov/
  Research)

- www.sci.washington.edu/
  (Rehabilitation, Information and Links)

- www.spinalcord.uab.edu/show.asp?durki=77527&site=10
  21&return=19751
  (Eat Right® Home-Based Weight Management Program
  for Individuals with SCI)

- www.ricability.org.uk
  (Unbiased consumer reports, for people with a disability/
  aged)

- www.pwd.org.au
  (Rights and advocacy of people with a disability, Aust.)

- www.argomedtec.com/FAQ.asp
  (Technology that helps people walk again)

- www.outsiders.org.uk
  (Providing information and networks since 1979, UK)

- www.ableize.com/products-and-services
  Disabled products, services, sports, holidays, clubs,
  groups and charities in the UK.

- www.dialuk.info/
  (160 local organizations with info and services for and by
  pwad)

- www.scope.org.uk
  (Supports people living with cerebral palsy)

- www.capability-scotland.org.uk
  (Supports pwad, Scotland)

- www.enabledpeople.co.uk
  (Info on assistance, entitlements and schemes, UK)

- www.e-bility.com
  (Resources, information, services and products for pwad,
  Aust)

Publications

- www.disabilitynow.org.uk
  (E-zine, UK)

- www.linkonline.com.au/
  (A cross-disability magazine, Aust)

- www.disabilityworld.org
  (International disability news and views)

- www.newmobility.com
  (Disability lifestyle magazine)

- www.paralinks.net
  (E-zine for people with SCI)

- www.spinalcord.uab.edu/
  (Newsletter of the SCI Information Network)

- www.raggededgemagazine.com/
  (Disability Rag's E-zine)

- www.pvamag.com/sns
  (Wheelchair sports magazine)

- www.sci.washington.edu/info/newsletters/
  (Northwest Regional Spinal Cord Injury System)

- www.mobilewomen.org
  (Website by women in chairs for women in chairs)

- www.chloemagazine.com
  (E-zine written by and for pwad, USA)

- www.disabilitynow.org.uk
  (E-zine based in the UK)

- Fashion101
  (Written by a chick in a chair, for women in chairs, Tiffany Carlson, USA)

- Moving Violations
  (An excellent memoir by an award-winning journalist in a chair)

Get into Life!

- www.toiletmap.gov.au/
  (Locate toilets, Australia)

- www.datingdisabled.net
  (Dating, USA)

- www.cupidcalls.co.uk
  (Dating, UK)

- www.cupidcalls.com
  (Dating, USA)

- www.disabledhearts.com
  (Dating, USA)

- www.disabledlove.org
  (Dating, Worldwide)

- www.workability.org.au/index.php?page=22
  (Employment website, Aust)

- www.wheelchairs.com/
  (Custom work is their specialty, USA)

- www.activeplaces.com.au/
  (Sports and general links, Aust, UK and USA)

- www.d-ability.org/main.php
  (Links – worldwide)

- www.projectwalk.org
  This is an exercised-based recovery program for people
  with spinal cord injuries. There are centers available in
  eight countries around the world.

- www.tac.vic.gov.au/jsp/content/NavigationController.do?a
  reaID=26&tierID=2&navID=D9BBFBB77F00000100BCE
  28A1027C58F&navLink=null&pageID=1270
  (a tonne of links on travel & disability, nationwide Australia)

- www.leanneschairworkout.com – A woman who has an
  amputation herself has created an exercise video for
  people who use a chair.

There are (as far as I know, to date) three national pageants for women with disabilities in the United States of America. They are Ms. Wheelchair America, Ms. Wheelchair USA and Ms. Ability USA.

- www.mswheelchairamerica.org

- www.mswheelchairusa.org

- www.msabilityusa.org

Fashion

- www.versaaccesswear.com./Outerwear.html
  (USA)

- www.rollimoden.de
  (GERMANY)

- www.wheelchairjeans.com/
  (USA)

- www.izadaptive.com/
  (CAN)

- www.wheeliechix-chic.com/
  (UK)

- www.spokeguardart.com/
  (fashion for your chair, USA)

- www.cheekydogs.com.au/
  (T-shirts, Bags and cards, Dion Beasley – Deaf & MD, Aust)

- www.anaurora.co.uk/
  (Fashion & Beauty, gardening, health & wellbeing, UK)

- www.heelswithwheels.com/
  (Clothing designed by a woman in a chair, USA)

- www.beautyability.com
  (is a website created by a fashion-ista who uses a chair herself, USA)

Lightning Source UK Ltd.
Milton Keynes UK
UKOW04f1129010813

214741UK00008B/330/P